IMAGE, WORD AND SELF

The International Conference on *Image, Word and Self: Recent Receptions of Freud on Both Sides of the Atlantic* (New York City, 25-27 October, 1990) has been organized by the Italian Cultural Institute and by The New School for Social Research, New York.

Conference Steering Committee: Sergio Benvenuto, *Consiglio Nazionale delle Ricerche,* Massimo Cellerino, *The New School,* Gianclaudio Macchiarella, *Italian Cultural Institute,* Maria Letizia Proietti, *University of Rome "La Sapienza",* Margherita Repetto-Alaia, *Italian Cultural Institute,* Joel Whitebook, *The New School.*

European Coordinator: Maria Letizia Proietti, *University of Rome "La Sapienza".*

Academic Sponsors: Richard Bernstein, *The New School,* Vincenzo Cappelletti, *Istituto della Enciclopedia Italiana,* Sergio De Risio, *University of Chieti,* Ira Katznelson, *The New School,* Eugenio Lecaldano, *University of Rome "La Sapienza",* Ignacio Matte Blanco†, Achille Tartaro, *University of Rome "La Sapienza",* Gianni Eugenio Viola, *Istituto dell'Enciclopedia Italiana,* Alan Wolfe, *The New School.*

IMAGE, WORD AND SELF

Proceedings of the International Symposium on Recent Receptions of Freud on Both Sides of the Atlantic

Edited by

MARIA LETIZIA PROIETTI

PETER LANG
New York • Washington, D.C./Baltimore
Bern • Frankfurt am Main • Berlin • Vienna • Paris

Library of Congress Cataloging-in-Publication Data

International Symposium on Recent Receptions of Freud on Both Sides of the Atlantic (1990: New York, N.Y.)
Image, word, and self: proceedings of the International Symposium on Recent Receptions of Freud on Both Sides of the Atlantic/
[edited by] Maria Letizia Proietti.
p. cm.
Includes bibliographical references.
1. Psychoanalysis and philosophy—Congresses. 2. Imagination—Congresses. 3. Imagery (Psychology)—Congresses. 4. Freud, Sigmund, 1856–1939.
I. Proietti, Maria Letizia. II. Title.
BF175.4.P45I58 150.19'52—dc20 96-30184
ISBN 0-8204-1630-4

Die Deutsche Bibliothek-CIP-Einheitsaufnahme

Image, word, and self: proceedings of the International Symposium on Recent Receptions of Freud on Both Sides of the Atlantic/
[edited by] Maria Letizia Proietti.
– New York; Washington, D.C./ Baltimore; San Francisco; Bern; Frankfurt am Main; Berlin; Vienna; Paris: Lang.
(American university studies: Ser. 20, Fine arts; Vol. 28)
ISBN 0-8204-1630-4
NE: Proietti, Maria Letizia: International Symposium on Recent Receptions of Freud on Both Sides of the Atlantic <1990: New York, NY>

The paper in this book meets the guidelines for permanence and durability of the Committee on Production Guidelines for Book Longevity of the Council of Library Resources.

Printed in the United States of America.

Publication of this Volume was made possible by the generous grants of:

– The Ministry of Foreign Affairs, Republic of Italy
– The Istituto Italiano di Cultura, New York, New York
– Fondazione SIGMA TAU–Rome, Italy
– "Villa Pini d'Abruzzo" Clinic for Mental Illness–Chieti, Italy

Table of Contents

Preface

Maria Letizia Proietti
Editor

> Anything that happens, happens.
> Anything that in happening, causes something else to happen.
> Anything that, in happening, causes itself to happen again, happens again.
> It doesn't necessarily do it in chronological order, though.
> Douglas Adams, *Mostly Harmless**

To whoever, these days, would want to focus "sur l'état présent de la question de l'imagination . . . je ne vois pas d'oeuvre tout à fait récente dans le domaine de la philosophie ou de l'ésthetique qui puisse être considerée comme une contribution majeure".[1]

For *image* and *imagination* one goes back to the Indoeuropean *mei*, which indicates all that is mutable and intermittent, and seduces our attention.[2]

The sanskrit *maya* springs from it, the all-mutable, insidious and inevitable play of appearances, up to the Old German *mein*: deception.

Examining the synonym: *phantasy*, the Indoeuropean root is *bha*, which signifies *light*, *vision*, as well as *sound* and *magic world*. *Fable*, *fame*, and *fate*, as well as *phenomenon* and *phantasm* derive from it.

---

*Cit. in Danis Nobus, *Studi internazionali del campo freudiano*, no. 14, July-December 1993, p. 27.

Imaginatio vel phantasia? Philosophers were asking themselves during the last International Colloquium on the topic[3]: the imagination in fact immediately recalls the other Greek term from which it derives: φαντασια, so as to underline their historically demonstrated interchangeability.

At the time of that Colloquium it was said that, due to reasons of historical and cultural tradition, the related family, that of the imaginary, had been excluded from discussion, which otherwise would have immediately shifted the results to other areas of inquiry.

Since there was a need for it, one thought of including in this Symposium, precisely this related family, purposely inviting psychoanalysts as well as philosophers to a discussion, that should take place in the West, but beyond the context of European traditions.

Thus, if during the proceedings of the last International Colloquium, the philosophers had not only captured the polysemous valences present in *imagination*, but had also reconstructed that western Latin tradition that transliterates or translates the Greek φαντασια, this New York Symposium has captured, or rather privileged, precisely that function of *imaginary* and *phantasmatic* excluded in the other, starting from which–ever since the Unconscious–a relapse on the function of language (Word) and on the function of subject (Self) is produced–hence the title of this Symposium–which determines a radical transformation, subversion or dissolve, as in the words of René Major, when he reminds us that *the Unconscious from Freud according to Lacan would be a chain of signifiers which somewhere (in another scene) is reflected and insists on interfering in the cuts offered to it by effective discourse and the cogitation it informs.* And when he reminds us that it is only *in-between these signifiers that 'a subject' can be still supposed: but in any case, the one that does the thinking, calculating and judging is not 'a subject': it's more la Jouissance.*

Then, if the Ego talks *in several voices of the constitutive and deconstitutive desistance of the subject, it's because the dis-location of the subject brings with it a dis-locution of thought.*

The unsuppressible complexity of terms is thus immediately reimplicated, as it is in the concluding words of Eugenio Garin at the International Colloquium: "There is agreement on the mediating function of the *imaginatio*. Just as with *spiritus*, which mediates between bodily matter and soul, on the plane of the structure of the human aggregate, so on the cognitive plane the *imaginatio* mediates between sense and intellect. There is a continuous reference to the Aristotelian text of the *De Anima* (III, 3 427 b): fantasy is different from αἴσθησις and from διανοἰα; it presupposes the first, and is presupposed by the second. If it were not for the fact that the apparent simplicity of the Aristotelian thesis is complicated as soon as one attempts to specify the character of the mediation and what those *phantasmata* and those *noemata*, which are not *phantasmata*, but neither *sine phantasmate*, are".[4]

What's more, in that same colloquium, Jean Starobinski had recognized that "le doublet *phantasie–imagination* s'est transporté dans nombre de langues modernes. Ce qui était en équivalence, d'une langue à l'autre, du grec au latin, a ainsi perdu son aspect bilingual pour devenir, à l'intérieur d'une seule et même langue, un couple synonymique".[5] But synonymic couples for this very reason are prone to a differentiation, a desynonimization thus allowing the oppositions of thought.

Significantly, it is only once one gets closer to medical observation, that the synonymic couple seems to tend more effectively to differentiate itself, as, for instance, in the words of the English doctor Willis, author of the *De Febribus* and the *Cerebri Anatome*, studied and read in the context of the Viconian tradition.

For Willis the imagination belongs to the circle of passions, while fantasy belongs to the circle of actions and therefore constitutes a *vis*.

Vis fantastica, therefore, and *passio imaginaria*: we are caught in the imaginary. And in fantasy?

It is just as significant that some philosophies tend to bring desynonymization back to resynonymization: their comment to doctor Willis'important observation is this: "Let it be clear: the recognition of the *vis imaginativa*, of the therapeutic effects of the same, of its force, both evocative and creative of events, are lines all traceable to the Avicennian influence, they are . . . a commonplace of doctors and philosophers from the Quattrocento on".[6]

Is it not precisely in this reconnection of a *vis fantastica* to a *vis imaginativa* that the indifference of some philosophies with regard to the body, which in an imaginary passion suffers, is revealed?

For those philosophies the idea which seems to have to prevail is that this *vis*–instead of *passio*–should no doubt be ascribed to the imagination: an idea that does not take Willis's distinction into account.

It is for this reason that Starobinski concluded, in that Colloquium, that, notwithstanding its relative decline as far as frequency of usage is concerned at the beginning of the XIX century, the imagination remains, in the context of French and European culture, a *philosopheme*, whereas *phantasia* is not, to the extent that the language of literary criticism itself, today so closely tied to that of philosophy, does not use it much any more, even though its linguistic value is not in the least negligible.

So that Colloquium tied itself to a function of the *imagination*, mostly understanding it as, for instance, Montaigne could have, when he wrote: "Je nourissais des *imaginations* hardies et des opinions au dessus de mon age"[7]: *cogitationes*, in other words, of which it is practically certain that they are not subject to the 'jeu déreglé des rêveries imagées', the imaginary passion, in other words, so feared as to have to be denied.

It is, however, a passion that passes through philosophical reflection and, continuously, makes itself noticed: when it enters the game the philosopher knows he no longer belongs to himself, that he is living "hors de lui, hors de la pure présence. Autant dire qu'il devient la proie de l'inquiétude, la victime du vain desire" within an ideal that "qui nous porte sans cesse au-delà de nous et souvent nous place où n'arriverons point".[8]

In this sense the imagination is always potentially *laesa* by way of that subtle distinction that runs in it, between its power to invent (*invenio*) and to experience the powerful and secret connections between things, the correspondences, the analogies; and, instead, *imagine them*, in other words simulate them, through the 'figures trompeuses' precisely because they derive from a lively persuasion. To the point of admonishing oneself thus "le monde réel a ses bornes, le monde imaginaire est infini:

ne pouvant élargir l'un, rétrecissons l'autre; car c'est de leur seul différence que naissent les peines qui nous rendent vraiment malheureux".[9]

The effort of a correct imagination is therefore also immediately one of the motives of reflection on the imagination: unequal effort, because within her we are continuously carried beyond ourselves and placed where we shall never arrive, or where we believe we are and are not, or where we do not notice we are such and such, and where, moreover, the implicit latent or unconscious phantasms are already playing with derisory, if not dramatic or tragic, cogency?

We have been reminded, in this Symposium, what the consequences of the capture of the Papin sisters by the imaginary were: they estirpated the eyes of their victims with whom they had so totally identified that they had no other means to escape a confusive and annihilating collusion which the violent destruction of what they saw as double, understood as a self-punishment analogous to a self-castration, correlated, among other things, to an intolerable–but unconscious–homosexual desire.[10]

As one can see the games are complex and they move from and on multiple levels: who and how could by now maintain that, as in the words of Rousseau: "Je suis le maître des comparaisons et j'empêche aisément l'illusion des objects réels"?[11]

The complexity that psychoanalytic knowledges introduce around this theme goes beyond that of a philosophic or linguistic nature.

The power to form–and de-form–of the imagination and fantasy is no longer a metaphor when hallucinatory formations and deliriums are admitted to constitute their more consistent and persistent 'contents' in every lived experience.

When psychoanalysis appears on the scene, and notwithstanding its own declared, inevitable and special attention to the image and imagination–*Imago* was the name of its first journal–something interesting happens contemporaneously which Starobinski shrewdly indicates: "Commençons par constater que dans *Studienausgabe* de Freud qui comporte des index très scrupuleusement établis, le mot *Einbildungskraft* cède la place à *Einbildungen*. Il est absent, notamment, du *Sachregister* de la *Traumdeutung*. Procédons à une contre-épreuve: ouvrons le *Vocabulaire de la psychanalyse* de J. Laplanche et J.B. Pontalis: le mot *Imagination* n'y figure pas. Que c'est il passé? Tout simplement, au long du XIX siècle, le mot *Imagination* a déserté le vocabulaire médical. Il appartient peut-être trop au vocabulaire commun, pour perdurer dans un vocabulaire spécialisé".[12]

The removal of the word *imagination* from a terrain it had previously occupied forces one to interest oneself in the lexical evolution that had occurred at that time in the two fields of medicine (psychiatry included) and of philosophy. Confronted with phenomena such as deliria, hallucinations, different functional disturbances, the medicine of the XIX century, if it had made recourse to the *concept* of imagination, would have deluded the expectations of it's own public, desirous to see psychophysiological 'explanations' offered to it?

And, on the other hand, while a *Naturphilosophie* that cosmologizes the imagination ceases to prevail, does 'positive' science have to talk in its own terms?

Or maybe because it is closer to literature and philosophy than to medicine, psychoanalysis preserves the other aspect of the imagination: *fantasie*?

The German *Fantasie* will be translated into French with *fantasme*, from which the adjective *fantasmatique* and the neologism *fantasmer* are derived.

Therefore, if in the Freudian topics, there is no place for the imagination, psychism is however dominated by the *Imago*. This term, proposed by Jung in 1911, taken up by Freud designates "une survivance imaginaire de tel ou tel des participants de la situation de l'enfant dans son milieu *familial* ou *social*".[13] But also and above all *intrapsychic* and *unconscious*.

Imago is one of its persistent and structuring traces; to understand it one needs to make recourse to the adjective *imaginaire*, but the imagination does not play a role as a faculty here.

"Marthe est possedée par *l'image* d'une mère suicidaire, alcoolique, defigurée par un accident. Dès notre premier éntretien cette femme m'a glacé."

The psychoanalyst has 'never' encountered a harder, more desperate woman, without any tie, if not of contempt. Marthe complains,

> but harshly, of 'the emptyness of her existence' and does not let one see anything live around her, or inside her. She seems instead to be possessed by a single fixed vision, a single immobile passion, eternalized, the image of this mother who seems *entirely* visible, and even more insofar as it has been her gaze that always attracted Marthe as a child: an empty gaze, in other words full of something which, as her daughter she would never have access to. Is there no other way out for Marthe than losing sight of her mother? To see her–and not to have her–in an absent presence? Is it necessary for the image in its obnubilating presence, to be erased and preserved in its absence?
>
> Marthe therefore, does not *imagine of, about* her mother. And the *imago* and the phantasms of her which, unbeknownst to Marthe, possess her and around which Marthe inaugurates and replicates the cipher of the drama of her own lived experience.
>
> That which Marthe *knows* and of which she *'harshly speaks'* is only the 'emptyness of her own existence'.[14]

Imaginaire qualifies the mode of representation, of re-presentation of/in the lived experiences, without implying a mental faculty that is specifically tied to it and by excluding implicitly any possibility of general definitions, of monocausal explanations starting with the invention of: the *Unconscious*.

Freud had had an intuition of its importance and difficulty when, against any approach which sought to exorcise by considering it only as a latent psychic content or as that which is not yet known, but is so potentially, he had always sustained its *only indirect* knowability through the analysis of traces: dreams and symptoms.

For this reason he had written: "The material for my hypotheses was collected by the most extensive and laborious series of observations. The decidedness of my attitude on a subject of the unconscious is perhaps specially likely to cause offence, for I handle unconscious ideas, unconscious trains of thought, and unconscious impulses as though they were no less valid and unimpeachable psychological data than conscious ones. But of this I am certain–that any one who sets out to investigate the same region of phenomena and employs the same method will find himself compelled to take up the same position, howewer much philosophers may expostulate."[15]

It was in and on this point that J. Lacan–the most reread by philosophers and psychoanalysts (also American) present at this Symposium, of the European psychoanalysts–had returned to Freud since his famous interpretation of the saying "*Wo Es war soll Ich werden*".[16]

And by now, after him, as Starobinski also remarks, in a more or less conscious manner "nombreux sont ceux qui recurrent aux effects de sens suscités par l'opposition *imaginaire* vs. *réel*. Sans rompre avec l'etymon séculaire, une nouvelle géneration lexicale vient de répartir d'une autre manière les oppositions differentielles".[17]

When, in the realm of philosophy, in the same period, this seems to resound as well, one could say, simplifying, in Starobinski's words, that now the attention of philosophers is directed to the status of the *image* without trying to situate the imagination in a set of more or less integrated and hierarchized faculties, as does, for instance, Paul Guillaume, when he underscores the difficulty of every attempt at general definition and resorts to a remark already proposed by Ribot[18], concerning the "sens du mot *image*" maintaining that the field of the imagination is difficult to circumscribe . . . in the sense that the image *increasingly detaches itself from perception*, increasingly develops on its own, *instead of being subordinated to it*.

He emphasizes a dynamic which takes one from the recognition of (or refusal to recognize) 'objects' to the evocation (or suppression) of memories which, with the necessary reservations, he calls the *reproductive (or destructive) imagination* , and, in this aspect, also constructive or *creative*.

However on the ambiguity of such a creativity a lot has been written since Freud's time.

From the boundless proliferation of this type of contributions[19], ambiguity emerges as the prevailing persistence to understand creativity as the production of 'objects' in the privileged areas of science and art.

'In the hellenic and judeo-christian tradition creativity is always and in any case based on an actual premise'[20] and, as such, also communicative.

Independently of this tradition one does not even consider the hypothesis of a non-working, unexpressed and improductive creativity, such as for instance, every contemplative stasis and many manifestations of non- or poor adaptation, which are, instead, creative par excellence, compared to the discomfort or oppression of the civilizing process.

In western cultures, moreover, being forced to metabolize the materials of an information that has by now become hypertrophic, depotentiates or impedes every psychic search and elaboration of energy, which, in an absolute sense, occurs only in the intrapsychic 'space'.

It is in the repeated listening and reiterated recuperation and elaboration of one's 'lived experiences' and desires that imagination and phantasy are, par excellence, creative, even if not, finally, either communicative or productive.

Psychoanalytic knowledges have stressed this aspect, unlike those philosophical knowledges, above all of idealistic ascendancy, which in various forms and with various modalities, have insisted prevalently or only on the aspects and the 'objects' expressed and transmitted through a communicative technique.

Their misunderstanding, 'along an unending chain of idle talk'[21], on their probably significative or signifying nucleus, continues: nucleus that remains irrecoverable, as is instead obvious for the psychoanalytic knowledges, because it goes back to a *preexpressive and unconscious* 'motivational' moment.

That which, starting with Freud, the psychoanalytic knowledges point to, is that, *every creativity that results from the imagination and phantasy is first of all connected to a lack of satisfaction of one's drives or to an, either active or passive, destructive drive, towards which it functions as autoremunerative or reparative indemnification.*

In his book *The legend of Timur* H. Papworth's intention is to question whether the miracle of Samarkand is Timur's (also known as Tamburlaine) work. It is not conceivable, the author writes, that a city of such beauty, where the structure directs man's mind towards mysticism and contemplation, could have been built by a cruel demon, a pillager and despot, such as Timur.

However one can not deny that what gives Samarkand its glory was built between the XIV and XV c.'s, in other words during Timur's reign. Timur's figure is one of the most surprising paradoxes of history. His name terrorized the people for decades. He was a great sovereign who kept Asia under his heel, and such greatness did not prevent him from taking care of the details as well. Timur attributed great importance to particulars. His armies were famous for their cruelty. Where Timur arrived, so writes the Arab historian Zaid Vosifi, blood gushed forth from the people as from a fountain and the sky had the color of a field of tulips.

Timur personally assumed command of his enterprises, he controlled everything. He had the conquered decapitated, and with the skulls he built towers, walls and roads, personally keeping an eye on the work.

> He had merchants' stomachs gutted to look for gold... He had opponents and adversaries poisoned, he himself preparing the brews.
>
> He brought death, a mission that absorbed half of his day.
>
> During the other half he *was captured by art.*
>
> Timur dedicated himself to the diffusion of art with the same passion that he devoted to the diffusion of death.
>
> In Timur's consciousness there was a very thin borderline between art and death, and this is precisely what Papworth does not understand.
>
> Yes, it is true, Timur decapitated, but it is also true that he did not decapitate everyone.
>
> He ordered those who possessed creative qualities to be saved.
>
> In Timur's empire there was no safer haven than talent: he attracted people of talent to Samarkand, pulled strings to get hold of an artist... Creators flourished and so did Samarkand. The city was his pride. On one of the doors he had the following inscribed: "If you doubt our might, look at our buildings" . . .
>
> Timur personally checked every construction. Those that had worked out badly he eliminated, he had perfect taste. He discussed the decorative variants, he took care of the delicateness of design and the purity of the lines. After which he dove back into... the slaughter, the blood, the fire, the screams . . .
>
> Timur's work can be summed up in a sentence of Saint-Exupéry's: "That which I did, an animal never would." . . .[22]

It is for this reason that a motivational analysis of 'creative' processes maybe in some way indifferent, if not extraneous, to the 'objects' expressed and, eventually, communicated, which it mostly considers as pre-texts or screens defensive of 'contents' to jealously subtract from a direct confrontation with the 'exterior'.

It is an encounter towards which there always seems to have existed, because of human *Hilflosigkeit*, a more or less frustrating precocious experience from which a sort of preventive disillusionment towards all subsequent experiences of socialization and/or communication, more or less intense, more or less conscious, was derived, which by now appears, first of all, as a frustrating menace.

The ideology of a creativity understood *tout court* as productivity, elevated to the power of value and become, therefore, competitive—which has dominated western, including not recent, culture—has moreover built a "pyramidal verticalism of the creative genius and the ensuing discrimination among artists-scientists and a large anonymous mass of common mortals predestined by a so-called 'poorly endowed' nature to live of reflected light, in other words in a resigned and deferent inferiority."[23]

From this one would want to infer, within the psychoanalytic knowledges, the consequent necessity to make use of parameters of judgement that eschew the tendency to rationalize and homologize every theory of the experiences of the imaginary, since, beneath the fortuitous variety of the epiphenomena, the free energy maintains equal potentialities and preexpressive valences among the resources of the *primary process*, whose inventive richness is, potentially, incomparable as compared to every productive experience, carried to its completion according to the technical modalities of communication and therefore in the sphere of the *secondary process*.

If these remarks could conclude with a speculative synthesis of a systematic nature—but this is not foreseeable, starting from the invention of the *Unconscious*—the published materials could be sufficient to determine some revolutionary deductions, if they were examined comparatively from an epistemological point of view.

Can one in the meantime consider precisely the awareness of the impossibility of taking stock of the question of the imagination as a major contribution?

Maurizio Bonicatti's observations, during this Symposium, then become particularly relevant, when he once again puts the sense and function of *imaginary* into question, making Freud and more generally psychoanalytic thought responsible for having forgotten something which still concerns the contemporary psychism, and in other words that *in the remote origin of the archaic psyche, the ideation of images did not presume a gratuitous use of the imaginary: images were created for rituals and for specific addresses*.

The image therefore—*ritually*—is not the reproduction of a prototype, *but an identification inseparable from it: therefore also idolatry, in other words cult of an appearance perceived as a real presence of a superior instance that is manifested in it*.

In the contemporary acception of idolatry, however, a misunderstanding of the etymon always creeps in which changes it—the Author warns—*into a cult of simulacra*.

That the imaginary could thereby become a synonym of illusion and psychoperceptual deception then becomes the most incumbent consequence, which would seem to cast its shadow on Freud himself and in most cases on all psychoanalytic thought.

It is therefore a question of continuously distinguishing image from image, illusion from illusion and keeping in mind that—as the Author believes—the epistemological disparity created by modern intellectualism regarding *primordial* experiences is measured by the incapacity to understand them by currently defining them as *primitive*, even in recent studies of a presumed scientific authoritativeness.

When one reflects on the function of *imaginary* and/or *fantastic* it will then be of no little import to be once again made aware of the fact that the experiences of our origins have not become heterogeneous and incomprehensible because of their archaicness: rather, because of the prevailing incapacity to escape from the schematic conventions of a civilization that mostly identifies totally with the present and is afraid of discovering its own precariousness and fragility outside of the frame of reference in which it considers itself inscribed.

This—significantly—appears to whoever comments and listens from beyond the ocean, as an illegitimate nostalgia for unknowable and by now unknown aspects of psychic reality, as in the words of Laurie Wilson: "I wonder if that very distance makes it impossible for any of us, including as erudite a scholar as Professor Bonicatti, from garnering the truth about the 'archaic psyche' ".[24]

But if one thinks of eras (for example the Pleistocene) or of lived experiences for which representability is the only means of communication or identification of and with one's visionary formations, immediately the complex and dramatic nature of the problem, of wanting to assign it a plausible meaning for systematic thought, becomes evident.

It can then happen, just as it does in actuality, that, for instance, mixed theromorphic morphologies, that in the archaic experience clearly dominate the zoomorphous taxa of the biome, can be marked as monstrosities.

In the same fashion the affabulation of fairy-tales remains, according to Maurizio Bonicatti, an archaic *Erlebnis*, by definition alienated and irrecoverable for the consciousness of contemporary man analogously to other intrapsychic 'matrixes' of which one is no longer 'cognizant'.

That which preserves a dynamic sense in each person's illusionism, cannot coexist with a demythologized thought, or better, with a thought for which each illusion becomes a synonym of the *non real*: at best it can subsist beneath conscious life and despite a civilizing process in which the dialectical presupposition true/false has established an authoritarian norm of thought, forcing every psyche infans (non talking) into a minority isolation which finds solidarity with the condition of animals because always 'infantile' (non talking), as Freud himself observed: "the gulf which men established later between themselves and animals did not exist for primitive people; nor does it exist for our children".[25]

And, as the Author provocatively and suggestively reminds us, not even for someone who, like Saint Jerome, wanting to undertake a monumental exegesis of the biblical texts, started by first of all bracketing his own doctrinal identity: then, in the three years of *anacoresis* passed in the Syrian desert of Chalcis, east of Antioch, the empathy which he established with the lion *does not take place through the domestication of the feline, brought to the ideal level of 'speaking' animal. It takes place because he re-discovers the primigenial condition in which the anthropos loses his uni-specific differentiation for the sake of integrating his roots with the wildness of other species: the never to be repeated equilibrium of Eden with the ecological system.*

Starting from the consideration of the Unconscious, the historian[26], who reflects on the 'split of the Ego in the unconscious processes of defense', poses this problem to the psychoanalytic approach in general, as to every form of knowledge: how the unconscious split cannot be controlled by the consciousness of the split, so every analogous event cannot be controlled by the historian's or anybody else's knowledge of it. In fact, the part of the writing–thinking I that is eventually split, just as it does not join the conversation (and doesn't know this) in the analytic setting, does not join the conversation (and doesn't know it) in the consideration and writing of history remaining repressed in the *Real*.

The *Real* is to be understood as the function introduced by J. Lacan, in other words as that which, for the subject, in his psychism, assumes a value of reality such that it eludes symbolization and imagination. It is essentially a question of *unconscious* desire and related phantasms.[27]

Is it these split parts, repressed and run off into the *Real*, that are really 'History', finally understood as every material and event which eludes symbolization and which—as repressed—tends to return when the defenses are weakened or fallen?

Is the writer of history only whoever can capture the return of such a repressed and de-scribe it as a hypothetical construction?

Even if a certain confusion is produced between whoever observes and whoever suffers/acts (psychoanalyst-patient, historiographer-history), between repression and foreclosure, Cynthia Chase remains convinced that the material of historiographic (as of the psychoanalytic) investigation is basically constituted of hallucinatory visions and experiences and by constructs *around* their relative *non discursive, opaque to consciousness, unbearable* contents.

The non symbolized, that constitutes the *Real*, would in short be the condition of impossibility of historical events and *therefore* of their historiographic consideration/construction.

However many of the observations that Cynthia Chase extracts from the idea of history as trauma (shock), seem, to Gianni Vattimo, to contain the risk of perpetrating the metaphysical attitude of the 'nostalgia of the origin'.

Is perhaps—writes Vattimo—*the very idea of history (historiography) insofar as it is based on a trauma, in its very foundation, the expression of a nostalgia of realism, origin, absolute beginning?*

Psychoanalytic hermeneutics has shown that—analogously to philosophical hermeneutics—the idea of origin, foundation, etc. has lost meaning.

In the idea of history as trauma, Vattimo senses a sort of realistic and objectivistic nostalgia.

The trauma is, in other words, still an image of 'origin' or of 'real' that resists.

Nietzsche, Heidegger and Freud, Vattimo again reminds us, opened the way for the recognition of the absence of meaning of 'origin', of *Grund*, of foundation, characteristic of foundational metaphysics, unmasking it in its violent and authoritarian character. Why on earth should one return to it?

According to René Major the function of reason (*ratio, logos, Vernunft, Grund*) is also complicated, in fact, *'since the unconscious', entirely displaced from the continent of consciousness to the archipelagus of the unconscious. Reason since Freud, then.*

By means of a thread which ties Freud, Wittgenstein, Lacan and Derrida together, if 'Es' thinks where 'I' am not, or where there is no Ego–Major reflects–this will not take place without committing desire in a very different and new fashion: if there is thought that can escape the illusion of thinking, it must certainly be on the side of the excess of desire, never definitely fulfillable.

Therefore, the importance of the work of the authors considered consists, for Major, in the tendency–even if formulated differently–to divest metaphysics and linguistics of the illusion that the signifier should correspond to a function of representation of the signified *or even respond of its very existence: for it's existence under the title of any signification at all.*

More particularly for Lacan and Wittgenstein–compared to the aporia represented by the non univocal correspondence of word and thing, or signified and signifier *by virtue of the arbitrary nature of the sign*–the necessity to suppress 'the question of reference', understood as a determination of the position of the signified, emerges.

The *non-correspondence of signifier and signified institutes a cut in the discourse* through which the 'subject' is inscribed as *discontinuity in the real.*

So, *the Unconscious from Freud according to Lacan would be a chain of signifiers which somewhere (in another scene) is reflected and insists on interfering in the cuts offered to it by effective discourse and the cogitation it informs.*

It is only in the in-between of these signifiers that 'a subject' can be still supposed: but in any case, the one that does the thinking, calculating and judging is not a 'subject': it's more la Jouissance.

This is why the role of the *possibility of figuration (Rücksicht auf Darstellbarkeit)* takes on special relevance: the attention in other words, to the means of stageing and with the awareness, by now, that the processes (also unconscious) that take place there are not influenced either by the relation with time, or by that with 'reality'.

One is dealing *with a production so originary, so idiomatic*, that it is capable *of scrambling all codes and outplaying all translations*, to the point that every graphic, pictorial, plastic or theatrical elaboration, with all its rules and tropes, could if anything seem a metaphor of it.

If the Ego therefore speaks in several voices of the constitutive and deconstitutive *desistance* of the subject, it is because the *dis-location of the subject brings with it a dis-locution of thought: this is also to mark the non-unicity of the unthought or of the unknown that an unconscious knowledge would speak and the non-unicity of truth, its disinstallation and unsealing in a de-steling (déstèlement), and to say the place where it masks itself on its stele.*

Doubling or disinstalling reason in all its modes of tension or appropriation of the non-proper is not an appeal to the 'subject's' irresponsibility, *but to another responsibility* that answers for its desistance and its dislocution and it is a saying of the reason of the unconscious as *anasemic reason of reason*.

What is more, Major reminds us, since it is *not something, Being cannot be said metaphorically*.

One cannot speak of it properly or literally, but only with a supplementary *trait* articulating the trace which Being's *retrait* will have left.

Pietro Bria and Sergio De Risio also agree on the centrality and complexity of the image and the imaginary, once they are considered within the psychoanalytic knowledges and are correlated with the function of the unconscious, psychic 'place' where *negation, doubt, degree of certainty would not exist. The processes of the system Unc are timeless, they are not ordered temporally, are not altered by the passage of time; they have no reference to time at all*, and all this within a psychic reality which, as in the words of Freud: *is extended: one knows nothing about it*.

What relation is then possible between an external reality rigorously contained within the normal four-dimensional coordinates (of space plus time) and an internal reality where space-time is so radically disconnected that, according to Freud, it disappears entirely?

According to the Authors, J. Lacan has answered by elaborating a sort of imaginary topology based on classic figures of general, algebraic and combinatory topology, such as the *Moebius Strip*, the *Torus*, the *Klein Bottle*, the *Cross-cap Sphere*, and the *Borromean Knot*.

These figures should allow the analyst to perceive the disconcerting presence of the Unconscious with greater ease and clarity, *supplying a 'visible' conceptual background, a rigorous reference for the imaginable, and allowing him or her to 'calculate' the effects*.

The thought of Matte Blanco would be situated, according to our Authors, in this crucial area. The Unconscious would be, first, a *system*, a *structure*: and would be no longer merely the site of repressed mental contents, but a group of structural laws that define a particular syntax for its contents.

This level of being one with the Other comes into conflict with the limits of the conscious thought that divides, separates and puts individuals in relation to each other.

This dimensional discarding–structural in the human–creates a tension that is destined to remain unsolved and is at the base of our symbolic creativity and of our particular mental suffering.

For Diego Napolitani, the imaginary universe is made of images, by which he does not mean simple mnemonic traces of sensible impressions, but configurations of relational complexes in which a 'subject' has been from the beginning of its existence, a constituent element. And where a 'subject' has instead become, according to the Author's definition, *Autòs: I use the term Autòs*–he writes–*for what E. Morin says/calls (1982) the auto-organizational component of the Self, a sort of 'author' of the human world's occurrence, who could be referred to that mysterious subject of autonomy and originality which Freud contrasted with the subject subordinated to his 'collective souls'*.

The Author thus transforms the sub-jectus into a pro-jectus: the subject in-process, which is the subject of its own original symbolic narration, into a, in one word, *aesthetic* subject. The *Autòs* can, in fact, reorganize the configurations of meaning that the imaginary function orders in its living archive as a function of its own existential transformation.

All this also implies that intimate transitional experience from sub-jectus to pro-jectus which may become a historical 'fact' or which may be denied, since this experience, opens an intolerably catastrophic horizon of freedom and solitude.

A counterpoint to the *Autòs*, for the Author, is what he calls *idem*, in referring to which he wants to talk, not so much of a conception, but of a preconception, of a configuration of meaning installed in it at its origins and confused with it, which remains outside recollection, time, every transformative dimension, every possible decay and death, since, because of its intrinsic ordering power the preconception cannot enter the circuit of symbolic responses, but dominates them by subordinating every other configuration of meaning.

Alan Bass dissents vehemently regarding the hypothetical construction of Napolitani, trying to show that Napolitani's interpretation, which seems obvious, is not so at all.

Its 'metapsychological' flavour would seem to reveal the seduction of the idealizing presupposition, that psychoanalysis consists of a peculiar and given pragmatic-cognitive order, exercising its influence on an unaware Napolitani; while Freud himself believed and declared that metapsychology represented a reconversion to the ideal of the scientist: a renewed submission to parental authority, to Prussian discipline.

Why would Napolitani need to–Bass asks himself–seduce us away from what Freud always said about metapsychology? And above all that the scientific foundation of every saying, theorizing, is, instead, only observation (1914)?

It is for this reason that Freud was ready, according to Bass, to compare metapsychology to metaphysics and mythology from the beginning to the end of his work, to the point of calling his theory of drives "my mythology".

Moreover, as Bass observes, Napolitani himself writes: "Freud himself gives us, in *Constructions in Analysis* (1937) a particularly suggestive example of his own metapsychological construction characterized by an invasive and hegemonizing thought, that inhibits his creative liberty as in those who are prisoners of their paranoid constructions.

Certainly Freud's tone is not that of someone who uses theory in a hegemonizing, homologizing, fashion: "If we are asked by what methods and means this result is achieved, it is not easy to find an answer. We can only say: 'So muss den doch die Hexe dran!'–The Witch Metapsychology. Without 'metapsychological' speculation and theorizing–I had almost said 'phantasying'–we shall not get another step forward".[28]

So, therefore, if Freud, towards the end of his life puts himself in the position of Faust when he is reasoning metapsychologically, his quotation from Goethe means, according to Alan Bass: "I know that metapsychology is my pact with the devil."

The point is that precisely because he wanted to be a man of science and could not have easily allowed metapsychology into his own conception, though Freud simultaneously found it necessary to do so, that he was ready to compare himself to Faust in his subjecting himself to Mephisto.

Certainly, Bass reflects, Freud thus declares his ambivalence in comparing the theoretical structure he had developed up to that point to a pact with the devil.

But Napolitani's interpretation, that for Freud metapsychology represents the rigid, paranoic certainty, that conforms to the ideal of science, seems inadmissible to Bass.

If anything Freud's gesture seems much more radical than Napolitani seems willing to grant: Freud would instead be an old, rather impenitent, Faust, practically completely detached from the paternal order, who still bargains with the devil.

In this way–Bass laments–Napolitani does not seem to consider that Freud's work *has done a lot to dissolve the subject-object opposition on which the opposition hermeneutics-science is based.*

Freud was simply consequential when he compared metapsychology to a mephistophelian witch whose alchemy would attenuate the distinctions between induction/deduction and fantasy.

Aldo Giorgio Gargani too–after Freud–accuses the despotic dominance of logicizing methods assumed by the constitutive processes of the dominant knowledge in the analytic terms of schemes, formulas and concepts that replicate in uniform and invariant manner, thus presupposing that everything can become known, that all answers are symmetrically coordinated to the questions and that thinking, calculating, knowing are all modes of *retracing tracks which have been forever traced.*

All this may, perhaps, fulfill the needs of certainty, or of an unambiguous style of thought which tries, in this fashion, to exorcise the terror of the new and the risk of the present, as if for an anguish of becoming.

One thus repeats oneself in the illusory but reassuring operation of relating one intelligibility to another already known one: the present to the past?

And yet–Gargani asks himself–is this repetition really the monotonous and invariant repetition of an identical content, as it is understood by 'common sense' and in a certain logicizing tradition?

Whether it is the constraint to repeat, or the repetitive schemas of a certain type of philosophy and epistemology, no, writes the philosopher, evoking from the psychoanalytic knowledges the function of *signifier* and of *other scene*.

It is then that, repeating oneself, one would intend procedures that no longer consist in 'doing the same thing'. But, on the contrary, they become constructive elaborations, a progression of further reactions and variants on a theme, new decisions as in the instance of that boy in the clinical case of the *Wolf Man* (1914) who fills one with dismay with his obsessions, but also with admiration because of the immense delirious structure which he built since pain entered his life, condemning him to repetition.

The philosophical work 'touched' by psychoanalytic work, is one in which, one step after the other, one asks for the radical ethical reflection within which a human being has to pitilessly come to terms with him/herself.

As for L. Wittgenstein, when he writes that the role of the philosopher is, properly, work on oneselves, on one's own conceptions, on how one sees things: to capture false images, to upset superstitious presuppositions, break with solidified schemas that crush us.

And, however, considering that it is not possible to write and/or think in a fashion that is truer than one is true: "one writes as much on oneselves as one is tall. Here we are not on stilts or on a ladder, but on bare feet".[29]

Philosophical theories would be, precisely, those stilts from whose fictitious elevation new fictitious ideals on life's circumstances, on linguistic practices, would want to descend: but theory and ideal models, even if necessary, do not respond but of themselves, and not of the circumstances of life, of experiences.

Psychoanalytic work—Gargani reminds us—highlights the illusory nature which overshadows the having/wanting to say something more elevated than one is oneselves.

Is renouncing such an impulse as difficult as restraining tears or anger?

The phantasm which the philosopher here evokes is that of pityless and radical research on oneselves, of the coming to grips with oneselves, while, on the 'table' of psychoanalytic knowledges, one performs the technical analysis of one's philosophical grammar.

However, in our opinion, because of the everpresent excess of unconscious, there is no analysis that does not residue—again—in an unaware factor, once again ready to be the implicit and silent 'origin' of other nonsenses, false problems, illusions and researches.

That which the philosopher does not seem to be able to accept, in his impassioned confrontation with the psychoanalytic knowledges, is the idea that *no* knowledge is meant to definitely end the false rationalizations, nonsenses, false problems, illusions and researches.

And so, as if possessed by a prescriptive god, he/she is not aware of prescribing a paradox: and namely that *the repressed element which generates nonsenses and intellectual discomforts, needs to be made manifest and self-evident.*

But the repressed element knows that no *have to* can be prescribed it: if, repressed, it returns, it is because it *can*, because of an unconscious, unpredictable and indomitable 'will'.

Then, the philosopher too, dazzled by too much light, could see that he has remained on stilts, and that the adjective 'pityless' which appears and reappears in his text is a signifier that pursues him and which has already outwitted him and won him, because, without his knowledge, it would display again the tragedy of a will disabled and unable—by definition and not because of a lack of courage—to descend into the depths of the problems of life and/or grammatical foundations?

In fact it is not he/she who *wants* who descends, just as it is not he/she who wants who becomes mad, as in the warning of J. Lacan to analyzers.

And this is what—fundamentally—describes a non-affinity of knowledges?

One, the philosophical, 'pityless', when it dictates that, whoever indulges in philosophical illusions, climbing on the stilts of philosophical theories, instead of descending into the depths of himself, is lacking in courage and is destined to remain false and superficial.

The other, the psychoanalytical, 'compassionate', while it recognizes that which, in the philosopher, dictating voluntaristic intentions and idealizing models, once again illudes him.

However, the philosopher had also written: "I think I can sum up my position with regards to philosophy by saying: properly philosophy should only be *composed poetically* . . . and I have thereby also recognized that I am someone who *does not completely manage to do what he desires.*"[30]

And yet, once one has dropped—as Wittgenstein wished—the philosophical superlanguages, there would no longer be the need to evoke terms such as 'unmask', 'unveil', to arrive at that which 'really' or 'pitylessly', is?

As viewed by Richard Rorty, as he reflects on Gargani, already this adverb 'really' (and/or 'pitylessly') is still, once more *a hang-over from those superlanguages.*

Rorty is not interested in that which *really* is, but in that which is *better*, or rather, more *useful.*

As applied to Freud, he gave us a set of tools for describing ourselves and we have found them useful. But he did not substitute health for madness or reality for appearance, nor did he once again formulate truth *as an object, as a determinate presence.*

But Rorty, the philosopher, talks from the side of consciousness, of notions, of concepts of which he thinks he can serenely and ironically dispose, when they *have turned out to be more useful for some of our purposes*: what is more, what consciousness, concept or notion can ever exist *out of the practices to which it contributes*?

However, outside whose practice?

The philosopher implies and takes for granted, a subject that is simply an 'us' (*us*), and which, thus posed, seems to be, once again, a *truth as an object, as a determinate presence*, presupposed and not founded, does it not?

To the pathos of one corresponds the imperturbable rationalization of the other: but both have denied or repressed the fact that, at the heart of the psychoanalytic knowledges, the '*us*', the '*I*', the '*subject*', the '*people*' that they take for granted, are dissolved.

Thus, it sounds reductive and unintelligible, to capture the dialogue with the psychoanalytic knowledges as an *impersonal libidinal hydraulics . . . useful for doing other things such as linking the agent's actions up with certain biological or neurological facts about her*.

And it sounds selfdeluding to say: *there is no tension to be overcome*.

Moreover, dis-tension is not more useful than tension, when one cannot confront them as such.

What there is or is not to be overcome, what one should or should not be or do: is this not really a vain appeal in the name of ideas or opinions ? For example, that one should be coura geous, that one should pitylessly descend into the depths of ourselves, or that there is no tension, no drama to be overcome?

Joel Whitebook is busy with the issue of the status and the function of the subject that Freud, demonstrating that the Ego is not in charge in his own house, has put into question again.

He asks himself what 'the precise significance' of the decentering of the subject is. And he sees this question embedded in a larger controversy, tied to the destiny of the Enlightenment and to the complex relation that Freud would have had with it, as an 'apollinean explorer of the dionysian' and in the wake of the kantian formulation, critical of traditional, dogmatic, paternalistic and heteronomous authority.

Considering that: *maturity in the Kantian sense of thinking for oneself presupposes separation from one's parents . . . in the deep intrapsychic sense of relinquishing one's libidinal ties to incestuous objects, Whitebook thinks that, analogously, Freud's dictum–Where*

Id was, there should Ego become–can be taken as a programmatic statement for the Kantian move from eteronomy to autonomy.

He thus implies–before considering the game within which J. Lacan had instead interpreted the Ego's destiny as it's possibility of returning *there where the Es was*–the conception of an Es as a foreign internal territory, primitive, unreflected and an agent of an ultimately menacing heteronomous determinism.

But, is it not precisely according to J. Lacan that Freud's 'copernican revolution' consists in the "subversion of a psychoanalytical notion of the Ego . . . vis à vis the Unconscious, which means that the Unconscious, or the subject of the unconscious . . . and not the Ego constitutes the core of our being (*der Kern unseres Wesens*)"?[31]

And why has this provoked *such powerful resistances that later analysts have continually been tempted*–according to Whitebook–*to recoil from this utterly subversive discovery and to rehabilitate the pre-analytic Ego, and in other words a centered, self-present and transparent Ego*, which only with difficulty could do justice to, or at least account for, the other, understood both as different, and as Other.

It is for this reason, Jacqueline Mehler Amati reminds us, that J. Lacan, rereading Freud, refused to ally himself with this deceitful and deceived Ego, and rather addressed, so to speak, the unconscious *through the interpretation of dreams, the play of words, the parapraxis, etc.*

For Mehler, however, there is still a Freudian term to employ so as not to *counterpose* the Ego to the Es: reconciliation (*Versohnung*) that appears to be a mechanism *of acceptance of repressed material, and a regulating principle of the whole complex psychic system mediating between reality and fantasy.*

But not as a function of the Ego, but rather as a principle specifically connected to the functioning of the whole psychism that "does not necessarily function in the service of progress or growth".[32]

What seems very interesting is therefore that, in this sense, *reconciliation* can lead to a cure, but also to a state of equilibrium with illness becoming a part of the whole personality.

For Martin Jay also, in the light, or the shadow, of the psychoanalytic knowledges, seeing with the eyes of an 'I see' becomes suspect leading to the paradoxical warning of J. Lacan—and on which he founds his own hypothesis of a crisis of oculocentrism having taken place—"The eye is maleficent. In the Bible and the New Testament there are no good eyes but evil eyes all over".[33]

Thus, before all others, it is really Freud and his special attention to representation (*Rücksicht auf Darstellbarkeit*) that dreams recommend to, please, close both eyes, or, at least, to close one.

It is precisely around this node that, according to Jay, the fundamental attitude towards vision on the part of budding psychoanalysis is organized.

Later J. Lacan would radically reformulate it as "antivisual".

Yet, and Jay reminds us, Freud was a born observer and raised at the school of extraordinary and admired observers (*visuels*) as was, for instance, his teacher Charcot.

However, if for this reason Freud remained an 'Enlightener', also in Jay's eyes, he also appears the most aware of the limits of such an episteme and of its 'oculocentric' premises.

His thought, therefore, remains sufficiently distant from that of a 'visuel' like Charcot, so much so as to constitute, for the French thinkers and psychoanalysts who looked up to his thought, an indispensable point of reference for their critique of the absolute predominance of the eye.

What is more Freud was the most explicit in pointing out that even the profoundest exegesis of dreams needed to confront itself with a *blind spot: the navel of the dream.* A place that was going to be left dark there where it pushes "towards the unknown".[34]

Some modes of presentation of the 'evil' eye and of its speculative violence, with subsequent pathogenic consequences in lived experience, seem therefore to be established for Jay's reflection: from scopophilia to blindness, from pathological narcissism to the complex of intrusion, from the con-fusion of oneself with one's specular image, to the scotomization of sight, and in other words to foreclosure.[35]

In Jay's reflection the thread of the voyage into the 'evil eye' occurs all around both the tie of psychoanalysis to Jewish iconoclasm and to the idea of J. Lacan when, in his return to Freud, he takes the antivisual and antimimetic aspects of the thought of the Master to their extreme consequences through his own formulation of the 'mirror stage' as formative of the function of the Ego.

Jay reminds us of the initial and special attention to the study of paranoia, probably also because of the suggestion of a teacher such as Clairembault, in whose clinic the cult of observation reached paroxysm. Clairembault spent his life perfecting his eagle's gaze, manipulating and observing sickness without ever listening to it and reserving for himself the last and most dramatic 'visual act': having lost his sight in old age, he decided to commit suicide by shooting himself in the mouth in front of a mirror.

In his will he had even left his eyes to be examined by any interested scientist.

Jay's reflections remain problematic however, when they finally aim at establishing a primacy of word and language over the image, which does not seem either authorized nor derivable from Freudian thought, nor, in fact even less so, from Lacanian thought, if one only deepens the sense of Lacan's comment on Freud's saying "Wo Es war, soll Ich werden", with regards to which, among other things, he asked himself what demon had inspired the author, whoever it was, to translate it into French in these terms "Le moi doit déloger le ça: the Ego must dislodge the Es".[36]

On the refusal and overturning of this translation which by now sounds "Where Es was, there should Ego become", Lacan also founds the peculiar meaning of his own return to Freud and, as one knows, all his thinking around the function of *Other*, understood as "celui que nous sommes forcés d'admettre au délà de la relation du mirage, celui qui accepte ou se refuse en face de nous, celui qui à l'occasion nous trompe, dont nous ne pouvons jamais savoir s'il ne nous trompe pas, celui auquel nous nous adressons toujours".[37]

Jay's explanation of the formation of a secondary identification that supplants the primary one, based on a specular projection, in the mother–child relationship, remains reductive, when it does not take into account the fact that the Other has already before intervened in the mother's desire.

One cannot seriously believe that the father's 'no', as a spoken act, can by itself bar the son's desire in her regards: that he may accept, or better, intercept, the condition of his own desire as infinite, in other words never definitely exhausted, does not seem to depend as much on the 'no' spoken by the father, as rather on the mother's non answer to his calls, when she is occupied "a répondre à son conjoint".[38]

In other words the mother–son dyad has a structuring sense for him only if the mother is also a woman, in other words if she maintains and continues to express interests and investments towards adults that are her peers and in particular, the physical and emotional attraction (real, imaginary and symbolic) towards her partner.

Jay's faith that *in sum, only when the unconscious functions like a language and not like a mirror can the healthy subject, split and introjecting the other rather than projecting itself on to it, be achieved* thus proves to be problematic and schematic.

In fact, Freud's thought, as that of J. Lacan, even though it remains, as Jay indicated at the beginning, in many ways still tied to the Enlightenment, does not defend itself from the contradictions and enigmas that are born as a result of a close confrontation with therapeutic practice and experience, since it tends above all not to throw itself, as Wittgenstein would have said, against the limits of language.

In this can be captured that richness and novelty which should by now impede generalizing and homologizing theories as results and games of a rationalizing function that requires unification, coherence and comprehensibility from *every* material of experience and which does not hesitate, in its name, to produce false coherences.

Jay's conclusion to his reflections which he draws with the words of J. Copjec that *Semiotics, not optics, is the science that clarifies for us the structure of the visual domain* and this precisely because the field of vision *is neither clear nor easily traversable* does not end up being convincing. *It is instead ambiguous and treacherous, full of traps*, if it is true, as Jay himself writes, that *the gaze I encounter . . . is not a seen gaze but a gaze imagined by me in the field of the Other* and that, as in the words of J. Lacan, "desire as unconscious–man's desire is the desire of the Other".[39]

The diabolical capture by the evil eye therefore seems, rather, the loss of belonging to the Other and of the memory of the Other, to be understood, lacanianly, as the only antidote to the reifying split of one's self-image in the image of oneself in the mirror: therefore alienation of one's image into the other, reflected, one.

It is in this circumstance that "the evil eye operates as the *fascinum* . . . which has the effect of arresting the movement and, literally, of killing life".

Notes

1 J. Starobinski, *En guise de conclusion*, p. 581 in *Phantasia Imaginatio. Atti del V Colloquio Internazionale del Lessico Intellettuale Europeo*. Roma, 1986. For the linguistic uses of Imagination and Phantasy cf. also: S. Battaglia, *Grande Dizionario della Lingua Italiana*. Torino: UTET, 1961.

2 E. Zolla, *Verità segrete esposte in evidenza*. Venezia: Marsilio, 1990, p. 69.

3 M. Fattori, *Phantasia Imaginatio*, Introduzione agli *Atti del V Colloquio Internazionale del Lessico Intellettuale Europeo*. Roma, 1986, pp. I-XXX.

4 E. Garin, *Phantasia Imaginatio tra Ficino e Pomponazzi*, in *Atti*, cit., p. 5.

5 J. Starobinski, cit., p. 571.

6 M. Fattori, cit., p.XXXIV and J. Starobinski, cit., p. 565.

7 E. Montaigne, *Essais*, I, XXVI, it. ed. Milano: Mondadori, 1970, p. 174.

8 J.J. Rousseau, *Discours de l'inegalité*, in J. Starobinski, cit., p. 567.

9 J.J. Rousseau, *Emile*, in J. Starobinski, cit., p.568.

10 M. Jay, ibid., pp.

11 J.J. Rousseau, *Emile*, in J. Starobinski, cit., p.570.

12 J. Starobinski, cit., p.576.

13 J. Laplanche and J.B.Pontalis, in J.Starobinski, cit., p.178.

14 J.B.Pontalis, *Perdre de vue*, pp.231-48, in *Nouvelle Revue de Psychanalyse*, Paris: Gallimard, 35, Printemps 1987. Cf. also J. Lacan, *Al di là del principio di realtà* in *Ecrits*, Italian edition by G. Contri, Torino: Einaudi, 1974, p. 82: ". . . we will reveal the inspired use that he <Freud> made of the notion of *image*. And even if, with the designation *Imago*, he did not fully isolate it from the confused state of common intuition, he however made masterful use of its concrete capacity . . . discovering the process of *identification* in experience: a process very different from that of imitation, characterized by its form of partial and groping approximation, identification is opposed to it not only as global assimilation of a structure, but as virtual assimilation of the development implied by that structure in its still undifferentiated state." (*translation by M. E.*)

15 S.Freud, *Fragment of an analysis of a case of hysteria*, S.E., VII, 113. What is more, Freud was aware that "Probably very few men can have realized the momentous significance for science and life of the recogni-

tion of unconscious mental processes" as he wrote in 1917 in *A difficulty in the Path of Psychoanalysis*, S.E., vol. XVII, p. 143.

16 J. Lacan, *Ecrits*, ed. cit., pp. 407-8, 417 and note, 519, 580 note, 803, 845, 860.

17 J. Starobinski, cit., p. 579 and cf. J. Lacan, *Lo stadio dello specchio come formatore della funzione dell'Io*, pp. 87 and ff. and *Al di là del principio di realtà*, in *Ecrits*, ed. cit., pp. 67 and ff.

18 J. Starobinski, cit., ibidem.

19 M.Bonicatti, R.Ferretti, A.Panza, M.L.Proietti, *Per una critica motivazionale all'antropoanalisi della creatività*. Roma: Bulzoni, 1978, pp. 9-14, and M.L.Proietti, *La 'cosa' poetica e il cammino verso sè in M. Heidegger*. Roma: Bulzoni, 1984.

20 M.Bonicatti, *Per una critica . . .* cit., p.16.

21 M.Bonicatti, cit., pp. 18 sgg.

22 R. Kapuscinski, *Imperium*.Milano: Feltrinelli, 1994, pp.72-73. Cf. also M. de M'Uzan, *De l'art à la mort*.Paris: Gallimard, 1977.

23 M. Bonicatti, cit., p. 38.

24 L.Wilson, *Comment on Maurizio Bonicatti's: The Primordial, the Fantastic, the Imaginary: new observations on Freud's thought*, ibid. pp. 45 and ff.

25 S. Freud, *A Difficulty in the Path of Psychoanalysis*, S.E., Vol. XVII.

26 C.Chase, *Psychoanalytic History*, ibid., p. 3.

27 J. Lacan, *Ecrits*, ed. cit., above all pp. 7, 8, 22, 28-9, 48, 49, 50, 143-4, 269, 375-90, 457-8, 546, 650-1, 643-5, 666, 667.

28 S.Freud, *Analysis terminable and interminable*. 1937. S.E., vol. XXIII.

29 J.L.Wittgenstein, *Culture and Value*. Oxford, 1980, p.33.

30 J.L.Wittgenstein, op. cit., p.24.

31 J.Lacan, *Ecrits*, ed. cit., pp. 513, 521, 582.

32 J.Mehler Amati, S.Argenteri, J.Canestri, *La Babele dell'Inconscio*. Milano: R. Cortina, 1990, and ibid. p. 157 and ff.

33 J. Lacan, *Les quatre concepts fondamentaux de la psychanalyse*. Paris: Seuil, 1973, ed. A. Sheridan, New York, 1981, pp. 118-119.

34 S.Freud, *The interpretation of dreams*. 1900. S.E., vol. V.

35 Scotomization: from σκοτος: darkness, obscurity. In the visual field it is a *lacunar* defect caused by a lesion of any point of the optic system. In the course of the signifying chain, J.Lacan will call this analogous disturbance *foreclosure*: the Freudian *Verwerfung*, translated in Italian by Giacomo Contri with: *preclusione*, translation which he justifies as follows: "We preferred *preclusione* to other terms (such as *reiezione, rigetto, ripudio*) since it is the one which corresponds to foreclosure in juridical terminology, and which designates an impeding situation which prevents the subject of a right from exercising it. The recourse to juridical terminology is not rare in Lacanian usage. The preclusion with which we are dealing is that of a key signifier . . . which does not manage to occupy the place it deserves in the unconscious. Psychosis is tied to the preclusion of such a signifier." In *Ecrits*, ed. cit., p.7. In the same text see also pp. 171, 180-1, 527-79 and by the same author, *Les Psychoses*. Paris: Seuil,1981. Cf. also J.Laplanche and J.B.Pontalis, *Vocabulaire de la Psychanalyse*. Paris: PUF, 1967 and S.Freud, *The Psychoanalytic View of Psychogenic Disturbance of Vision (1910), S.E., Vol. XI.*

36 J. Lacan, *Ecrits*, ed.cit., p. 580 and note.

37 J. Lacan, *Les Psychoses*. Paris: Seuil,1981.

38 F. Dolto, *La difficulté de vivre.* Paris: Carrère, 1986, p. 135.

39 J. Lacan, cit. in M. Jay, cit., ibid. p. 169 and ff.

Editor's Note

Thank you!

To Gianclaudio Macchiarella, who wanted this event to take place; to my son Francesco, for the happiness and strength that were his gift to me; to the impatient patience of Margherita Repetto; to Michael Moore, for having reviewed the 'language' of all texts with agile competence; to the extraordinary and unforgotten intuition of Mrs. Richard Bernstein; to Mark Epstein's 'faithfulness' in translating me; to Joanna Kaczinska for her fine listening.

Maria Letizia Proietti
University of Rome "La Sapienza"
June 1994

Acknowledgements

It has not been the easiest of enterprises to organize this Conference, bridging Europe and the United States, on philosophical and psychoanalytic themes as fundamental as they are often complex and controversial.

And yet it has been a genuine cultural experience, one in which you confront your limits and aspirations daily, to the point that, when everything is finished . . . you feel a certain nostalgia about it. These Acts are then, perhaps, a final farewell. Or, hopefully, the beginning of some other 'thing'.

The idea for the Conference was Maria Letizia Proietti's, the Editor, who traced its fundamental outlines and followed its development, and editing its Acts that we now present, preceded by a more than interpretive essay on the debate that took place here during the days of the Conference, and of that, ideal debate that preceded, accompanied and followed it.

My colleague Margherita Repetto, with her robust competence, was always at my side in the daily task of elaborating and mediating between the different positions vying for attention.

I think we are all indebted to the wisdom and humanity of Prof. Richard Bernstein, Chair of the Philosophy Department at the New School, who steered us into port without too many shocks. We are also very grateful to all the other Members of the Steering Committee and to the Academic Sponsors, for the great commitment they showed, through significant acts or decisive advice, in helping the realization of this rare encounter.

Neither the Conference nor these Proceedings would have been possible without the financial support of the Italian Ministry of Foreign Affairs. Our most heartfelt thanks go to the enlightened availability of the private sponsors: the SIGMA-TAU Foundation in Rome, the "Villa Pini d'Abruzzo," Clinic for Mental Illness and the Istituto dell'Enciclopedia Italiana, particularly its Vice President, Prof. Vincenzo Cappelletti.

New York, July 1994

Gianclaudio Macchiarella
Director of the Italian Cultural Institute in New York (1988-1991)

About the Editor

Maria Letizia Proietti is Senior researcher of History of Art Criticism at the Department of Art History and at the Department of Philosophical and Epistemological Studies of the University of Rome "La Sapienza."

Her formation includes extensive studies in Art criticism, Philosophy and Psychoanalysis at the University of Paris I (Sorbonne) as well as at New York University.

She is also a member of the roster of the Italian psychologists, and of the Italian psychotherapists.

Among her publications are: *Lettere di Claude Monet*, Roma: Beniamino Carucci, 1974; *Per una critica motivazionale all'antropoanalisi della "creatività,"* Roma: Bulzoni, 1977; *La "cosa" poetica e il cammino verso sè in Martin Heidegger*, Roma: Bulzoni, 1985; *Quando l'elaborato grafico o pittorico diventa un doppio persecutorio*, Milano: Sipiel, 1987; *Figure della differenza in margine a Nietzsche e Derrida*, Roma: Lithos, 1995; *Figure del destino in Martin Heidegger e Friedrich Hölderlin*, Roma: Bagatto, 1995.

About the Contributors

Jacqueline Amati Mehler achieved her medical degree in Buenos Aires and specialized in Psychiatry and in Child Neuropsychiatry at Harvard University. She is a member of the "Società Psicoanalitica Italiana" and for several years she was a member of its Executive Committee. Among her essays on psychoanalysis are: "Sessualità maschile e transfert," Londra: Weekend Conference of the Società Britannica, Oct. 12-14, 1984; *Rivista di Psicoanalisi*, XXXI,1; "Oggetti transizionali, fenomeni transizionali e area transizionale," *Rivista di Psicoanalisi*, XXXI,3, 1985; "Polylinguisme et polyglottisme dans la dimension intrapsychique," *Revue Francaise de Psychanalyse*, 2, 1988; "Hope and Hopelessness. A Technical Problem?" *International Journal of Psychoanalysis*, 1989.

Alan Bass is a Ph.D. at John Hopkins University. He has an intense activity as a member of study groups in Psychoanalysis (among many: Chair, Study Group on Current Trends in Psychoanalytic Thought, sponsored by N.Y.C.P.T., Member of the Interdisciplinary Colloquium on Psychoanalysis and Literary Criticism). He has published many books and essays on Philosophy and Psychoanalysis and annotated translations of Jacques Derrida's works: *Writing and Difference*, Chicago: University of Chicago Press, 1978; *Positions*, 1981, *Margins of Philosophy*, 1982; *The Post Card: From Socrates to Freud and Beyond*, 1987.

Maurizio Bonicatti is currently Full Professor of History of Art Criticism at the School of Humanities of the University of

Rome "La Sapienza." He is also a psychologist at the "Istituto di Formazione in Psicoterapia Analitica" (Training Institute in Analytic Psychotherapy) in L'Aquila, Italy.

Since 1982 Professor Bonicatti serves as Editor-in-Chief of the serial publication *Esperienza prelogica e pratica terapeutica* (*Prelogic Experience and Therapeutic Practice*), published in Milan, Italy, by Nuova Italia-Sipiel.

Among his many publications, Maurizio Bonicatti is the author of *Il caso Vincent W. Van Gogh*, Torino: Boringhieri, 1977 and of *I "sogni letterari" nel mondo classico–Un' interpretazione freudiana*, Firenze: La Nuova Italia, 1995.

Pietro Bria has a degree in Medicine and Surgery and a specialization in Psychiatry. Former Professor of Psychiatry at the School of Medicine of the "Università Cattolica del Sacro Cuore" in Rome, he also taught Clinical Psychiatry at the School of Specialization in Psychiatry. He is Associate Member of the "Società Psicoanalitica Italiana." His area of interest spans from clinical and therapeutic research to the epistemology of psychiatric science and psychoanalytic theory. Bria has published works on the clinics of psychosis and neurosis, the methodology of psychotherapeutic treatment, the nature of emotional processes, and the psychoanalytic theory of the mind. With respect to the latter, he contributed to Ignacio Matte Blanco's theory of bi-logic and edited with an introduction the Italian edition of Matte Blanco's work *L'inconscio come insiemi infiniti.*

Cynthia Chase is Professor of English at Cornell University since 1988 and is member of the Executive Committee of the MLA Division on Comparative Studies in Romanticism and the Nineteenth Century. Her publications include: "The Ring of Gyges and the Coat of Darkness: Reading Rousseau with Wordsworth" in *Romanticism and Language*, ed. Arden Reed, Ithaca: Cornell University Press, 1984; *Decomposing Figures: Rhetorical Readings in Romanticism*, Baltimore: Johns Hopkins University Press, 1986; "Anecdotes for Fathers: The Scene of Interpretation in Freud and Wordsworth" in *Textual Analysis; Some Readers Reading*, ed. Mary Ann Caws, New York: Modern Language Association of America, 1986; "The Witty Butcher's Wife: Freud, Lacan and the Convergence of the Resistance to

Theory" *MLN*, December 1987; "Primary Narcissism and the Giving of Figure" in *Abjection, Melancholia, and Love: The Work of Julia Kristeva*, ed. John Fletcher and Andrew Benjamin, Warwick Studies in Philosophy and Literature, London: Routledge, 1990.

Sergio De Risio has a degree in Medicine and Surgery and a specialization in Psychiatry. He is Professor of Clinical Psychiatry at the School of Medicine of the "Università Cattolica del Sacro Cuore" in Rome. He is Associate Member of the "Società Psicoanalitica Italiana" and a Member of the "Società Gruppoanalitica Italiana." He is also a Full Member of the American Group Psychotherapy Association. Professor De Risio has published several scholarly works on psychosis, and on the theory and clinical methods of group psychotherapy. De Risio's studies have also focused on problems related to the psychoanalytic concept of the mind and on a comparison between the thought of I. Matte Blanco and of J. Lacan.

Aldo Giorgio Gargani is Full Professor at the Department of Philosophy of the University of Pisa, Italy. He is a member of the "Österreichische L. Wittgenstein Gesellschaft" and of the "Wissenschaftskolleg zu Berlin." Professor Gargani has carried on an intense activity in conferences and seminars in Italy and abroad, both in Europe and in the U.S. His areas of resarch include the philosophy of the XVII century, logical positivism and analytical philosophy, as well as philosophy of language (with particular reference to the theories of Ludwig Wittgenstein and the philosophical schools of ordinary language of Oxford and Cambridge). He has been concerned with some central topics of the recent debate in contemporary philosophy in Europe and in the United States (Nelson Goodman, H. Putnam, R. Rorty), as well as with the significant and emerging connection between philosophical method and literary criticism. Gargani has also carried out extensive research on the Viennese and Central European culture with particular reference to E. Mach, S. Freud, H. Von Hofmannsthal, A. Schönberg, R. Musil, F. Kafka, I. Bachmann. He is the author of many publications, which include among others: *Hobbes e la scienza*, Torino: Einaudi, 1971; *Introduzione a Wittgenstein*, Bari: Laterza,

1973; *Il sapere senza fondamenti*, Torino: Einaudi, 1975; *Language and Community of Life in Wittgenstein's Later Philosophy*, Vienna: Hölder-Pichler- Tempsky, 1985; *Lo stupore e il caso*, Bari: Laterza, 1985; *Friction and Thought*, in *Recoding Metaphysics*, Evanston, Ill.: Northwestern Univ. Press, 1988; *Regard et Destin*, Paris: Éditions Du Seuil, 1990.

Martin Evan Jay is Professor of History at the University of California, Berkeley since 1982. Recipient of several awards for his publications, Martin Jay is the author, among others, of the following books: *The Dialectical Imagination: A History of the Frankfurt School and the Institute of Social Research*, Boston: Little Brown and Co., 1973; *Adorno*, London: Fontana Modern Master Series; Cambridge, Mass.: Harvard University Press, 1984 and of numerous studies published by international specialized magazines. Among these: "The Textual Approach to Intellectual History" in *Fact and Fiction: German History and Literature, 1848-1924*, Karen J. McHardy, ed., Tubingen; "Ideology and Ocularcentrism: Is there Anything Behind the Mirror's Tain?", in *Intellectuals and Politics: Social Theory beyond the Academy*, Charles Lemert, ed., Newbury Park, CA: Sage Publications, 1990.

René Major has a degree in Medicine, with a specialization in Psychiatry and Psychoanalysis. He is former director of the "Institut de Psychanalyse" in Paris and President of the "Societé Internationale d'Histoire de la Psychiatrie et de la Psychanalyse," Director of the "Programme au College International de Philosophie," and Editor-in-Chief of "Cahiers Confrontation," published in Paris by Aubier.

Among the many books and essays he has authored are the following: *Le discernement. La psychanalyse aux frontiers du droit, de la biologie et de la philosophie* , Paris: Aubier Montaigne, 1984 and *De l'éléction. Freud face aux ideologies americaine, allemande et sovietique*, Paris: Aubier Montaigne, 1986.

Diego Napolitani has a degree in Medicine and a specialization in Psychiatry. He has been an Associate member of the Italian Psychoanalytic Society since 1963, a full member of the Group Analytic Society of London from 1980 to 1985. He is the Co-Founder and formerly President of the "Società Gruppoanalitica Italiana." Dr. Napolitani founded and headed two therapeutic community centers for psychotic patients, from 1964 to 1976. Besides publishing several essays in French and Italian scholarly journals, he has written: *Di palo in frasca. esperienze transizionali dai fatti quotidiani alla relazione analitica*, Milano: Corpo 10, 1986; *Individualità e Gruppalità*, Milano: Boringhieri, 1987.

Richard Rorty is Kenan Professor of Humanities at the University of Virginia since 1982. He was visiting professor at Pittsburgh, Catholic University of America, at the University of California at Santa Barbara, at Frankfurt and Heidelberg. He also served as President of the Eastern Division of the American Philosophical Association. He has published numerous books translated into many languages. Among them: *Consequences of Pragmatism*, Minneapolis: University of Minnesota Press, 1982; *Contingency, Irony, and Solidarity*, Cambridge, Ma: Cambridge University Press, 1989; *Objectivity, Relativism and Truth: Philosophical Papers I*, Cambridge: Cambridge University Press, 1991; *Essays on Heidegger and Others: Philosophical Papers II*, Cambridge: Cambridge University Press, 1991; *Verité et Solidarité: Le Pragmatisme ou la Philosophie sans Authorité*, Paris: Éditions de l'Éclat, 1991.

Gianni Vattimo is a well known, leading Italian philosopher. He has focused on the crisis of historicism and the great philosophical systems of the nineteen century. As a result of his intellectual insights into the correlation between hermeneutics and the recent American pragmatic issues, he published (among others): *Ipotesi su Nietzsche*, 1967; *Introduzione a Heidegger*, 1971; *Il soggetto e la maschera*; *Le avventure della differenza*, 1980; *La fine della modernità*, 1985. Such a diversified contribution has culminated in the proposal of more tolerant rationality, coupled with an effective and concrete individual commitment in daily life. Said approach, reflected in his contributions to daily papers and to philosophical publications, such as "RES," inspired his next works: *Il pensiero debole*, 1983, edited with P.A. Rovatti: *La Società trasparente*, 1990. He also has translated, with comments, numerous texts of primary importance to philosophers around the world: Schopenhauer, Bergson, Heidegger, Lowith, Gadamer, Apel, Bleicher, Derrida, Rorty, etc. Professor Vattimo currently teaches Theoretical Philosophy at the University of Turin, Italy and is the editor of *Rivista di Estetica.*

Joel Whitebook is a Faculty member at the Department of Philosophy of the Graduate School of the New School for Social Research, New York. He is a member and supervisor of the Metropolitan Institute for Psychoanalytic Psychotherapy, the Associate Editor of *American Imago*, and *Telos*, and supervisor of the Clinical Psychology Program of the City University of New York. Beside numerous scholarly publications and essays, he has recently published *Perversion and Utopia: A Study in Psychoanalysis and Critical Theory*, MIT Press.

Laurie Wilson is Professor of Art at New York University where she directs the Graduate Art Therapy Program. She has published widely on Art Therapy. As an art historian, she has written a book on Louise Nevelson and a monograph on Alberto Giacometti.

SESSION I

Chapter 1

Reading Disavowal: Psychoanalysis and the Construction of History

Cynthia Chase

How much of the history of psychoanalysis, and of history-writing, is the history of disavowal disavowed?

Freud begins his very last article, "The Splitting of the Ego in the Process of Defence," in a curious way.

> I find myself in the interesting position of not knowing whether what I have to say should be regarded as something long familiar and obvious or as something entirely new and puzzling. But I am inclined to think the latter. I have at last been struck [he continues] by the fact that the ego of a person whom we know as a patient in analysis must, dozens of years earlier, when it was young, have behaved in a remarkable manner in certain particular situations of pressure. We can assign in general and somewhat vague terms the conditions under which this comes about, by saying that it occurs under the influence of a psychical trauma. (*S.E.* 23:275)

Freud describes himself in a peculiar position here in relation to his own understanding. He describes himself as having "at last been struck" by something: as registering with a start, as if it were a blow or a jolt, a "fact" of the reality disclosed in an analysis, a "fact" about the past that it supposedly makes manifest. This fact—the splitting of the ego, the very agency supposed to compel psychical unity—only now imposes itself as the explanation for the patient's behavior in analysis. It is as though Freud's belated acknowledgment had to struggle against a disavowal like that involved in the splitting of the ego itself, the disavowal of an impression that occurs as a trauma, a cognition intolerably at odds with "a powerful instinctual demand" or wish. Freud had to contend with a powerful wish for the integrity of the ego and for the integrity of the *concept* of a psychical agency defined by the "synthetic function of the ego" he describes as "of such extraordinary importance" (*S.E.* 23: 277). That wish would have operated like a new edition of the child's disavowal of castration, like another version of the child's wish for an invulnerable bodily integrity unendangered by the shattering pleasure of *jouissance*: it would have motivated Freud's disavowal of a perception and inference that now "at last" take place with a force something like that of the past "psychical trauma" he infers. It is as though the fact that the ego's synthetic function can be "disturbed" presents itself as a "trauma," like the possibility of a mortally wounding blow.

Freud's description of his deferred cognition of the phenomenon of splitting therefore repeats, in another respect as well, the phenomenon he goes on the describe, since his awareness of the phenomenon leaves him still uncertain of its status—uncertain, he says, whether it is something that has been known to him, already something "long familiar and obvious" within the parameters of psychoanalytic investigation, or on the contrary "something entirely new and puzzling." The article's opening paragraph suggests that, like "the patient in analysis," he has maintained and still maintains "two attitudes . . . side by side": that the splitting of the ego is and that it is not consistent with long-established psychoanalytic knowledge.

My reading of these two opening paragraphs does not aim to establish that Freud the theorist, like the patient he goes on to describe, adopts the fetishist's solution to an unacceptable reality. It aims rather at something Freud's opening gives us to read, a disturbing "fact" about psychoanalytic knowledge: that being "struck" "at last" by a piece of that knowledge does not mean that one knows its status, or knows whether one had it before or not, and thus knows the extent to which one's own knowledge is implicated in the splitting ego's strategy of simultaneous acknowledgement and disavowal. Freud's text implies that splitting cannot be mastered by the knowledge of splitting.

What makes the splitting of the ego so disturbing or ambiguous a phenomenon that it provokes this delayed and am-bivalent characterization on Freud's part—as "something long familiar and obvious" from psychoanalytic observation, as well as "puzzling and new"? Whence the uncanniness of this "fact" about the ego in analysis? And a remarkable feature of Freud's final article is that defense against psychical trauma by means of the splitting of the ego is here given a radical generality: it is said to characterize not one sort of patient, but "the ego of a person whom we know as a patient in analysis." What analysis as such discovers, or constructs—so Freud would belatedly register—is the history of a splitting of the ego.

If Freud's recognition of the splitting ego repeats the gesture he describes, this may have to do with disturbing implications for the possibility of treating the transference-neurosis. These, would mean disturbing implications for history writing, as well: trouble for the writing of history that interprets the past with a view to affecting the future. In "Analysis Terminable and Interminable" (1937), "alterations of the ego" are called fundamental obstacles to completing an analysis. The "rift in the ego" (*S.E.* 23:276), the detachment of a portion of the ego from reality, deprives the analyst of his collaborator and interlocutor. For the historian, the phenomenon of splitting implies that the current conception of the past, with which he has to work, embodied in institutions and discourses that necessarily bear upon the historian's own practice, constitutes in unpredictable ways not only a disavowal of crucial elements of the historical past but the converse of the very symbolization of reality, the "symbolic abolition" (Lacan, 388) of crucial conditions of discourse or experience. Establishing the history of a splitting of the ego—the model of history-writing that psychoanalysis offers—raises difficulties which emerge dramatically in the history of one such construction: in the history of the Wolf Man case. This involves at least three case histories of disparate status: Freud's, from 1915 and 1918; Ruth Mack Brunswick's "Supplement," from 1927; and Nicolas Abraham and Maria Torok's extraordinary book of 1976, *Cryptonomie: le verbier de l'homme aux loups* (published in English as *The Wolf Man's Magic Word*), the history of their own *rehearing* of the case through a multilingual reading of the Wolf Man's recorded words. It is the last swerve in the history of the case, that I will want especially to stress, to reflect on the conception of historical experience implied in the remarkable reading practice its authors derive from an example of multilingual reading in Freud, drawn from his article on the most observable instance of ego-splitting: fetishism. Already, the first case history of the Wolf Man, Freud's, brings to the fore difficulties for historiography. "From the History of an Infantile Neurosis" comes to focus on the question of the phenomenal status of the trauma—the question of the Wolf Man's recollection or fantasy of the primal scene. Addressing that question of the ego's history turns out to be inseparable from addressing such history-writing's history: Freud places the question of the status of the primal scene in the context of his conflicts with Adler and Jung over the significance of the castration complex and "the importance of the infantile factor". Throughout its history, the Wolf Man case history carries with it the most disconcerting implications, of Freud's emphasis on an actual belatedly traumatic event (the sight of the parents' copulation) and of his construal of a traumatizing fantasy. Freud's highly deliberate non-decision between these alternatives—"I intend on this occasion to close the discussion of the reality of the primal scene with a *non liquet*" (*S.E.* 17:60)—insists on and accepts the peculiar character of the knowledge of history allowed by the concept of trauma. The consequences of the child's psychical trauma are summarized in a passage in which what will become the notion of the splitting of the ego, and its bizarre implications for the nature of "knowledge," are fully apparent. The Wolf Man "rejected (*verwarf*) castration," Freud writes (*S.E.* 17:84), then explains that the phrase must be understood in two ways. The child "repressed [castration]," yet later, in a "second reaction which did not *do away with* the first," he "recognized [it] as a fact." Then, from this split structure another splitting splits off: in another and stricter sense, Freud goes on, the word *verwarf* describes "a third current, the oldest and deepest, which did not as yet even raise the question of the reality of castration" (*S.E.* 17:85). Freud's wording evokes the omission of the very conditions of integration into psychical reality.

The nature of repudiation or disavowal described by Freud remains ambiguous, however, because of the dubious status of what it is disavowed, the "reality" of "castration." The lucid commentary of Laplanche and Pontalis suggests that this "disavowal of reality," common to "the child, the fetishist, an the psychotic," is the refusal to accept . . . what?—not a perception but a theory, castration being a theory, an "infantile sexual theory," albeit one privileged by Freud as a crucial mode of access to "reality" (Laplanche and Pontalis 1973, 168). This elucidation of "foreclosure" or disavowal is worth bearing in mind as one takes stock for instance of those indictments brought by new historicist literary historians against writers of the Romantic and Revolutionary period for their "disavowals" of history. Such "disavowal" would then be simply the refusal to accept a concept of history tantamount to the castration theory as an infantile sexual theory. It would mean a refusal invariably to think in terms of a narrative of loss and endangerment derived from a highly interpretive "perception" of absence dependent on its binary opposition to the presence of a significant trait.

Lacan resolves the ambiguity of Freud's account of disavowal by reconstruing it as belonging to a "primary process" made up of two complementary operations, "the *Einbeziehung ins Ich*, introduction into the subject, and the *Ausstossung aus dem Ich*, expulsion from the subject." Lacan calls the first of these operations "symbolisation"; the second" constitutes the Real inasmuch as this is the domain which subsists outside symbolisation" (Lacan, 388). The category of the Real radically reorients the notion of "reality" in Freud's text. Whereas Freudian "reality" is constituted by "symbolizing what ought to be symbolized (castration)," in Laplanche and Pontalis's revealing paraphrase (Laplanche and Pontalis, 168), the Real is what can enter psychical experience only through hallucination. "What has been foreclosed from the Symbolic reappears in the Real" (Lacan, 388). Disavowal would then be a mode of access to, as well as defense against, "history"—now construed as that which eludes symbolization. According to Freud, what eludes symbolization is once again castration, or more literally, the possibility of one's own dismemberment. Freud cites Wolf Man's recollection of his hallucination at age five—"I had cut through the little finger of my (right or left?) hand, so that it was only hanging on by its skin" (*S.E.* 17:85)—and concludes strikingly: "We may . . . assume that this hallucination belongs to the period in which he brought himself to recognize the reality of castration and it is perhaps to be regarded as actually marking this step" (*S.E.* 17:85). This is no less than an acknowledgment of hallucination as a mode of recognition of reality, a move Freud will make once again in another text we shall examine, his 1937 paper "Constructions in Analysis." Thus the first installment in the history of the Wolf Man's case histories, Freud's 1915 text, already brings into play the difficulties posed by the hypothesis of *Verwerfung* or disavowal for the construction of the history of a subject or the history of experience and interpretation. "From the History of an Infantile Neurosis" is perhaps chief among the texts in which Freud sketched the idea that would recur to him as "new and puzzling" in 1949 in "The splitting of the Ego."

Abraham and Torok's construction of Wolf Man's infantile history necessarily takes place inseparably from their reinterpretation of his case histories. In Freud's 1927 essay on "Fetishism" they descry an unidentified allusion to Ruth Mack Brunswick's treatment of Wolf Man for (as she had written) "a hypochondriacal *Idée fixe*" about his nose (Brunswick, 264). It is Freud's prime example of the selection of a fetish.

> For obvious reasons the details of these cases must be withheld from publication; I cannot therefore show in what way accidental circumstances have contributed to the choice of fetish. The most extraordinary case seemed to me to be the one in which a young man had exalted a certain sort of "shine on the nose" into a fetishistic precondition. (*S.E.* 21:152)

Freud's text goes on to explain that the fetish was the nose; but that it had come to be so could only be understood by hearing the patient's words—"*Glanz auf der Nase*"—not in German but in English, the language he had spoken with his governess as a child, and thus hear them as "glance at the nose" rather than "shine on the nose," the words' translated meaning. Through this extraordinary passage, Freud's and Abraham and Torok's altogether disparate interpretations of this case touch. Freud here shares the procedure of multilingual decrypting, that Abraham and Torok will employ, whereas they depart entirely from his centering on the fear of castration, Abraham and Torok note: "Freud grasped the verbal mechanism of the fetish and its metapsychological import in this particular case: 'The Mother has no phallus'" (32). To them the mother's lack of a phallus means precisely her lack of the father's phallus because "he deprived her of it by diverting his desire elsewhere" (32) in sexual play with Sergei's elder sister, a scene she would have replayed for her younger brother. The little brother verifies her account with adults; and it is the scandal following this event–*that* danger, not castration–that motivates the Wolf Man's singular way with words. It motivates his repetition, all but indecipherably reinscribed, of the magic word *tieret* (to rub), productive of the father's or rather of the little brother's pleasure. The primal scene is a scene between the father and the sister which truly *takes place* in the *replay* that impels the decisive disaster: a dialogue (whose words Abraham and Torok decrypt in the dream of the wolves) in which the Wolf Man's identity as witness to this scene (which he first recounts to the governess) threatens the family with scandal–at his mother's appeal, the Wolf Man suppresses and silences forever the words in which his desire is lodged. The social, legal, institutional character of this catastrophic situation contrasts with the perennial, natural, transhistorical Freudian primal scene of parental intercourse. In Abraham and Torok's rehearing of the Wolf Man, his history turns, like "history," on a conflict of power within an institution (here, the family).

Yet their reconstruction of a specific, contingent episode at the origin of the illness keeps faith with the profound historiographic imperative of Freudian analysis, present independently of the polemic with Jung and Adler when Freud defends his hypothesis of the Wolf Man's childhood recollection–rather than fantasy–of an actual specific scene of parental coitus *a tergo*. Freud's defense of his hypothesis of the actual occurrence of a specific primal scene is not, I think, simply a theoretical regression, a literalistic insistence on discovering an origin in an external event. Its insistence needs to be heard as the obscured responsiveness to an enigma, to the enigmatic fact, fundamental to psychoanalysis, of the status of words as *events*.

The "fact" of a dream (or of the *Verbal mechanism* of a fetish); the fact of the existence of a dream-text: these *words* are the event from which Freud's interpretation starts, and

Abraham and Torok start there, too. But by exercising a reading *technique*—the multilingual listening Freud practiced in hearing *Glanz* as "glance"—they arrive at a radically new interpretation of the role, in the Wolf Man's history, of words. "It is not a situation *including* words that becomes repressed; the words are not dragged into repression by a situation. Rather, *the words themselves, expressing desire, are deemed to be generators of a situation that must be avoided and voided retroactively*" (Abraham and Torok, 20; their emphasis). Whence the elaborate lexical operation legible in the words the Wolf Man speaks, exercised upon the word itself rather than on the meanings they represent. The effect is both to stifle and save, mutilate and repeat, words that *in themselves constitute* the catastrophic satisfaction of desire or the event of its prohibition and burial. The operation consists in displacement to a lexically contiguous meaning, to its synonym, and to the synonym's translation or inversely its homonym in another language. An unpredictable combination of lexical, semantic, and aural displacements encrypts the original "magic word" in an inscription by its apparent intelligibility as part of a discourse that invites the full gamut of psychoanalytic interpretation. Here is one example among many, atypical insofar as Abraham and Torok's decrypting for once takes fewer steps than Freud's. The Wolf Man reports his feeling of terror as a child on the occasion of seeing a swallow-tailed butterfly open and fold its wings. This memory is linked by Freud to an early castration threat from a nursemaid, Grusha, whose name is the same as the name for a certain sort of striped-not-butterfly, but a pear, also recollected by the patient (*S.E.* 17:90-1). Abraham and Torok hear in the English name of the butterfly (which his patient of course spoke to Freud in German) the words "Swallow the tale": "*Cry out? No! I must swallow it. . . . I swallow the tale* (of the tail)." What is tragic within this tale is that my desire must be eradicated within myself (Abraham and Torok, 45). Thus within a richly multidimensional text the relics of an entirely other drama appear.

Abraham and Torok's hypothesis of a traumatic danger constituted by certain words could be seen as a new way of understanding the peculiar "more radical" "flight of the ego" taking place in that more untreatable condition than the neuroses:

schizophrenia, the strangeness of its symptom due to "the predominance of what has to do with *words* over what has to do with things" (*S.E.* 14:200). As Freud writes, "What has dictated the substitution is not the resemblance between the things denoted but the sameness of the words used to express them." Whereas in dreams what is subjected to the primary process are the "thing-presentations to which the words have been taken back," in schizophrenia it is "the words themselves in which the preconscious thought was expressed" that are so manipulated (*S.E.* 14:201, 229). Freud, in these passages, presumes the priority of "thing-presentations" or "preconscious thoughts" over words, conceived as their expressions or representations. Abraham and Torok instead conceive of words as *forces* "generating" a catastrophic situation which therefore will have to be undone by work upon the words themselves. The symptom Abraham and Torok call cryptonomy takes its origin in a particular *kind* of danger rather than, as Freud suggests (*S.E.* 14:233), in the radical *degree* of the ego's withdrawal from an insupportable reality. Their hypothesis would be profoundly pertinent to the reinscription of history that we can assume informs historical or literary texts. Texts reinscribe traumatic social change inhering in the production of discourses composed in crucial part by precisely, words—change "generated" by words, to the extent that ideology rather than economics impels the disjunctions that make up historical time, historical event. Abraham and Torok's hypothesis would imply that the displacements and "disavowals" that psychoanalytically informed deconstructive and new historicist critics have been learning to construe are in fact supplemented and undercut by encrypted repetitions and undoings of historical catastrophes lodged for the archive (which must mean, at some point identified by individuals who write and speak) in words that have to be silenced.

Abraham and Torok's construction of encrypted words intensifies an imagination of words as the *generators of situations* which is monumentalized in Freud's concept of the transference. Freud of course came to locate the difficulty—if also the hope—of analytic treatment in the fact that the analyst uses language to repeat rather than recollect and represent. Ruth Mack Brunswick conceived her work with the Wolf Man as treating symptoms of Wolf Man's unresolved transference onto Freud. Abraham and Torok take up the complications of the treatment and the concept of transference posed by Freud's distinction between mourning and melancholia, between the introjection and the incorporation of a lost object. The piecemeal, painful work of mourning introjects the desire that linked one to the person lost, reintegrating it, dissolving it, into the self. The spell of melancholia incorporates the lost other within the self when and because one cannot introject the desire, make it newly one's own, and also in order not to have to dissolve it. Wolf Man suffers a melancholia brought on by the impossibility, the prohibition, of symbolizing his loss of those who are his objects of love as exemplars of the fulfillment of desire, his sister and his father.

Since Wolf Man's desire must neither be fulfilled (since its expression has been identified with the catastrophe of the family's destruction) nor sacrificed (which cannot be done without a substitution, that is, a symbolization), its objects are incorporated or encrypted in "an inside heterogeneous to the inside of the Self" (Derrida 1986, xvi)–a sort of crypt or closed-off passageway. Wolf Man's melancholia is an *Ichspaltung* of a kind in which there is no transference in the usual sense, no address to the analyst that is simultaneously an address from the infantile self to the loved object. The patient's relation to the analyst does not repeat his own relation to a former loved object; instead it covertly replays the imaginary relationship *between* the incorporated objects: Freud is the father, his patient is the sister. Abraham and Torok postulate: the Wolf Man "'repeated' nothing of his own. He was simply not himself. He *was* his sister" (write Abraham and Torok (75). The apparent transference only camouflages an imaginary rapport between incorporated objects that precludes the patient's utterance of the words embodying desire. Yet in the production of the cryptonyms, there does take place a form of writing that "manages somehow to pass over the heads [of the incorporated guests] and address external Objects" (21), that include the possibility of being read. The difficulty is that the two modes in which the repetition of the past takes place are thoroughly heterogeneous and mutually contradictory, occurring at incompatible levels and coming from two different positions or "selves." One repetition (itself unrecognized) blocks out the other. If the outcome of a traumatic loss of libidinal objects is incorporation, the premise that analysis can proceed through treatment of the transference breaks down.

As "the work of the only authentic area remaining in an alienated ego," the cryptonymic procedure deserves, as Abraham and Torok suggest, "the respect due any attempt at *being* in spite of everything" (21). One could put its significance in another way: as an unmitigated outcome of the conflict between representation and enactment—between the semantic, cognitive, constative dimension of language and its performative status, its ability to "do" something (in the first instance, simply to occur at all). The production of a sign breaks with the given array of significations, interrupts relationship and meaning. The words the Wolf Man swallows and encrypts have this disruptive force. The word *tieret* embodies the threat to meaning posed by a sign that signifies by the *event* of its production (the event of maximum libidinal "pleasure"), not by referring to a signification. The threat to the conditions of meaning posed by the endangerment of the position of the father, in the scandal inaugurating Wolf Man's illness can be seen as secondary to or as a figure for this "linguistic predicament." By the fact that it is a quotation, the Wolf Man's "magic word" *tieret* has another dimension that exemplifies the paradoxical condition of the performative power of words that Derrida calls "iterability." Only as repeated and repeatable does the "event" take place. A sign's or an event's identity depends on being iterable, quotable; this means that its meaning or identity is never whole or complete. This lack of self-identity of the sign appears conspicuously in the Wolf Man's story in the lack of a moment when the word *tieret* spoken for the "first time," carried its libidinal charge or performative force. It has force as an "event" only as a quotation. The Wolf Man's cryptonymic procedure seeks to meet the contradictions of these fundamental conditions of (im)possibility. The composition of the hidden "rhymes" corresponds with the imperative both to produce and not to produce the mark in which is vested the very force of language to occur, the very possibility of an inscription or mark, and at the same time the interruption and potential destruction of language's capacity to mean.

Freud's writings on the transference thematize the tension between the cognitive and performative aspects of language as the tension between the patient's "impulse to remember" and his "compulsion to repeat." "The patient *remembers* nothing of what is forgotten and repressed, but . . . he expresses it in *action*. He reproduces it not in his memory but in his behavior. . . . As long as he is under treatment he never escapes from this compulsion to repeat; at last one understands that it is his way of remembering" (*S.E.* 12:150). Repetition can be assimilated to remembering insofar as it can be construed as a mimesis of past conditions in some sense addressed to the analyst to behold and comprehend. Freud's texts oscillate between this notion of memory and a more performative one. The same essay more explicitly describes the transference on the one hand as a continuation of the patient's illness–"we must treat his illness, not as an event of the past, but as a present-day force" (*S.E.* 12:151)–and on the other as an "artificial" illness, "conjured" into existence by the analyst's resisted insistence on recollection. The analysts' work is described not as inducing the patient to resume recollection (an aim thereby implicitly acknowledged to be impossible), but rather as enforcing the view of the patient's statements *as* actions that are repetitions, that are, in effect, representations, thus "tracing [the illness] back to the past" (*S.E.* 12:152), even while it is lived through by the patient "as something real and contemporary." This sort of recuperation of repetition is undercut dramatically in the remarkable final sentence of "The Dynamics of the Transference": "For when all is said and done, it is impossible to destroy anyone *in absentia* **or** *in effigie*" (*S.E.* 12:108). The *reality*, as actions, of the patient's repetitions is central to the opportunity they offer for the treatment: the opportunity not to transform performed actions into cognitive content as representations, but rather to enact new outcomes of scenarios carried over from the past.

Neither of these models of the analyst's task–straight cognition or straight "performance," action–would meet the necessity of dislodging the Wolf Man's incorporated Objects, the "guests," whose conflicts he plays out in his present relationship, especially with the analyst. Doing away with them would involve the peculiar process described by Benjamin in an introduction to his translation of Baudelaire's *Tableaux Parisiens*—"The Task" (or "the giving up": *die Aufgabe*) of the Translator." As Paul de Man puts it: for Benjamin, translation "kills" the original "by discovering that it was already dead" (de Man 1986, 84). Freud refers to "destroying" destructive or pathological affective structures, an unsurprising aim for psychological treatment; de Man, however, refers to killing the object that translation is usually thought to value and to aim to preserve: the original text. Such a seemingly perverse or pessimistic account of translation derives from an estimate of "the original" as a structure without integrity, like the psychoanalytic conception of the "origin" of a psychical illness—not an intrinsically meaningful event, but the deferred action of an initially insignificant occurrence lent "meaning" retroactively. Translation, de Man argues following Benjamin, has to do with "what in the original belongs to language, and not to meaning as an extralinguistic correlate susceptible of paraphrase" (84). Benjamin is evoking the translator's engagement with individual words and syntactical structures—the text's devices for the production of meaning—instead of with the meaning inferred from the text (and experienced as the identity of the text) at its reception. From this perspective, the notion of "the original" delusorily conflates and identifies the production and the reception of a text. The disjunction between the syntax and the semantics of a text, the incommensurability between its devices and its meaning, makes for an ultimate "giving up" of translation, renders translation impossible.

The original is "already dead" in the sense that it consists in "language" that does not contain its meaning and "meaning" that does not inhere in its language. This is the case, too for those performances of a relationship between his incorporated objects (the father and the sister) that are Wolf Man's substitute for a transference. Those performances, the Wolf Man's exchanges with his analyst, are merely the means or pretext for the mechanics of the production of the magic word; its significance does not inhere in them. Such a situation invalidates standard assumptions about treating the transference-neurosis—above all, the expectation of gaining access to the original illness through interpreting the interpersonal bearing of the analysand's present discourse.

"Killing the original by finding it already dead": what de Man's strange formula *does* readily describe, unlike the canonical (and pious) view of translation (including the translation of the transference back into the terms of the past), is the work of mourning. This is the analyst's task confronted with a melancholia such as the Wolf Man's incorporation of his father and sister. Freud writes of the bitter work of melancholia, "Just as mourning impels the ego to give up the object by declaring the object to be dead and offering the ego the inducement of continuing to live, so does each single struggle of ambivalence loosen the fixation of the ego to the object by disparaging it, denigrating it and even as it were killing it" (*S.E.* 14:257). But what if ambivalence–say, the tension between rapt pleasure in and aggressivity toward the primal scene–strengthens rather than loosens the fixation, sustains, as in the Wolf Man's case, the structure of the crypt? In place of melancholia's work would have to come a killing" by finding already "dead": devalorizing the significance of the "original" scene, demystifying the father's pleasure, crime, and endangerment, through a disclosure of the limited, illusory validity of "the juridical code that permitted the [English] nurse's blackmail in the first place," that rendered the father-daughter scene a crime. The patient's freeing from fixation on the incorporated objects and the "original" structure of their relationships could happen through a process as Abraham and Torok's peculiar labor of "translation," which is also the renunciation of translation: their attention to the material elements of the *language* of the illness, not to its reception or ostensible meaning (i.e. what is understood by Freud and by the Wolf Man who accepts his interpretations) nor finally even to the *latent* "meaning" of Wolf Man's exchanges with his analysts, the replayed scenario of seduction and prohibition. For the nucleus of the illness is not the illicit asymmetrical sexual relationship, but rather the attachment of explosive force to certain words. An analysis concentrating on the peculiar labor of "translating" the reinscriptions finds the original characters (in both senses) "already dead" by disclosing what in them belongs to language, after all, "and *not* to meaning." Considering texts from the perspective of "the task of the translator" involves attention to their materiality in a way that is profoundly congruent with psychoanalytic theory, and particularly with reflections around the motif of "trauma." *Nachträglichkeit* (deferred action), the syntax of psychical trauma, of experience subjected to repression, is one version of the disjunction between "language" and "meaning," between the production and the reception of an experience or text. Another way of thinking about trauma, which arises very early in Freud's thought and recurs very late, is the model of a psychical apparatus combining separate systems for perception and consciousness and for memory. Freud's speculation on the origins of life, in an organism for which *warding off* is far more important than receiving stimuli, leads to the counterintuitive notion of consciousness as a "defensive shield" or "screen." This line of thought's implications for the historiographical status of literary and other texts, its consequences for a conception of how history impinges upon writing, were explored by Walter Benjamin in "On Some Motifs in Baudelaire" (1972, I.2: 605-654; 1969, 155-200). Benjamin focuses on some remarkable assertions in *Beyond the Pleasure Principle:*

> On the basis of impressions derived from our psychoanalytic experience, we assume that all excitatory processes that occur in *the other* systems [than the perception-consciousness system] leave permanent traces behind in them which form the foundation of memory. Such memory-traces, then, have nothing to do with the fact of becoming conscious; indeed they are often most powerful and most enduring when the process which left them behind was one which never entered consciousness. . . . (*S.E.* 18:24-5)

The limits set upon "the system's aptitude for receiving fresh excitations" by retaining "permanent traces" suggest that any "excitatory process becomes conscious in the system *Cs.* but leaves behind no permanent trace there; . . . the excitation is transmitted to the [other] systems and it is in *them* that its traces are left" (*S.E.* 18:24-5). These inferences thus "lead one to suspect," as Freud writes, "that becoming conscious and leaving behind a memory-trace are processes incompatible with each other within one and the same system" (*S.E.* 18:25).

Where an impression was conscious it leaves no record, and where it leaves a record, it was never conscious: strange inspiration for a theory of history, but it accords with Benjamin's conception of history in terms of shock or trauma. Unlike Bergson, who "rejects any historical determination of memory," Benjamin describes a writing which "has as its basis an experience in which shock experience has become the norm" (Benjamin 1969, 157, 162). "On Some Motifs in Baudelaire" sketches how Baudelaire exemplifies and thematizes writing as a form of consciousness, as the parrying of shocks. In its own resolute negativity, Benjamin's essay resembles Freud's "Papers on Technique." "On Some Motifs in Baudelaire" should be read with "Constructions in analysis" as an account of how historiography may proceed in conditions in which consciousness and recollection fail.

The key image in Benjamin's description of these conditions is Baudelaire's figure of "M.G.," a portrayal of his friend Constantin Guys in which Benjamin's reading also describes Baudelaire himself, engaged in the "fantastic combat" of "parrying" impressions (Benjamin 1969, 163-4; Baudelaire, 553). Guys was a draughtsman who produced pictures and sketches of such ephemera as Parisian fashions, performances of opera and ballet, travels in Spain and Turkey, and episodes in the Crimean War. Painting or writing is here consciousness as shock defense, *preventing* impressions from entering the (involuntary) memory by *noting* them as they occur. These images do not attain nor aspire to the fullness of recollection or the past recaptured. They are dating notes. The more efficiently consciousness screens against stimuli, Benjamin writes, "the less do these impressions enter experience (*Erfahrung*), tending to remain in the sphere of a certain hour of one's life (*Erlebnis*). Perhaps the special achievement of shock defense may be seen in its function of assigning to an incident a precise point in time in consciousness *at the cost of the integrity of its contents*. This would be a peak achievement of the intellect; it would turn the incident into a moment that has been lived (*Erlebnis*)" (Benjamin 1969, 163; my emphasis).

Crucial in this description is the impoverishment, abstractness, reductiveness, of what counts as (psychical and aesthetic) achievement; it should not be obscured by the misleadingly positive sound of the word *Erlebnis*. Baudelaire's attention to consciousness parrying shocks can be found in a different form in a shrewd and suggestive recent account by Robert J. Lifton of "traumatic syndrome," the "compulsion to repeat" in survivors of accidents or combat that Freud addressed in *Beyond the Pleasure Principle.* Lifton describes it as the state of being haunted by images that can "neither be *enacted* nor cast aside" (Lifton, 172; my emphasis). Lifton locates the origin of the accident neurosis in "the gap between image and enactment" (172) and much of his book *The Broken Connection*, is given to arguing for the significance and value of feelings of guilt about such a disjunction, not because the survivor is really guilty, but because his sense of guilt reflects his commitment to humanistic values and a norm centrally including the assumption of *continuity* between "image and enactment," "feeling" and knowledge" (Lifton, 175), perception and cognition, "language" and "meaning." What is made clear by Baudelaire's essay, however, is that this norm reflects an *aesthetic* ideal, or rather a mistakenly idealist conception of the aesthetic. His text both evokes and decisively undoes an operation of consciousness that is at once an action and a work: human being as *the* work of "art." This operation of consciousness is rather of the order of M.G.' sketches or notations, dating impressions they reduce rather than restore: premised—like Freud's model of the "psychical apparatus"—on the *non*-integrity of perception, on the disjunction and heterogeneity between the impression and its knowledge.

Benjamin reads Baudelaire' description of M.G.'s sketching as an account of the successful functioning of the "shock defense": operation of *consciousness* rather than memory, though Guys draws, of course, from memory. (Baudelaire's essay describes him as *looking* during the day and drawing at night.) Yet we need to read this as a description—not only an allegory—of the functioning of consciousness "itself." Benjamin's interpretation as "consciousness" of the frenetic sketching of M.G. has the same significance as Freud's conception of the psyche as a writing machine in "Note upon the Mystic Writing Pad" (*S.E.* 19:227-234)—namely, that consciousness in Freud's conception, is always already supplemental, technical, a material process. Stressing "the disincarnation and reduction of meaning" that consciousness entails—its way of assigning an incident a precise point in time "at the cost of the integrity of its contents"—brings out the close proximity between "presence" or "presence of mind" and its "incomplete substitutes" (*S.E.* 23:283): notes, writing, the sketches or notations of others.

It brings out the proximity between the successful operation of the shock defense and the measures that must meet its failure: the *constructions*, to which Freud concedes a crucial role in a psychoanalytic reconstrual of the past. The historiographer, for Benjamin, is a figure like M.G., or like the analyst confronted with the bizarre, abstract "images" in which the patient repeats his past (hallucinations, rebuses, scenes that stage magic words). "History in the strict sense," he writes,

> is an image from involuntary memory, an image which suddenly occurs to the subject in the moment of danger. The historian's credentials rest on a sharpened awareness of the crisis that the subject of history has entered at any given moment . . . Historiography . . . has to test its presence of mind in grasping fleeting images. (Benjamin 1972, 1.3: 242-3)

Techniques for producing schematic sketches of what "suddenly occurs" (the image, as much as the traumatic incident, "occurs to" the subject of history): such are the resources of the historian; and the artist, "the painter of modern life," the subject of history fully "present" to historical experience, has no resources of another order (more immediate, natural, or complete).

Such would be the reasons for what Freud puts aside as another issue "for a later inquiry" in "Constructions in Analysis":

> Quite often we do not succeed in bringing the patient to recollect what has been repressed. Instead of that, if the analysis is carried out correctly, we produce in him an assured conviction of the truth of the construction which achieves the same therapeutic result as a recaptured memory. The problem of what the circumstances are in which this occurs *and of how it is possible that what appears to be an incomplete substitute should nevertheless produce a complete result*—all of this is material for a later inquiry. (*S.E.* 23:266).

The construction is a schema or a figure; it is in this way, *like* the image achieved by consciousness and like the recollection that association in the absence of resistances may produce.

"Constructions in Analysis" introduces an "analogy" between two sorts of texts, constructions and delusions, both of which include hallucinatory memories and an attempt to contextualize them. "The delusions of patients appear to me to be the equivalents of the constructions which we build up in the course an analytic treatment–attempts at explanations and cure," writes Freud, and further, "Just as our construction is only effective because it recovers a fragment of lost experience, so the delusion owes its convincing power to the element of historic truth which it inserts in the place of rejected reality" (*S.E.* 23:268). The persuasive power of the construction is a function of the power of disavowed impressions to return and of the totalizing tendency that extends their felt authenticity to contiguous elements of the analyst's discourse. Freud's theory of the disjunction between consciousness and memory here shows its power as a dialectical model. "Constructions in Analysis" extends the argument of the earlier papers on technique, that it is the transference–the compulsive repetitions that are the patient's "way of remembering"–that makes analysis possible. Hallucinations and delusions are here considered to involve the return of the repressed, to which the hallucinatory return of the "disavowed" is assimilated. The past *failure* of the shock defense is here envisaged as a crucial condition for cognition.

Freud's comment ". . .I have not been able to resist the seduction of an analogy" calls attention to the not necessarily trustworthy allure of the comparison between constructions and delusions, which enlists a dialectical model of tremendous recuperative power, through a chiasmus ascribing to delusions the cognitive content of constructions and to constructions the persuasive power of delusions. But if Freud's paper implies that delusions (i.e. psychosis) are subject to analytic treatment, it also suggests that the material of analysis' quest for "historical truth" is delusions: constructs around the opaque, nondiscursive contents (like the Wolf Man's word-things) of disavowals. Freud is explicit, if brief, about the constraints under which the analysis of disavowal will labor: these "attempts at explanations and cure," he writes–delusions *and* constructions–"under the conditions of a psychosis, can do no more than replace the fragment of reality that is being disavowed in the present by another fragment that had already been disavowed in the remote past. It will be the task of each individual investigation to reveal the intimate connections between the material of the present disavowal and that of the original repression" (*S.E.* 23: 268). The intricacy of such connections—their reliance on a different mode of repetition than either transference or manifest hallucinations or hallucinatory memories—is exemplified in the Wolf Man's re-heard case. The promise of the dialectical model (disavowals are involuntary memories, they contain the past) is betrayed by the dependence of analytic interpretation upon *technique*, which is to say, upon chance, in the absence of continuity between consciousness and memory, the absence of predictable correspondence between the "repetition" and what it repeats.

There is a *caveat* for historians in Freud's sentence quoted above. For if "mankind as a whole" may be functioning "under the conditions of a psychosis"—as Freud's closing generalization from individuals' delusions to mankind's suggests (*S.E* 23:269)—then the most the historian could do would be to replace "the fragment of reality that is being disavowed in the present by [one] that had already been disavowed in the remote past." At best, the historian would provide knowledge of past historical events (reading through the disavowals *in* the past *of* the past) without thereby preventing their displacement onto the present; at worst—reproducing the delusions claim to read—the historian would unknowingly replace historical events of the present with belatedly experienced events of the past. Freud's reflections point to a permanent lag in the "experience" of history, to the "inherent latency" of historical occurrences.

Is there a sense in which we could assert, like Benjamin, the "historical determination of memory," the historical determination of such a relation to history? Freud's hypothesis about memory and consciousness proves fruitful in explaining "situations far removed from those which Freud had in mind when he wrote" (160), says Benjamin, because impressions too excessive, too sudden, or "insupportable" in their contradiction of the self's integrity become part of daily adult life. But rather than the mark of a historical period this could be said to be the character of history as such: change, incommensurate with and never fully explainable by preceding conditions.

Derrida ascribes a kind of historical determination to Freud's model of the psyche, and a fundamental historicity to the psyche as such. In the first place, Freud's analogy between the psyche and a writing apparatus would not be possible without the historical existence of such an apparatus: without "the historic-technical production" of "a supplementary machine, *added* to the psychical organization in order to supplement its finitude" (Derrida 1978, 228). Freud's conception of memory is, in this sense, historically determined: by the historical, not "natural," occurrence of a machine. But in the second place, that process of supplementation is *not* itself historical in the sense of being limited to a specific era. "The very idea of finitude is derived from the movement of this supplementarity." There is no such thing as the psychical without it. This is what we saw in the proximity of consciousness to the activity of historiography, and in Benjamin's deft appropriation of Baudelaire's account of Guys's sketching to Freud's conception of the workings of consciousness. Derrida writes:

> Far from the machine being a pure absence of spontaneity, its *resemblance* to the psychical apparatus, its existence and its necessity bear witness to the finitude of the mnemic spontaneity which is thus supplemented. [. . .] This resemblance [of memory to the machine]—i.e., necessarily a certain Being-in-the-world of the psyche—did not happen to memory from without, any more than death surprises life. It founds memory. (228)

The psychical is defined by an "original" possibility and necessity of supplementation, an openness of the psychical to the non-psychical, which constitutes the *historicity* that is the condition of possibility of historical events. That materiality of the psyche is what Abraham and Torok accept and acknowledge in giving up the transference and displacing the possibility of meaning to untranslatable but writable words. Historiography would have to start, as they do, from Freud's avowal of the inevitability and uncertainty of "constructions."

References

Abraham, Nicolas, and Maria Torok. *The Wolf Man's Magic Word.* Translated by Nicolas Rand. Minneapolis: University of Minnesota Press, 1986.

Baudelaire, Charles. *Oeuvres complêtes.* Paris: Seuil, 1968.

Benjamin, Walter. "Die Aufgabe des Uebersetzers. *Gesammelte Schriften.* Frankfurt: Suhrkamp, 1980. vol. 4:l, pp. 9-21.

---."On Some Motifs in Baudelaire." *Illuminations.* New York: Schocken, 1969. pp. 155-200.

---."The Task of the Translator." *Illuminations.* New York: Schocken, 1969. pp. 69-82.

---."Ueber einige Motive bei Baudelaire." *Gesammelte Schriften.* Frankfurt: Suhrkamp, 1980. Vol 1:2 pp. 605-54.

Brunswick, Ruth Mack. "A Supplement to Freud's 'History of Infantile Neurosis.'" In *The Wolf Man by the Wolf Man.* Edited by Muriel Gardiner. New York: Basic Books, 1971. pp. 263-310.

Caruth, Cathy. "Unclaimed Experience: Trauma and the Possibility of History." *Yale Journal of Criticism* (1990).

Chase, Cynthia. *Decomposing Figures: Rhetorical Readings in the Romantic Tradition.* Baltimore: Johns Hopkins University Press, 1986.

De Man, Paul. "'Conclusions'" Walter Benjamin's 'The Task of the Translator.'" *In the Resistance to Theory.* Minneapolis: University of Minnesota Press, 1986.

---. "Literary History and Literary Modernity." In *Blindness and Insight.* Second edition, with five additional essays, edited by Wlad Godzich. Minneapolis: University of Minnesota Press. 1983.

---. "Sign and Symbol in Hegel's Aesthetics." *Critical Inquiry 8.4* (Summer 1982): 761-75.

Derrida, Jacques. "*Fors*: The Anglish Words of Nicolas Abraham and Maria Torok."

Foreword to Abraham and Torok. *The Wolf Man's Magic Word.* Translated by Nicolas Rand. Minneapolis: University of Minnesota Press, 1986.

----. "Freud and the Scene of Writing. "In *Writing and Difference.* Translated by Alan Bass. Chicago: University of Chicago Press, 1978.

----. Signature, Event, Context." In *Limited Inc.* Evanston: Northwestern University Press, 1988.

Freud, Sigmund. *The Standard Edition of the Complete Psychological Works of Sigmund Freud.* Edited and translated by James Strachey. 24 Vols. London: Hogarth, 1953-74.

"The Dynamics of Transference" (1912), vol. 12.

"Remembering, Repeating, and Working Through" (1914), vol. 12.

"From the History of an Infantile Neurosis" (1918), vol. 17.

Beyond the Pleasure Principle (1920), vol. 18.

"A Note upon the "Mystic Writing Pad'" (1925), vol. 19.

"Fetishism" (1927), vol. 21.

"Constructions in Analysis" (1937), vol. 23.

"The Splitting of the Ego in the Process of Defense" (1940), vol. 23.

Lacan, Jacques. "Réponse au commentaire de Jean Hyppolite sur la "Verneinung' de Freud." *Ecrits.* Paris: Seuil, 1966. 371-8.

Laplanche, Jean, and J.-B. Pontalis. *The Language of Psychoanalysis.* Translated by Donald Nicholson-Smith. New York: Norton, 1973.

Lifton, Robert Jay. *The Broken Connection: On Death and the Continuity of Life.* New York: Basic Books, 1979.

Chapter 2

Comments on Cynthia Chase's Paper

Gianni Vattimo

Let me try, first of all, to define the point of view from which I am going to comment on Cynthia Chases's text. My point of view is that of philosophy: not only because of my profession, but also, and more importantly, because of the theme of this conference. It is very likely that one of the differences between North American and European interpretations of psychoanalysis is the greater impact that psychoanalysis has had in Europe on the general culture (literature, art), and specifically on philosophy.

As I see it, a philosophical approach must be ontological; it must attempt to place a specific "science" like psychoanalysis within the framework of the notion of Being and the transformations that that notion has undergone and is undergoing in our epoch. Philosophy—at least in the sense I give the word—doesn't aim to contribute actively to the development of the specific sciences whose results, methods, etc., it discusses. It is a "reflective" discipline (not a science); it cannot even be considered as the epistemology or the logic of the sciences, though many philosophers of this century have at least tried to practice it as if it could be. My view of philosophy has its basis in the hermeneutic of Heidegger and Nietzsche, which is at the same time an ontology. From this point of view, philosophical and ontological, what I'll try to read in Mrs. Chase's text, is first: a series of observations on the hermeneutics of history, based on a reconsideration of some aspects of Freud's experience and theory, and, perhaps more significantly, the implications of these hermeneutical theses for a "theory of Being."

What I think I have understood in this sometimes highly technical and sophisticated text is that historiography's (re)construction of history–like the (re)construction of the split neurotic ego in psychoanalysis–has to deal with the problem of the "reality" of the original fact, trauma, experience. Both the experience of the neurotic–disavowal–and the experience of the historian– oblivion or forgetfulness–are forms of foreclosure. In other words, the historical "ignorance" that the historian wants to correct is like the neurotic's foreclosure of something he wants to forget, void and avoid. Now, the "therapy" of the neurosis involving disavowal–according to Freud as interpreted by Ms. Chase–does not, and cannot, aim at a re-construction of the foreclosed original situation. The central function of the word in the cases Ms. Chase discusses means that the interpretative effort to retrieve the disavowed event or traumatic experience finds at its end not a fact, but words. The analysis doesn't retrieve an ultimate origin; words are always traces, repetitions, quotations. Of course, those words may also constitute an origin: they may be the starting point of the traumatic situation that gives birth to the neurosis. But their status as words changes the relation of psychoanlaysis and of history to the idea of reconstruction. Neither historiography nor psychoanalytic therapy may be thought of in "realistic" terms. There is no health in literal, *objective reconstruction* of past events.

Moreover, realism, objectivity, and a literal representation of the original scene are exactly what characterizes the neurotic *(the neurotic during the therapy* according to Freud; but perhaps not only in this phase of transition, given the weight that the compulsion to repeat has in many neurotic forms). Mrs. Chase quotes Freud: "The patient remembers nothing of what is forgotten and repressed . . . but he expresses it *in action*" (S.E. 12:150). Is this not a form of "realism," illusion of going back to the "thing itself," even beyond the mediation of words? The notion of truth as the correspondence of sentences to things is the logic of the neurotic, the expression of his inability to remember. And the neurotic's realism goes even farther: he takes as facts the words which were at the origin of his neurosis, and *refuses any translation of them.*

Translating seems to be the way of coping both with the neurosis and with the problems of reconstruction in historiography. It may not be a coincidence that only a few years before Freud elaborated his theory, Nietzsche and Dilthey worked on the same problem of the "reconstructive" and objectivist ideal of historical science. From this point of view, psychoanalysis does not constitute a radical novelty, but appears more as an expression of its time, which, in Heidegger's words, must be called the epoch of the culmination and end of metaphysics—i.e. not only of the end of belief in the correspondence theory of truth, but also and above all, the end of the belief in the foundational strength of the "origin." Nietzsche began *Human all too human* with a proposal to dissolve, through chemical analysis, all the appearances of eternal values, absolute truth and so on. In the end, he discovered that the very idea of reaching a true, non-mythical and unmystified *basis* for all those "human all too human" values was itself a mystification, a final form of the belief in eternal truth. May psychoanalysis be considered another form of the same experience? Nietzsche expressed the meaning of his experience in *The Dawn* (*Morgenröte*): "The greater the knowledge of the origin, the greater becomes its meaninglessness."

My proposal of a connection between psychoanalysis and the epoch of Nietzsche—the epoch of the end of metaphysics—does not aim at a historicist reduction of Freud's theory. And by the way, as to a non foundational interpetation of Freud and psychoanalysis let me remind you that this is one of the most interesting aspects of Richard Rorty's last book, *Contingency, Irony, Solidarity*. Like Rorty, I want to argue that a recognition of the deep "zeitgeistlich" connection between Freud and Nietzsche (and later, Heidegger) brings with it a 'historical' re-statement of psychoanalysis which might not be whithout its uses, since psychoanalysts are generally reluctant to situate their "science" historically: it is not clear for example, whether they agree that psychoanalysis is a "modern" science, perhaps even in the sense that its very subject is *modern* man, and not man in general. Moreover, recognition of this connection to history may also furnish the means for an evaluation (not technical, but philosophical) of the current psychoanalytical debates. From a Nietzschean-Heideggerian standpoint, to situate oneself within the horizon of the end of metaphysics means also to assume this end as a sort of guiding thread. It has even become fashionable to claim that your philosophical adversary is still too metaphysically oriented, that he has not fully understood Heidegger's doctrine. There are, I think, good reasons to adopt this criterion: my philosophical approach to psychonalysis will, then, be to interpret it as one example of the dissolution of the notion of origin in our time. However, some aspects of psychoanalytical doctrine seem to betray this vocation.

All of this, I believe is relevant to the concluding part of Mrs. Chase's paper. Many of the observations she draws from Benjamin's idea of history as shock seem to me to risk repeating a "realistic" or metaphysical attitude of nostalgia for the origin. Take, for example, her preference for involuntary memory over "Bergson's sanguine category of voluntary recollection." To quote Benjamin: "Perhaps the special achievement of shock defense [voluntary recollection, consciousness, etc.] is the function of assigning an incident a precise point in time, *at the cost of the integrity of its contents*" (Chases's emphasis). Voluntary intellectual reorganization brings with it "impoverishment, abstractness, seductiveness." But isn't Benjamin's idea of history (historiography) as based on a shock fundamentally an expression of nostalgia for realism, origin, absolute beginning?

Despite the novelty of his intuition, Freud sometimes (or more than sometimes) displayed a tendency to interpret his own theory in positivist terms; psychoanalysis probably repeats this tendency to underestimate the novelty of Freud's "discovery." Psychoanalytical hermeneutics, like philosophical hermeneutics, has shown that the idea of origin has lost its meaning. But, as Heidegger often said, it is not that easy to overcome metaphysics, or, as Nietzsche would put it, to assimilate all the consequences of God's death. In Mrs. Chase's reference to Benjamin's idea of history as shock, trauma, drastic change, and in her related observations on voluntary and involuntary memory, I sense a sort of nostalgia for realism and objectivism. The *shock* is another image of origin, or the "real," that resists: see also her allusions to the materiality of the signs. To conclude, these seem to me to be the undiscussed ontological implications of the last part of Mrs. Chaser's paper. Nietzsche, Freud, and Heidegger have opened the way to recognize the meaninglessness of the origin, of the *Grund,* of the foundational metaphysics–revealed in its authoritarian and violent character. Why should psychoanalysis, even with Benjamin's legitimization, return to this realistic metaphysics? The cult of the shock seems a way of foregoing *remembrance—translation–* in favor of a neurotic repetition of the (supposedly) original scene.

SESSION II

Chapter 3

The Primordial, the Fantastic, the Imaginary: New Observations on Freud's Thought

Maurizio Bonicatti

Meanings and metaphors related to the concept of the imaginary are particularly complex in the Freudian tradition; they share a common deritualized value that has radically modified their original meaning. In the remote origin of the archaic psyche, the ideation of images did not presume a gratuitous "use" of the imaginary: images were crated for rituals and for specific addressees. Plastic images were originally linked to devotional themes and, therefore, to mythical thought. The archaic psyche preserved some memory of the ritual origin of images. In ritual an image does not reproduce a prototype; it is inextricably identified with the prototype.

To identify the image and the prototype is the principle of idolatry; the idol is the significant opposite to the *simulacrum* (from Latin, *simulacrum - simul - ac*; verb: *simulo - are*; adjective: *similis -e.*).ειδωλατρεῖα, on the other hand, derives from the remotest symbolic function of the εἶδος: when, in the prelinguistic phases of the Pleistocene, representation was the *only* means of communication for ritual messages.

"Idolatry" in its strictly etymological meaning is the cult of a perceived similarity that is worshipped, because the image itself is sacred; it is not considered a reproduction, but a revelation of the actual presence of a superior entity. The contemporary meaning of "idolatry", instead, derives from a false etymology that confuses the stem "essence" with the figurative "cult of simulacri." Consequently, the imaginary can become a synonym for either illusionism and psychoperceptive deception, or for the alteration of the phenomenal world by comparison to the secondary process. For example, in thought disturbances the subject sheds all responsibility, as if he or she were not the author of his or her own visionary creations. A mixed morphology, heteronomous with respect to each *taxon* of life, and perceived through vision, is systematically interpreted as non-transferable from its epistemic frame. The same morphology cannot find the empathy that in the archaic psyche identified the *Imago* with a real presence. This also happens to the subject who created this morphology. In the archaic experience of the imaginary, mixed theriomorphic morphologies prevailed over the zoomorphic *taxa* of life. The experience of theriomorphism in the archaic psyche was not a synonym for monstrosity, unlike the broader contemporary definition, which no longer relates to ritualized monstrosity.

Aside from magic and animistic thought, manifestations of *subjective certainty* tend to be considered delirious because of their lack of reference to the phenomenal world; even the wandering of thought in the sphere of subjectivity can result symptomatically into "fantastic confabulations" (Jaspers). In classical psychiatric terms, "confabulation" refers to *thought disturbances*. In an etymological dictionary, *confabulate* is defined as: "to talk together, to converse about things of little relevance while keeping aside." In psychiatric usage, the intransitive verb *cumfabulare* is reflexive, since concentration presupposes abstraction from any contact with other people; consequently the verb presupposes a transitory choice of de-realization.

Freud defines the clinical term *depersonalization*, according to an analogous procedure, writing that:

> these phenomena are to be observed in two forms: the subject feels either that a piece of reality or that a piece of his own self is strange to him. In the latter case we speak of *depersonalization*.

Freud uses the noun, *Entfremdungsgefühl*, which was not a German neologism, unlike the English translation *depersonalization*. It is important to notice the assimilation of the two substantives in *A Disturbance of Memory on the Acropolis. An Open Letter to Romain Rolland on the Occasion of his Seventieth Birthday* 1936. (*S.E.* 22:245)

While writing *The Occurrence in Dreams of Material from Fairy Tales* (1913) Freud wanted to: "apply the psychoanalytic views derived from dreams to products of ethnic imagination such as myths and fairy tales." (He was referring to the researches begun by Abram, Rank and Jung.) (*The Claims of Psychoanalysis to Scientific Interest*, 1913. (*S.E.* 13:185.)

Freud notoriously interpreted the fairy tale materials condensed in dreams as adult memories that screened repressed childhood experiences. This confirms the principle that our infantile amnesia proves that we have grown estranged from our childhood. (*S.E* 13: 189.) Fairy tales are not childish in and of themselves, or in their role as 'legends' ("to be read" as textual transcriptions); in affabulation the adult frequently seeks what was typical in his or her childhood *Erlebnis*.

Originally refers to the archaic conception of oneirism: a presence manifesting itself as a person (for example, a dead person) does not represent a deritualized signifier, but a return-reappearance from a place that is inaccessible to human beings. Freud's axiom relates to ritual, and ignores the principle of sufficient reason; it implies that we can accept or refuse real existence to a representation. This could lead to a distinction between the *subjective-internal* and the *real-external* that is incompatible with primary process, because primary process admits the existence of "real" internal world. Moreover, the internal world considers the reality of "being (=going) out of [one's] self" to be a dangerous antagonist. Despite the coherence of Freud's thoughts on affabulation, later analyses of textual rather than mythopoetic fairy tales have created a monodirectional trend. If Freud had focused more on Ernst Cassirer's notion of the interdependency of myth and language in archaic man's psychic processes, *Moses and Monotheism* would have been a very different work.

In fairy-tales the archaic prevails over antiquity, not so much in the design of the story as in its formation. The material of a recent scene, like a dream, can represent a long past moment in an individual's experiences. A greater condensation or vivacity of images, on the other hand, can be related to the unexpressed latent content of the primary process. The words *fata* and *fabula* have a common etymological root: the perfect tense of the deponent verb *for-aris* is both transitive and intransitive, thus the narrating subject and the predicate form a single substantive. The fairies in Cathérine d'Aulnoy's *Contes de Fées* are *both* authors the fairies in and narrators of the affabulation on the basis of the subjective and objective form of the genitive "of the fairies." Their affabulations assume a magical belief which has not yet been "discredited." Affabulation remains an archaic *Erlebnis* that the contemporary psyche cannot retrieve, like other lost intrapsychic matrixes. The matrix that allows fairy-tales to retain their dynamism is their power as illusion. This root cannot coexist with a demythologized thought that considers every illusion as synonym of the "non-real."

The psychodynamic that can reproduce illusions and is vulnerable to demythologized thought may still be able to filter the subconscious life that the psychic processes cannot renounce, despite civilization. The phantoms that populate a child's psyche are no different from fairy-tales or religious hierophanies; their presence is symmetrical to that of interiorized "good objects". The dialectical assumption of truth or falsehood establishes an authoritarian norm for thought, creating conflict for the infantile psyche. The conflict is analogous to other conditions for which the dichotomy of true or false is inadequate, causing withdrawal. As a result the child is categorized as a minority, like some patients or animals who do not speak a logical language. Freud saw adults' lack of interest in his own previous experiences as a sign of their inability to understand childhood. (*The Claims of Psychoanalysis to Scientific Interest*, 1913).

This attitude derives from the dark threat perceived by systematic thought in every non-speaking—*in-fans*—existential situation (as referred to human infants, but not only to them.)

Structural knowledge of affabulation shows how the child's psyche, in the minority isolation imposed on it by the adult world with the true vs. false dilemma (logical/prelogical), is similar to the condition of animals, because it is infantile [=] "non-speaking":

> The child cannot tell the difference between his own self and the animals', he is not surprised at finding speaking and thinking animals in fairy tales. (*S.E.* 8:660).

This is a recurrent thesis in Freud, and he expressed it again twenty years later:

> A choice of this kind may be strange, but the gulf which men established later between themselves and animals did not exist for primitive people; nor does it exist for our children. (*Moses and Monotheism*: *S.E.* 23:82.)

The child's psyche and zoomorphic life correspond in the elementary "animation," which can be attributed to animals in the primary process. Only in the primary process is it legitimate to attribute thought and word–conventionally prerogatives of anthropomorphic intelligence–to different forms of life. There are also forms of animism. In the archaic psyche, thought and word gave origin to the various formulations of animism.

Freud did not think the remote origins of fairy tales had to be sought in their earliest texts. The Indo-Aryan group expresses a mythopoetic function different from that of the Hamitic-Semitic group, for whom the roots of affabulated symbols have parenetical purposes.

A recurring theme in historic religions from the axial period (both Aryan and non-Aryan) is the return to earth of the mystical progenitors who presided over the cosmogonies. According to Mircea Eliade, this theme describes their return to immanence; it expresses a collective elementary fantasy that also filtered into the anthropomorphism of Hellenic Olympus. Once established in archaic Greece, anthropomorphism made the gods' imagined promiscuity in the heroic events of ἔπος" more accessible to iconic and later literary representation.

The affabulation collected by bards and later written in the *Iliad* (7, 17-61) relates an anthropomorphic *descensus* of the *deus ex machina*: Apollo and Athena descend to the battlefield between Hector and the Achaians. In order to have a *Descensus*, mythical time must be reenacted when the city of Ilion is ritually "consecrated" (Ιλιον εἰς ἱερὴν) and the gods arrive there "by flying down" (αἴσσω). In this episode the two deities do not appear to Hector and Agamemnon; their anthropomorphism does not work as a hierophany. Apollo and Athena speak in human language, but only to each other: the warriors cannot hear them.

We must also consider a mythopoetic epilogue in which the gods' anthropomorphic immanence is resolved antithetically: the two deities seem to react to an Edenic nostalgia by means of a new metamorphosis, which gives them back the totemic zoomorphism of their ancestors. Thus in the original Aryan myths, anthropomorphism can become zoomorphism, yet the opposite is not possible. This process should not be considered a metamorphosis, but a "return" to the primordial anthropomorphic and zoomorphic community of Eden. The *Iliad* provides the first written narration of the same process; it elaborates unknown sources (both oral and iconological) which must have been adapted to the written word in different phases.

Two such sources are unconscious fantasies and "figurative language," which Freud defined as "the mode of expression of the dream-work as *archaic* or *regressive*" ("The Archaic Features and Infantilism of Dreams," in *Introductory Lectures on Psychoanalysis. S.E.* 15:199).

Figurative language has archaic origins, much earlier than the birth of writing. Despite its archaic nature, figurative language is secondary to the prelogical fantasies, which increased proportionally to their collective elaboration, in archaic thought, and were ultimately combined in mythopoiesis.

The first epigraphic texts were sacred rather than demotic writing in the Semitic-Hamitic linguistic group. Likewise the Indo-Aryan linguistic group had a sacred rather than a spoken language. Sacred language belonged exclusively to affabulation (in its Hellenic derivation it would become "myth.") The only proof of these differences lies in the roots of nouns referring to personal names; the roots of verbs referring to pragmatic functions are the only spoken items from the Indo-Aryan linguistic group. *In illo tempore* denomination had a proper sacred value; this is why personal names were derived from the archetypical identification between *nomen* and *numen*.

The first affabulation is a parable from book two of Samuel, which dates to the beginning of the 1st millennium, the pre-Homeric phase of the Semitic-Hamitic language group. This parable already has all the features of our axial tradition, confirming Freud's thesis that the essential characteristics of modern man emerge in the Judeo-Christian tradition. The most archaic narrative expression of this affabulation is a parable meant as prophetic mediation between man and *Verbum* (II-I millennium B.C.E.): King David receives a hortatory message after committing adultery with *Bathsheeba* and murdering her husband Uriah:

> And the Lord sent Nathan unto David. He came to him in a certain city, the one rich and the other poor. The rich man had very many flocks and herds; but the poor man had nothing but one little ewe lamb, which he had bought. And he brought it up, and it grew up with him and with his children; it used to eat of his morsel, and drink from his cup, and lie in his bosom, and it was like a daughter to him. Now there came a traveller to the rich man, and he was unwilling to take one of his flock or herd to prepare for the wayfarer who had come to him, but he took the poor man's lamb, and prepared it for the man who had come to him. Then David's anger was greatly kindled against the man; . . . but Nathan said to David, "You are the man." *(2 Samuel* 12:1-7. *Revised Standard Version*).

As motivational presupposition to the word of the prophet, David expresses supremacy in the "pause" of the solar hero (Rank): first in *Eros* for Bathsheeba, then in the destructive phase of *Thanatos* in the suppression of Uriah. The elaboration of Bathsheeba's mourning (2 *Sam.* 11: 26-27) is also pertinent to the solstice. The Lord, who finds an interlocutor-King in David, assumes the intermediary voice of the prophet Nathan: that is, an "indirect" communication, the parable, which is referable neither to μῦθοζ, nor to the λὸγος, but to a αἶνοζ, paraenesis. In Nathan's parable, since the king's subject is poor, he is the only one in the position to rediscover the primordial Edenic unity with animals: he seeks "election" through sacrifice, for he will be recompensed in a transcendental future. But the Lord sends a double punishment: lustral for the poor man, and vengeful for the rich man (the deadly disease which befalls the son born from the adulterous relationship between Bathsheeba and David (2 *Sam.* 15-18).

In Nathan's exegesis, the parable must induce David to contrition, revealing the royal-solar destructiveness: "in the sight of the sun" and "Amons sword" (2 *Sam.* 18, 10), emblems of divine anathema, accompany the christological prefiguration of a sacrificial death, where the *anthropos* (the son of David and Bathsheeba) will have to take the place of the poor man's lamb, and expiate the sin in a manner ritualized by the seventh day, *Dominica dies*: "on the seventh day the child died" (2 *Sam.* 18). Such connotations have as their common denominator the symbols of a patrilineal power, and thereby the destructive rather than creative relations of familial inclusion. These relations are not symbolized in the fanciful Aesopian personifications. In the Bible by contrast, they are experienced dramatically and sinfully in the Oedipus, in the constant deprecation of the feminine gender.

Oedipus is connected to the original formation of vicarious substitute fathers, such as Saul, who takes Jesse's place as David's projection. First Saul serves as an *alter ego* for Goliath, a "gigantic" father whose head must be cut off (*eviration*, castration), and then as a sovereign father who must be dethroned (as in the *mythopoesis* of the relationship Jove-Saturn).

The Edenic, "magical" aspect of an extra-specific language, re-proposed by the act of fabulation, may be examined more closely through a motivational critique. In a great number of fairy tales from around the world, friendly animals act as protagonists of the story. They help the hero to meet predetermined tasks or trials, thereby showing him their gratitude for having been saved from some danger or threat of the fundamental drives such as hunger (Lorenz). In other stories the animals give the hero a part of their body, such as a feather, so that the hero can summon the animal in a moment of need. In one variant of this theme, the female animal gives the hero a part of her body so that he can become that animal if necessary. In certain Baltic fairy tales, the hero can swim like a fish, run like a hare, or fly like a bird. Another wide-spread motif is the hero's exclusive capacity to know how "to speak" and understand animal language (a metaphor that leads us back to Aesop). Sociological criticism has examined this motif only superficially. In fact, sociological criticism did not include Phaedrus in its analysis of Aesopian fairy tales, because of the well known social connotation of his servile origins. This connotation was used to present the structure of the tale as a mouthpiece for the lower classes, and the animals as the satirical actors. However, sociological studies have neglected what is perhaps the most obvious characteristic of these fairy tales: the speech of animals. I wonder to what extent their numinous character, in the context of the fabulation, is incompatible with anthropomorphic language (which dominates all other cultural genres). That which is *ineffable* in the language of the conscious system can only be enunciated through *other* languages (*Ersatzbildungen*), which the psyche can use when it "makes its way" through the supremacy of consciousness. The speaking animals are endowed with repressed psychic material since, according to a *topos* of anthropomorphism, they are self-conscious (hence the impossibility of any conflicts with consciousness). There is therefore an obscure incompatibility between anthropomorphic intelligence (in its typical exponent–conceptual language) and the "innocent" Edenic condition. The first symbol of anthropocentric supremacy the Creator confers to Adam is the act of naming: "And Adam gave names to all cattle, and to the fowl of the air, and to every beast of the field" (Gen. 2, 20). The Edenic myth of the "speaking animals" conversely presents inanimate objects that become animals through transference: when a subject attributes a soul to them through a prelogical process based on the antithetic relationship between "animation" and "soulless/inanimate." In the third year of St. Jerome's seclusion in the Syrian desert, before undertaking the monumental exegesis of biblical texts, he placed his doctrinal identity within parentheses. The empathy between the hermit and the lion does not take place through the domestication of the feline, brought to the ideal level of "speaking" animal. It takes place because he re-discovers the primigenial condition in which the *anthropos* loses his uni-specific differentiation for the sake of integrating his roots with the wildness of other species: the never to be repeated equilibrium of Eden within the ecological system.

Chapter 4

Comments on Maurizio Bonicatti's Paper

Laurie Wilson

Professor Bonicatti immediately warns us that in the present we are far from using, or even considering the concept of the imaginary in the ways it was used in earlier times. The archaic psyche—with its memory of the ritualistic, mythic unity of the symbolic image and its original referent—is too distant from either our own culture, or Freud's. I wonder if that very distance makes it impossible for any of us, including as erudite a scholar as Prof. Bonicatti, from garnering the truth about the "archaic psyche."

Professor Bonicatti wants us to know how much we have lost by giving up the imaginary, from which he believes we have become estranged, and which enriches not only children's lives and literature, but most of the ancient world. He adds Freud to the group of those who consider the imaginary and fantastic outside the limits of acceptable adult thought, serving the purpose of escape or research in such locations as dreams, ancient literature, and the delusional fictions of the insane.

Bonicatti's nostalgia for the prelogical is coupled with his overriding concern that modern man has become alienated from it, and has thereby irretrievably lost an aspect of inner life essential to the human condition. This argument is not new, but it is perennially important. For example, Suzanne Langer has described the value of symbolic and discursive modes of apprehension and expression. But while she tied the symbolic to the arts, Bonicatti connects affabulation to fairy tales, to the mythopoetic, and to religion. More recently Bruno Bettelheim decoded fairy tales and showed their fundamental value of unpalatable but inescapable truths for children of all ages.

Perhaps Bonicatti comes closest to Freud in his discussion of various literary and biblical characters who face disillusioning truths: David and his protoanalyst, the prophet Nathan, who uses a parable to disclose a painful truth. As an analyst Bonicatti knows that his patients must eventually come to know themselves, but also that they may need the consolation of myth or art as enthralling illusions which simultaneously reveal and conceal necessary knowledge. A strictly logical approach which Bonicatti calls "demythologized" to such verities can neither contain their complex ambiguous nature nor help individuals or societies to come to terms with them.

We could usefully discuss his suggestion that what adults seek in affabulation is a means of dealing with and repairing the damage caused by repressed childhood experiences which appear in dreams and, I would add, in transference as well as other enactments. Adult use of affabulation is a worthy topic for any symposium. One of the tasks of psychoanalysis is to help individuals discover the myths to which they have been unwittingly subscribing (whether their own or their family's).

On this side of the Atlantic, we usually call such myths unconscious fantasies; we could rename them 'affabulations' to better bridge the dialogue across the ocean. For clinicians it may have become too easy to consider a patient's unconscious fantasies to be the carriers of warped and faulty conclusions that were reached in a state of immaturity (at moments of shock). Seen as such, they may be perceived as needing to be brought to light and excoriated. If I have understood Bonicatti correctly, these internal myths may also be carrying a wider range of messages, even benevolent ones, from the archaic past of our own childhood, our parents; our parents' parents', and so on. Thus nursery rhymes, which are passed from generation to generation, administer various doses of interesting information about life to children from their adult caretakers. So "Rockabye baby in the tree top" tells the carefully listening child about the ambivalence of parents, who can imagine a baby crashing down.

One of Bonicatti's most intriguing and heuristically useful ideas is his proposal that a representation is something whose existence we can accept or refuse. In contrast with the archaic or ancient response to representations as real presences, Bonicatti points to modern man's insistent dethronement of imagery as mere illusionistic distortion.

Though his premise is not overtly stated I think Bonicatti implies that it is through the arts that modern man can return to the possibility of accepting representations as having a real and really worthwhile existence. He wants us to regain this choice without embarrassment or without being called delusional.

In my work as an art therapist, art historian, and psychoanalyst, I have seen people respond to visual representations in various ways. Like Winicott's transitional object, the visual image can seem real to some and illusory to others, depending on their state of need and readiness to face life without a Teddy bear. The very fact that the *image* can either sustain or disappoint both viewer and maker in its relationship to both internal and external "truth" underlies the ambiguous power of the arts. Picasso's famous statement, "Art is a lie but a lie which tells the truth," condenses a part of Bonicatti's argument. Picasso knew that if he removed every referent to the recognizable world from his work, he would lose many members of his audience. Picasso's respect for magic and his ability to sense people's feeling would seem to support Bonicatti's notion that representation is for many people, a guarantee of the reality of the represented.

Professor Bonicatti indirectly critiques the long-standing privileging of logic and language over the prelogical and over images. It is perhaps inevitable that many societies equate older and wiser, but the accidental chronology of developmentally early occurrence of images and prelogical mental processes is no reason to consign them to the nursery and ultimately to the attic. As the Israeli psychoanalyst Pinches Roy has pointed out in his writings on art and primary and secondary process, many 'illogical' primary processes can be subject to conscious development throughout childhood and adolescence, and serve as sophisticated, useful tools for adult artists and other perceptive persons. He explains what should be obvious when we look at the highly complex and intelligent work of great artists, which cannot possibly be reduced to products of more primitive modes of apprehension and expression. Howard Gardner has also suggested that we reexamine the narrowness of our view of mental capacities; he proposes that human beings have multiple forms of intelligence, and sets visual intelligence on a par with linguistic, musical and other forms of intelligence. For an excellent description and discussion of the visual origins of much language, I refer you to the work of Werner and Kaplan on *Symbol Formation* (1962).

It is intriguing to wonder why so many analysts subscribe to the same privileging of words over images. This is an especially vexing question in the case of Lacan, who was himself surrounded by visual artists during his intellectually formative years.

I do not believe we have lost the fabulous in modern life. We have renamed it and given it contemporary shapes. Our relationship to the fabulous is not as simple as it used to be because of the pluralities of modern life. Not just in New York, Paris and Rome are we obliged to jostle shoulders with people of different faiths, who worship such different idols as Allah, oil, and the name of the father since instant worldwide communication can make and break idolatrous images in milliseconds.

SESSION III

Chapter 5

Reason From the Unconscious (Lacan, Wittgenstein and Derrida)

René Major

A title always induces proper name effects; it comes to be added to the name like another name for the name, exercising a function of designation independent of its meaning. The title I've chosen - "Reason From the Unconscious"- involves a cryptonymy which you will have unveiled as an epigraphisation or a reservation. A text of Lacan's, initially delivered as a lecture in 1957, is subtitled, "Reason From Freud."[1] This subtitle is a doubling of the title, "The Agency of the Letter in the Unconscious," followed by, "or Reason From Freud." However, the subtitle does not explicate the title; rather, we find in the title the reason for the subtitle and the reason for the duplication. After Freud, reason (*ratio*, *logos*, *Vernunft*, or *Grund,* untranslatable by each other or for each other) is no longer what one might have thought it was. It has been affirmed, under the proper name and title of Lacan, as the pressing demand of the letter, its insistence and its authority in the unconscious. Reason is entirely displaced from the continent of consciousness to the archipelagoes of the unconscious. "Reason *Since* Freud," then. But Lacan's motive is double: to make the Freudian letter return to Freud himself, and to refound psychoanalysis–with the help of linguistics–on the materiality (or the ideality?) of the letter, the correlative of a logic (or a strategy?) of the signifier.

The title "Reason From the Unconscious" suggests another questioning of reason. "From the Unconscious" introduces a double reference, to time and to space: reason from (i.e. since) the coming of the Freudian unconscious, and from the place that henceforth is designated by the term "Freudian unconscious," in an internal and external relation to Freud's name, or in relation of non-relation to this name. The ambiguous use of this preposition not only marks the *becoming-space* of time, but also introduces a *differentiation* which will trouble the Lacanian concept of metaphor, particularly the metaphors of *the unconscious as literality*, and of literality as the "reason of the unconscious."[2]

Another titular cryptonymy: two authors, Nancy and Lacoue-Labarthe, have, in the double sense of the title "Le titre de la lettre" (meaning either the "title of the Letter,"[3] or "The Letter's Entitlement"), proposed to read what Lacan says, in "The Agency of the Letter," as a science of the letter, a "destruction" of the Saussurian sign and a "translation" of the Heideggerian *logos*.

We shall return to this reading. But since Lacan takes the dream-mechanisms brought out by Freud and transposes them into figures of style—thus, through the materiality of the letter, giving the unconscious its reason—we should recall that for Freud the contents of the unconscious are more or less strongly cathected, and contradictory wishes can coexist in it. These contents consist of representatives of the drive and drive movements that fit together by their own logic. The unconscious knows nothing of negation, doubt and degrees of certainty. These are the work of censorships[4].

Take an example given in the *Traumdeutung*. A child of ten, told of the sudden death of his father, says, "I understand that my father is dead, but I can't understand why he doesn't come home for dinner."[5] There is no grammatical impossibility in saying or writing such a sentence, yet its two parts are, according to a certain rational logic, completely contradictory. According to an unconscious logic, however, this sentence expresses a wish that does not take into account the reality of a death which has, nonetheless, been recognized. The child has no doubts either about the father's death or about the possibility of his coming home for dinner. Notice that the sentence makes no use of metaphor, unless you discern an implicit metaphor of death as temporary absence. The metaphor in retrait would then make the sentence's logical contradiction or the contradiction of logics rational, but that rationality would be based on a negation of death or on a belief in life beyond death–a temporality which is entirely unrelated to the processes of the unconscious. They are not temporally ordered–time is just one way among others, of thinking–which accounts for the facts that another of the child's wishes, the wish for the death of the father, can only remain alive by reason of non-temporal space. However, in another order of reason, the child's desire is temporally linked to the father in his fantasy. So, the paradox of the logic(s) of the unconscious[6] arises only if the rational/irrational opposition is correlated to the opposition of conscious and unconscious processes - an opposition deconstructed by Freudian reason. Still, one must nevertheless run up against the boundaries of language in order to speak of the unconscious, or from the unconscious.

The unconscious may be rational, but it never stops banging its head against paradox. Languages propensity to get headstrong was the object of the epistemophiliac drive of an assiduous reader of Freud - Wittgenstein. In one of his Vienna Circle conversations, he remarks: "I can perfectly well conceive of what Heidegger means by Being and Anxiety. Man has a characteristic drive [ein *Trieb*] which makes him run up against the frontiers of language [*gegen die Grenzen der Sprache anzurennen*]"[7] If "everything happens in language," as the *Philosophical Grammar* asserts, one might wonder what the place of the subject in language games is if there is precession or contemporaneity of language for the "pragmatic" subject–and how language is articulated by means of the drive that makes the subject run up against its boundaries. The language-game, for Wittgenstein, is reminiscent of primitive behavior, the drive register itself. It is instinct made language, reflecting only the use the subject makes of it. But perhaps the drive's destiny is language? If, for Freud, there is an addressee–but perhaps destination is indistinguishable from errancy–the addressee must be double, given the internal alterity of the subject of language. In Wittgenstein, the Other is essentially the pole of learning and communication, while the subject is the pragmatic operator of discursive exchanges. Subjective specificity is gathered (in both senses of the word) in the aesthetic or the ethical. The passage cited above underscores this idea:

> Think for example of the astonishment at the fact that something exists. This astonishment cannot be expressed in the form of a question, and naturally there is no reply either. Everything we'd like to say can *a priori* be only nonsense. And yet, we run up against the limits of language. Kierkegaard saw this running-up against too, and described it in a quite similar way (as a sort of banging one's head aqainst paradox). This running-up-against is ethics.

We can understand from this why Wittgenstein insisted on contesting Freud's thesis that dreams are the distinguished fulfillment of repressed wishes—or, rather, on relativising its scope by restricting it to statements whose sexual tenor is obvious. The idea of a dream-language, even of a dream-language in painting, is not foreign to Wittgenstein:

> Once, in Vienna, I saw an exhibition of a young artist's paintings; one of the pictures showed a room as bare as a cellar. Two men wearing top hats were sitting on chairs. That was it. And the title: *Besuch* (visit). As soon as I saw it I said, 'It's a dream'.[8]

There follows a parenthesis, the second I have pointed out (the first concerned the "sort of banging one's head against a paradox"). "(Freud said to my sister who described the picture to him, 'Of course, it's a very banal dream, linked to virginity.')." For Wittgenstein the dream's beauty must remain intact. So he attacks the "meaning" Freud gives in the *Traumdeutung* to "a flower-dream"—again, a problematic of defloration—going so far as to imagine himself in the consulting-room on the Bergasse saying to the patient: "These associations do not make the dream beautiful. It was beautiful. Why should it not be?"[9]

During the period in 1919 when Wittgenstein is reading *The Interpretation of Dreams*, he reports, among others, the following dream:

> It was night. I was outside a house whose windows were resplendent with light. I went toward a window to look inside. There, on the floor, I noticed an exquisitely beautiful *prayer-mat* that I immediately wanted to examine. I tried to open the front door, but a *snake* shot out to stop me going in. I tried another door, but there again a *snake* shot out to block my path. Snakes also appeared at the windows and opposed any attempt to reach the *prayermat.*[10]

Do not expect me to attempt an interpretation of this dream. I can say no more about it than what the dreamer himself confides to Bartley. These confidences show that Wittgenstein could make his dream mean what everyone will have understood as to its sexual content—relying on a symbolic translation of the doors or snakes, or the substitution of one signifier for another to evoke a metaphor that the use of language makes us share. But Wittgenstein is well aware of Freud's chapter on symbolic figuration; it is highly probable that the symbols in his dream are an overdetermined ciphering. And this, he asserts, is the aspect of dream images which resembles linguistic signs or fragments of writing. His comparison to "a series of marks on paper or sand"[11] is worth recalling both because it hypothesizes that these marks are different from the conventional letters of the alphabet, and because it puts into question the existence of a stable semantic nucleus between signifier and signified or between the symbol and the thing it symbolizes.

Two remarks before proceeding. First, Wittgenstein thinks of the interpretation of dreams as a satisfying explanatory analogy rather than as a causal explanation. These are two different things. The rationality of the dream-interpretation can be judged from the point of view of a scientific objectification; however, the Freudian notion of a *divided subject* implies that the subject of science should be resituated in a more general understanding of subjective operations and in a relativisation of scientific objectification. As for the satisfaction supplied by the dream interpretation's "singular attraction," as Wittgenstein calls it, it is difficult not to establish a symbolic relation between this satisfaction and the one covertly accomplished in the dream. Interpretation's efficacity, if it has any, lies in its performance of the dream-narrative's constative. In this sense, we can understand that the work of interpretation still belongs to the dream, as Wittgenstein suggests, only if we consider the interpretation a symbolic accomplishment of what the dreamer brought about without realizing it.

My second remark concerns the language-picture and Wittgenstein's desire, disarmed before the beauty of the dream. He shows himself to be shocked, even outraged: "Freud gives what he calls the meaning of the dream. The filthiest sex, the worst sort of smut. . . . Was the dream not beautiful?" Of course it was. But why refuse to examine the relationship of the beautiful to desire, and, especially, the effect it can produce by leaving us speechless? In this respect, Freud's audacity, particularly regarding the works of Leonardo and Michelangelo, remains unprecedented. What he "runs up against" is not simply the aesthetic or the ethical: he bangs his head against the paradox of the ethical. For Wittgenstein, "being psychoanalyzed is a little like eating of the tree of knowledge. Knowledge thus acquired presents us with new ethical problems." He hastens to add that this new knowledge "brings nothing to their solution."[12] But this unveiling of ethical problems does constitute an ethics of analysis which engages the responsibility of the subject of unconscious thought, however difficult this new concept of "responsibility" may be for us to conceive. If "it" thinks where I am not or where ego is not, that ego comes to be there must engage desire quite differently. If there is a form of thought that can escape the illusion of thinking, for Freud it has to do with the survival of desire in "inflexible reason."

Let us return to the problematic of the sign. What particularly interests me today is if Wittgenstein prefigures Lacan as to the reason of the unconscious found in the agency of the letter. Both work to deconstruct the sign, but differently. For Wittgenstein, the logic of representation, which conditions the truth of a proposition, has no need to resort to any reference to the subject. "There is no thinking subject, capable of representation," asserts the *Tractatus*: "it is the nature of essentially necessary signs which speaks of itself." Without detaching itself from all reference to the subject, the Lacanian logic of the signifier seeks to rid metaphysics and linguistics of the illusion that the signifier answers to the function of representing the signified, or "better still," says Lacan, "that the signifier has to answer for its existence under the title of any signification at all."[13] There are concatenations of signifiers, but these signifying chains do not represent signifieds and are independent of all signification. Are they independent in Wittgenstein's sense, in that their relations remain a function of a *projection*, "a regulated coordination between the elements of a representing structure and those of a represented structure, without the nature of the representing elements or of the represented elements ever needing to be determined"?[14] For Lacan, as for Wittgenstein, the aporia represented by the non-univocal correspondence of word to thing or signifier to signified (by virtue of the arbitrary nature of the sign) requires that the question of reference, determining the position of the signified, be suppressed.

In "Subversion of the Subject and Dialectic of Desire," the text of a seminar from the same time as "The Agency of the Letter," Lacan asserts that "if linguistics promotes the signifier, to the point of seeing in it the determinant of the signified, analysis reveals the truth of this relation by making the gaps of meaning the determinants of its discourse."[15] While Wittgenstein sees a "precipitation of the ethical," Lacan sees a "precipitation of meaning as passage of the signifier into the symbolization of a law or as process giving rise to meaning." And, furthermore, Lacan adds, "the signifier is constituted only from a synchronic and countable gathering where not one is sustained other than by its opposition to each of the others."[16] Lacan radicalizes the non-correspondence of signifier and signified stressing the function of the bar that separates them and institutes the cut in the discourse through which the subject is inscribed as discontinuity in the real. The unconscious "from Freud,"—read, from Freud according to Lacan—would be "a chain of signifiers which somewhere (in another scene, he writes) is reflected and insists on interfering in the cuts offered to it by effective discourse and the cogitation it informs."[17] It is only in the in-between of these signifiers that the subject can be supposed, and "what thinks, calculates and judges" is not the subject but "jouissance." "The sign in return" produces *jouissance* by means of "the cipher permitted by the signifiers."[18] To repeat: signifiers make possible the cipher of the sign which produces thinking *jouissance*.

Indeed, it is worth asking whether the Lacanian signifier—which is nothing like the Saussurian signifier because, as Nancy and Lacoue-Labarthe have shown,[19] it keeps the word but over-invests it to the detriment of the thing, representing an elided subject only for another signifier—is, like the proper name, an insignificant mark designating a subject with no relation to any meaning. Does the differential chain behave like a differential series of proper names that refer to the place of the subject—the place where it is missing from its place—in the symbolic order that organizes its sequential linking? One of the strategies of the signifying logic that is put into place, and that puts into place an entirely calculable subject, has to do with the reason of the unconscious, the sense of non-sense, conceived from the letter and its indivisible nucleus. This strategy must pass through the folding back of the primary process mechanisms described by Freud—those which organize unconscious thought—onto the figures of metonymy and metaphor, and it must pass metaphor and metonymy off as primary effects of the signifier. The strategy is doubled by Lacan's assertion that "game-theory, or, better, strategy . . . benefits from the entirely calculable character of a subject strictly reduced to the formula of a matrix of meaningful combinations."[20] This subject is the Other, which "is none other than the pure subject of modern games-theory."[21]

My commentary on the concept of the *letter* and its authorization of a science of the letter as science of the unconscious, does not detract from an appreciation of Lacan's critique of naive symbolism. Lacan recalls that the snake—I call on Wittgenstein's dream again—could not be the symbol of the libido, nor, in any straightforward way, of the penis, but must instead be the symbol of the place where it lacks,[22] inasmuch as the relation of the subject to castration means that *knowing* does not prevent one from *not knowing that one knows*. "The prayer-mat" (but "who is prayed to do what?" we might ask) is an example (for *instance*, we can say in English, in a phrase that borders here on scholasticism) in support of propositions for which one can substitute a letter as symbol.

Freud, for his part, holds to a surprising notion he invents, that of *an unconscious concept* as the operator of symbolic substitutions. Freud himself is astonished by this concept as it emerges from his pen and adds, *Sit venia verbo*. The unconscious concept is that of "a small thing that can be detached from the body," like the penis, the faeces, or the child; it establishes, across the dissimilarity between the different things, a resemblance that makes them substitutable for each other in the sexual theories of children or in a chain of representations, and that conditions a whole logic of exchange, of the gift, or of keeping [*la garde*]. The symbolic representation of castration is linked to the logical process of unconscious equivalences like these, and any signifier such as "the little thing," "the little bit," or "the little one" is likely to set the process going, to the point that the part can be taken for the whole and the whole for the part.

What, then, of the letter - defined by Lacan as the material support borrowed from language by concrete discourse in which the subject is pre-inscribed through: his proper name[23]–when, for example, in the Wolf Man case, the word *Wespe* is deprived of its initial *W* as the wasp is of its wings, and the speaker thinks he can recognize in the resulting *espe* the initials "S.P.," which form the monogram that designates him? We can see how the sign of division under which the subject is manifested marks a division of the letter through which language can both signify subject and designate it. The same word (*Wespe*) behaves simultaneously like a common noun and a proper name—and as common noun it acquires a certain number of meanings from the proper name, itself a-semantic. This example, which Lacan uses to suggest that words can "accomplish imaginary acts of which the patient is the subject," shows that the proper name's imaginary properties can invade language to give singular meanings to words, but any resulting loss of the sign's rights, by which the subject remains symbolically inscribed in language while the real of the subject remains in "*retrait*" by the signifier. This does not keep the homonymy that allows the meeting of S.P. and the wasp from hitting the target for the supposed subject, or, to put it better, from engendering subject effects or effects of subject.

I speak of subject-effect, in the absence of another term, to indicate a distance from the problematical concept of the Subject, and to express a suspicion regarding the subject's literalisation as it is developed in a language-oriented determination of the unconscious. In the experience to which I have just alluded, the "subject" is not who is precipitated in a meaning [*vouloir-dire*], nor, who would assign a place *to himself* or *the other* "as such" although the horizon of this "subject" is always glimpsed by an Ego in me [un moi en moi]–but who, from this unknown being, holds in suspense the reply to the question "Who?". To Freud's question about the subject's eccentricity with respect to consciousness - its non presence to itself–Lacan responds in terms of the difference between the enunciation's subject and the subject of the statement, reinscribing the subject as subject of the signifier, instituted in and through the signifier. This makes us wonder what the word "subject" retains of the essential features of the *cogito*, and how it separates itself from it radically, while still keeping hold of it. We can also wonder whether the translation of the dream's mechanisms into the unique and complex opposition of metaphor and metonymy—in a rhetoric in which linguistics perceived the manifestation of the subject, which becomes the rhetoric of the unconscious—does not reintroduce the classical opposition of absence/presence and manifestation/retreat (even if, in order to produce itself while remaining unconscious, desire must impose an inevitable substitution or a displacement, which these figures can transcribe).

Lacan's operation consists, first of all, in recognizing in the analysis of the dream, the general laws of an unconscious logic, following, in this, the Freudian discovery; he recognizes, as well, a true system of writing rather than a symbolic imagery, but one whose model is phonetic, from alphabetic writing. Then, since only linguistics is in a position to define the topic of the unconscious and formalize its processes, it becomes a question of establishing the algorithmic formulae for metaphor and metonymy,[24] (24) the two aspects of the signifier's impact on the signified, which articulate a logic of the signifier and a logic of desire (the subject itself being the place—topic and tropic—of the signifier).

In order for this operation to succeed, certain notional equivalences would have to be secured. How sure are we that the discursive function of metaphor entirely parallels that of Freud's *Verdichtung* (condensation)? After all, one finds quite different figures of condensation, which, like the oxymoron, can also reconcile such opposites as temporality and intemporality. There might well be grounds for reservations about what Freud says of the very name of the metaphor which "by condensing in it *Dichtung* indicates the connaturality of this mechanism to poetry." Is *Verdichtung* a metaphor for *Dichtung* or vice versa, and what is a metaphor of metaphor? Does metonymy retranscribe the *Verschiebung* (displacement) observed in the dream? Does it exhaust its possibilities? This term is aimed at the very series of the terms of linguistic combination, the linking ~~of~~ signifiers; the contexture of their relations in *praesentia*, whereas the very broad use of the term "metaphor" places the entities of discourse in competition so as to substitute one signifier for another, which is relegated to the position of the signified. Is this a metaphorical usage of metonymy and metaphor?

We shall address these questions presently, but we should emphasize that, to the question of whether anything distinguishes the dream-work's two mechanisms from the functions presumed to be their counterparts in discourse, Lacan replies, "Nothing, except for a condition imposed on the signifying material, the *Rücksicht auf Darstellbarkeit*, generally translated as "the role of the possibility of figuration," and retranslated by the author as "attention to the means of staging." However, while the mechanisms that Freud assigns to the primary process are exemplary in the dream - and we must recall that through the process of displacement a representation *cedes* its investment to another; and through the process of condensation it appropriates the investment to another; and through the process of condensation it *appropriates* the investment of a number of others with the accent on depropriation, or on the appropriation of drive energy attached to the "signifier"—they do not comprise all the properties of the unconscious. The processes linked to the unconscious are not influenced either by a relation to time or by the test of reality (as we have seen in the example of the child able to recognize the reality of the father's death but unable to understand his absence). Should we speak of the time of metaphor, its *usure* (investment, use and using up surplus-value, wearing away), its intemporality, its problematic relation to reality?

No doubt this is why Lacan, using the hackneyed metonymy of "thirty sails" to figure as many ships, remarks that the "thing" of this metonymy is not "to be taken in reality" since a ship normally has more than one sail. So, since neither the reality of the signified nor the attachment to the referent produces the figure, the literality attributed to it will have little meaning or will be the *pas, not* or step, of meaning. If meaning is bound up with temporality (in Homer's age a boat usually did have only one sail), then metonymy undoes the relation.

"The Agency of the Letter" borrows a metaphor from Victor Hugo, "His sheaf was not avaricious nor hateful . . ."; one can recognize in it the exemplary "turn" by which an effect of figural meaning is designated, but the substitution of the sheaf for Boaz has as much to do with metonymy as metaphor: effect is taken for cause in the signification of paternity. And further, it is not insignificant that in this "sample" the signifier "sheaf" comes to abolish a proper name (Boaz). If, as we are told, "the formula for metaphor" is "one word for another," can one say that the proper name is a word like any other? For my part, I would only use the term signifier for the proper name (the "Agency" speaks expressly of the "signifier of the proper name") if the context referred to the imaginary properties of the name, i.e. to the proper name taken as common noun and, therefore, situated in a relation of meaning. But the line from Hugo takes the "not avaricious or hateful" sheaf as a real property of the referent, and the name Boaz can only be read in the register of its designation and thus as an "insignificant" mark. Moreover, Lacan, shows clearly that Boaz's generosity "is reduced to less than nothing by the munificence of the sheaf," whereby desire shows its metonymic "lack of being."

In truth, the idea developed in "The Agency of the Letter" that the figural meaning–here metaphor–can give the measure of the meaning produced by the unconscious is still much too logical; its logic still obeys that of phonematics and a principal of identity, the foundations of a philosophy of presence. Psychic writing, like the dream's writing, is so originary a production, so idiomatic, capable of scrambling all codes and outplaying all translations, that it is far more than a metaphor for ordinary writing: writing in the usual sense, with its rules and tropes, is, rather, a metaphor for it.[25] On the other hand, the substitution of signifiers might seem to be the essential activity of analytic interpretation, especially since, in the wake of Freud, the dream is untranslatable (not only into another language but into the very language it borrows to constitute itself as a narrative) and interpretation is a becoming-language of the oneiric idiom. No doubt one must resort to other concepts which refuse to be taken over by a logic of identity or a logical time. Freud's psychographic metaphor of the dream's writing and its decipherment–comparable to the decipherment of a hieroglyph–and of the psychic apparatus and the functioning of memory,[26] compels us to rethink the trajectory going from metaphor to concept, as well as the very concept of metaphor as function of the trace and its effacement. For this purpose, a graphematics would be more suitable than a phonematics.

I have waited until now to let you hear a short sentence I've had in mind since I began speaking. It is not really even a sentence, only four words separated by those marks, a bit longer than hyphens, called dashes. Four words and two dashes. Here they are: *Me–psychoanalysis - you know.* . . . I let these words be spoken. [Ces mots. Je me les suis laissé dire]. And here I must pause, because the phrase I've just used "I let these words be spoken" can mean that they were said to me, or that I allowed myself to say them, that I went so far as to speak them. The ambiguity of meaning here is a correlative of the subject's indeterminacy, the overdetermination which assigns the two figures, which cannot be opposed, even before it manifests itself as subject, before it receives its determination by the ego, by representation or by the signifier. I have never heard these words spoken, except by myself, mentally, and, as you would expect, with all possible intonations. It's enough to bang your head against tone, tonality and intonation, which alone would decide the meaning, a beginning of meaning. I heard myself speak them a moment ago, now attributing to myself the doubtful or ironic thought of them, now attributing it to one of you here, or to some absent person who is, for the time being, reduced to silence by my speaking which places him in the position of the analyst, or undertakes a long analysis of his silence. The four words I lend him could be the beginning of a dialogue, since they are separated by a mark that could indicate a change of interlocutor. They could also be the typed transcription of a dream since they drop every preposition, every conjunction, and every verb: a metaphor for the dream-writing itself.

But how must this sentence be interpreted? How should we interpret this fragment of discourse which was never "spoken," but slipped from Derrida's pen to punctuate the end of an introduction to the English translation of an article by Nicolas Abraham, "The Shell and the Kernel"?[27] Derrida's text speaks of the language of psychoanalysis, "which radically alters words, the same words, those of everyday language," and introduces a "scandalous antisemantics," of "concepts de-signified by the psychoanalytic context." The "semantic conversion" operated by psychoanalysis perceives the unconscious as absolutely heterogenous to the whole axiomatics of meaning that it makes possible, for it makes meaning possible through an a-semantic agency. The words of everyday language are called in to say something quite different, something also quite different from meaning: the anasemic conversion "does not concern exchanges between significations, signifiers and signifieds, but between the order of signification and what, making signification possible, must yet be translated into the language of what makes it possible."Anasemia is not a figure or, if it is a figure, it is a figure without figure, figuring as one of "those new figures which are absent from the treatises of rhetoric." How, then, are we to think, to include in our discourse "the very thing that, because it is its condition, escapes it radically"?

If I–me, ego–speak of psychoanalysis, I speak of the Ego that psychoanalysis has identified as the psychic place of the imaginary identifications which, calling on a plural that gives the illusion of a singular, make the subject say "I," but I also speak of the "Ego" of psychoanalysis, of its constituted and instituted discourse, "theoretical" and "practical," with respect to which "the subject," as it is re-interpreted and reinscribed by psychoanalytic language, destitutes and restitutes itself in the margin or at the limit of this discourse, in its interiority and in its exteriority. And I speak in several voices–voices you will recognize–of the constitutive and deconstitutive *désistance* (to use the word suggested by Derrida) of the subject, the place and the reflexive voice of the verb, from which the subject desists without stepping down *désiste sans se désister*], faced with a figure that is *at least double*. To say that the dis-location of the subject brings with it a dislocution of thought is also to mark the non-unicity of the unthought or the unknown that an unconscious knowledge would speak and the non-unicity of truth, its disinstallation and unsealing in a desteling [*déstèlement*], and to say the place where it masks itself on its stele. Doubling or disinstalling reason in all its modes of tension or appropriation of the non-proper is not an appeal to the "subject's" irresponsibility, but to another responsibility that answers for its désistance and its dislocation; it is a destabilization of the function of meaning or truth, of Being, described in Heideggerian language as truth of adequation *homoiosis*, and it is a saying of the reason of the unconscious as anasemic reason of reason.

Therefore, if, as "The Agency of the Letter" insists, metaphor unites the function of the subject and that of the signifier—which, like the fetish, is, with the letter's support, missing from its place [*manque à sa place*], and, with interpretation, comes back to the place where it is lacking - we might wonder what becomes of the signifier, whose place would be that of not having a place, resisting the substitution of one word for another under the sway of the metonymic turns of "word for word." We might also wonder what truth the letter serves, and we might, at the same time, question the theory of the subject as the theory of truth. The closing pages of Lacan's text, which attempt to articulate "the letter, being, and the other" [*la lettre, l'être et l'autre*], reply clearly to this. What Freud offers us, according to Lacan—and this is where "Freudian truth" resides—is not a revision of the empty adage "Know thyself," but the ways which lead to the *Kern unseres Wesen,* to the nucleus of our being,[28] to a "questioning of the situation of man in entities." And the text hastens to add: "When I speak of Heidegger or rather when I translate him, I attempt to leave the speech he proffers its sovereign significance." The reference to Heidegger's text "Logos," which Lacan had just translated, is certainly not indifferent, especially given that "Logos"—too—is entirely occupied with the problem of translation - the translation of Heraclitus, whose "sovereign word" Heidegger left sovereignly untranslatable[29]—and with the enigmatic and problematic relation of the *logos* to the idea of translation. So the Heideggerian motif of the *unthought* comes to serve in the "Agency" as a peg on which to hang the reciprocal translatability of Freud and Saussure, but at the same time the Lacanian reference of (Freudian) desire to (Heideggerian) truth could have made possible a reading of Freud—via Lacan—by Heidegger.

It is thus to meaning [*signifiance*] that the final appeal is made, for immediately after the recourse to Heidegger Lacan invokes experience and transmission: "If I speak of the letter and of Being, if I distinguish the other and the other, this is because Freud indicates them to me as terms to which efforts of resistance and transference against which I have had to measure myself for the twenty years that I've been exercising this practice. . . . It is also because I must help others not to get lost in them. It is to prevent the field they have inherited from falling fallow, and to that end make them understand that if the symptom is a metaphor, it is not a metaphor to say so . . ."[30] Let us stop for a moment. You will have noticed that, along with the inheritance received and the inheritance bequeathed there is a whole substitution of proper names accompanying metaphoricity, the proper name being the asemantic nucleus from which metaphors unfold. To say that Lacan is a metaphor for Heidegger or his symptom, would be to recognize that Heidegger is *literally* the truth of Lacan, the truth that would place the language of psychoanalysis, as well as the language of philosophy, under the sign of a basic literality to be understood, rather than under that of a metaphoricity to be deciphered.[31] But the proper name has a fixed referent, and the sign's distinction rules a homoiotic interpretation of truth. This is why Lacan not only adds that "it is not a metaphor to say so," but specifies that "the symptom *is* a metonymy . . .," which makes Being itself appear in its pure truth and *signifiance*, even if Being appears in its negative form in the text's final exhortation: "I ...invite you to be indignant that after so many centuries of religious hypocrisy and philosophical bluster, nothing has yet been validly articulated of what links metaphor to the question of Being and metonymy to its lack— . . ."

In conclusion, I shall make two remarks about this conclusion. The first is a question: what can have happened to make Lacan retreat from his discourse's metaphor about metaphor at the moment when his text could appear to be entirely metaphorical, when his turning of Saussure could be linked to the return, guided by the function of resemblance (*nemesis and homoiosis*)? Lacan's transformation of Saussure's schema into an algorithm by displacing the signifier to the position above the bar—the position where Saussure had placed the signified—could have been a mere substitution of one word for another, in this case using the same words. By saying that it is not a metaphor to say that the symptom is a metaphor, Lacan casts suspicion on everything that restricted his discourses's movement, its rhetoric and effects of style (the sheaf of his discourse substituting for his name) to the literality of metaphor and a generalized metaphoricity. In so doing, he mimics Heidegger, who, in the *Letter on Humanism*, after saying that "thought works to (construct) the house of Being, the jointing of Being coming to enjoin man to dwell *in* the truth of Being," asserts, a little later, that "the discourse on the house of Being is not a metaphor transforming the image of house towards Being, but it is from the essence of Being correctly thought that we will one day be able to think what house and dwelling are."[32] Should we simply think in terms of a tropic inversion between discourse and predicate and subject, signifier and signified?—or, if the language (*die Sprache*) is the house of Being, must we think differently about metaphoricity and its *retrait*, made possible by the *retrait* of Being: must we redefine the house's intimacy as the unhomelike site of the *retrait*? "The *Retrait* of Metaphor"[33] develops these questions to the fullest extent; however, I will add that our reservations about the metaphorical invagination of *Dichtung* in *Verdichtung*—the passage of one into the other in a distant proximity—could be removed by defying the usual use of metaphoricity, but undermining at the same stroke, through the law of the double, the Lacanian conception of metaphor.

My second remark (prelude to a long footnote to come) concerns metaphor's links to the question of Being. Since it is not *Something*, Being cannot be said metaphorically. One cannot speak of it properly or literally but only with a supplementary *trait* articulating the trace which Being's *retrait* will have left. However, the *retrait* of the metaphorical will have the meaning both of what retreats and of what returns, of what retraces in the *retrait* of the *trait* when the "subject" desists from the *estance* (the right for standing that is given to it by Ego (the "Me—you know . . . "), for I do not know what I mean before Being's *retrait* as the *retrait* of metaphor has been manifested. This *retrait* allows one to think less of what binds metaphor to Being than of what unbinds and broaches their *traits*.

The borrowed metaphor of the *retrait* comes to announce that I am leaving speech after drawing a dash - between Me and psychanalysis which, through my voice, will have been held to a rigorously unstable discourse, in a language that only speaks in translation. All I'll have done is interpret a silence, the silence I broke when I started to speak.

Notes

1 Jacques Lacan, Écrits, Paris: Seuil, 1966, pp. 493-528. Tr. by Alan Sheridan as "The Agency of the Letter in the Unconscious, or Reason since Freud," in *Écrits: a selection*, London: Tavistock, 1977, pp. 146-78 [Translator's note: We have translated the "depuis" of Lacan's title as "from" to allow the points that follow.]

2 As is later affirmed and reaffirmed: "could it be a dead letter that I put as the title of one of the pieces that I said were *Écrits* . . . , the agency of the letter as reason of the unconscious," "Lituraterre," in *Littérature*, 3, 1971.

3 Paris: Galilée, 1973.

4 "The Unconscious," *Pelican Freud Library*, Vol. 11.

5 *The Interpretation of Dreams*, PFL, 3

6 I refer here to Michel Neyraut, *Les logiques de l'inconscient*, Paris: Hachette, 1978.

7 *Wittgenstein und der Wiener Kreis*, Frankfurt-am-Main: Suhrkamp, 1984.

8 *Leçons et conversations*, Paris: Gallimard, 1971, p. 91.

9 *Leçons sur l'esthétique*, Paragraph 20.

10 William Bartley III., *Wittgenstein*, Philadelphia and New York: T.B. Liffincot Co., 1973.

11 *Leçons et conversations*, p. 94.

12 *Remarques mêlées*, p. 46.

13 *Écrits*, p.498; tr. p. 150.

14 According to Sylviane Agacinski's reading, in her "Découpages du Tractatus," in Agacinski et al., *Mimésis des articulations,* Paris: Aubier-Flammarion, 1975.

15 *Écrits*, p. 801; tr. p. 299.

16 *Écrits*, p. 806; tr. p. 304.

17 *Écrits*, p.799; tr. p.297

18 Ibid., p.10.

19 Op. cit.

20 *Écrits*, p. 860.

21 p. 806; tr. p. 304.

22 *Écrits*, p. 722.

23 *Écrits*, p. 495; tr. p. 148.

24 The formula for metonymy: f(S . . . S') S $\simeq$. For metaphor: F (S'/S) S(+) s.

25 "Freud et la scène de l'écriture" (1966), in *L'écriture et la différence* (Paris: Seuil, 1967; tr. Alan Bass, *Writing and Difference*, London: Routledge, 1979) must be re-read to appreciate the extent to which it responds, knowingly or not, to "The Agency of the letter. . ."

26 "Note on the Mystic Writing-Pad," PFL, 11, 429-34.

27 In French *Confrontation*. 8 (1982), and *Psyché: Inventions de l'autre*, Paris: Galilée, 1987, 145-58.

28 That of Philippe Lacoue-Labarthe ("L'Écho du sujet," in *Le sujet de la philosophie*, Paris:Aubicr-Flammarion, 1979, that of Jacques Derrida ("Désistance," in *Psyché*, op. cit., pp. 597-638).

29 *Écrits*, p. 526; tr., 173-4.

30 Here I rejoin *Le titre de la lettre*, pp. 136-8.

31 I refer, in a modified transcription, to *Le titre de la lettre*, note to p. 144.

32 The quotation is taken up by Derrida in "Le retrait de la métaphore," *Psyché*, pp. 63-93 (tr. in *Enclitic*, Vol II, Number 22, Fall 1978), a text I follow in my conclusion.

33 A reading that must be preceded by that of "La mythologie blanche," in *Marges de la philosophie*, Paris: Minuit, 1972, pp. 249-324

Chapter 6

The Imaginary and the Unimaginable

The Mathematics of the Imaginary and the Problem of the Unconscious in the Thought of Matte Blanco

Pietro Bria
Sergio De Risio

The term IMAGINARY is rarely if ever used in Freud's texts. Naturally, we cannot make the same statement as far as correlative terms are concerned. The role of the "psychic image" is fundamental in Freud, from the beginning, and is the basis for his ideas on the unconscious and on the relationship between the unconscious and the conscious. In Freud's works, the latter is connected to the relationship between image and word (for example, the relationship between "thing presentation" and "word presentation"). The role of the imaginary, so important for the psychic image, is expressed by the title of the first official journal of psychoanalysis: IMAGO.

In his *Studies of Hysteria*, Freud had a clear idea that pathological mental activity (and mental activity in general) was guided by a recurrence that holds together the threads of the complex mental fabric in order to construct the central nucleus of the neurotic complex. Originally Freud was drawn to the contents of these imaginary elaborations, but the extraordinary organization in Chapters VI and VII of *The Interpretation of Dreams*, focused on "The Means of Representation in Dreams," emphasizing the formal, logical processes that supervise the organization of oneiric work. Within the context of what he calls the conditions of representation of essential dream thoughts in oneiric images, Freud lists four principles: displacement, condensation, representation by symbols, and secondary elaboration. In his analysis these conditions are mainly connected to the problem of logical relations between elements. Within the sphere of "dream thoughts", the unconscious material that forms the starting point of the oneiric composition, Freud distinguishes certain forms known as *unconscious fantasies*, which he considers immediately usable by the formation processes of dreams (given their nature and structure.)

These unconscious fantasies, the main component of the imaginary dimension, may be studied for their content (for example, Kleinian studies, and object-relation's theory), or for their logical structure, which should bring us close to the intimate essence of the unconscious.

Freud dealt with this aspect of structural logic again in his 1915 work *The Unconscious*, where he highlighted the main characteristics of the unconscious system:

> There are in this system no negation, no doubt, no degree of certainty. The processes of the system Unc are timeless, they are not ordered temporally, are not altered by the passage of time; they have no reference to time at all. . .The Unconscious processes pay just as little regard to reality. . .To sum up: exemption from mutual contradiction of primary processes (mobility of cathexes), timelessness, and replacement of external by psychical reality–these are the characteristic which we may expect to find in processes belonging to the Unc system.

What emerges indisputably is the problem of space-time, to borrow terminology from Einstein's theory of relativity.

We have to underline the indissoluble bond between the conditions of spatiality and the conditions of any type of representation: every form of representation must possess some form of extension in space. The spatial problem is expressed implicitly in Freud's work from a topical point of view, and explicitly. Of the fragmentary notes Freud wrote in 1938, the penultimate states that:

> Space may be the projection of the extension of the psychic apparatus. No other derivation is probable. Instead of Kant's a *priori* determinants of our psychical apparatus. The psyche is extended; one knows nothing about it.

Lacan was one of the few theoreticians to deal with the psyche as a spatial extension, attempting to explain its extraordinary complexity by distinguishing between the Unconscious and the Conscious.

If we consider all the characteristics of the unconscious system elaborated by Freud in detail, our reflections consist entirely of paradoxical formulations that are initially unsurmountable. What relationship is possible between an external reality rigorously within the normal four-dimensional coordinates (of space plus time), and an internal reality where space-time is so radically disconnected that, according to Freud, it disappears entirely?

Lacan responds by elaborating an imaginary topology, based on classic figures of general, algebraic and combinatory topology such as *the Moebius Strip, the Torus, the Klein Bottle, the Cross-Cap Sphere and the Borromean Knot*. He aims for a single psychic reality that extends continuously between (and is therefore able to understand) the polarities of the internal an external worlds. For example, the *Moebius Strip* and the *Cross-cap* sphere show the divided subject (conscious/unconscious) and its relationship with the external in a way that depicts the effect of the divisions; thus he topologically accounts for the paradoxes implicit in those primary unconscious relationships where penetrating means being penetrated, attacking means being attacked, and desiring means being desired. These are what Lacan calls *specular* relationships (which we may call *symmetric* in Matte Blanco's terminology), whereby the object is included in the subject and the subject is included in the object in a seamless fashion. Furthermore, in the 1938 notes Freud elucidates the area we are attempting to define: having and being in children. Children like expressing an object-relation by an identification: 'I am the object'. 'Having' is the latter of the two; after loss of the object it relapses into 'being'. Example: the breast. 'The breast is part of me, I am the breast'. Only later: 'I have it'—that is, 'I am not it' . . . .

Freud refers to something which can be intuited, but as Lacan attempts to show, cannot be said. As Nasio states his geometric entities are singular artifices, time-space effectuations which, like a very particular theater, create drama out of paradox. In his Elements, Euclid associates a figure with every demonstration. According to J. Dieudonné, it seems somewhat surprising that every theory is accompanied by a figure. One might be led to think that this is simply an aid to help understand the demonstration better . . . But then we realize that some of the figures have a much more essential function, not very far from the methods of Indian or Chinese geometers who, once the figure has been traced, are satisfied with saying "Look!" as a demonstration. These figures should allow the analyst to perceive the disconcerting presence of the unconscious with greater ease and clarity, supplying a "visible" conceptual background, a rigorous reference for the imaginable (a rigorous background for speculative imagination, as Bion would say) and allowing him or her to "calculate" the effects. According to Lacan in the *Four Basic Concepts of Psychoanalysis* "Our conception (of the unconscious) implies that it is always established in an approach in relationship to what is imposed upon us as a form, the infinitesimal calculation . . . It (the concept of the unconscious) is only realized through a leap, a passage to the limit . . . We therefore need to state just how that conceptual elaboration, in the form of what I would call finite quantities, called the unconscious, transpires".

Matte Blanco is situated in this crucial area. The Unconscious is first a system, a structure, it is no longer merely the site of repressed mental contents, but a group of structural laws that define a particular syntax for these contents. But a fundamental level of the psyche is also concerned with the undivided being, completely alien from the time-space of the Conscious. Freud seems to have intuited the dialectic between mental levels in the note cited above: "having" and "being" in the child: the level of object-relation ("I have the breast") and the level of the being one with the object ("I am the breast"). According to Matte Blanco, this level of being one with the other comes into conflict with the (three-dimensional) limits of the conscious thought that divides, separates and puts individuals in relation to each other. This dimensional discarding–structural in the human creates a "tension" that is destined to remain unsolved, and is at the base of our symbolic creativity and our particular mental suffering.

We thus have two aspects of the psychic being that are incompatible but constantly entwined in every psychic manifestation. At the dawn of philosophy these aspects are expressed in ontological terms by Parmenides (Unity, Homogeneity, Immobility) and Heraclitus (Division, Difference, Becoming). Their co-existence gives rise to an antinomy situated at the base of our mental operation that characterizes our emotional being. Matte Blanco called it the "fundamental antinomy of being," and defined its single-minded structural character as the expression of a fundamental ontological fact:

> There is in human beings and in the world a mode of being which expresses itself in the distinction between things, hence in their division: and another mode which treats any object of knowledge as if it were non-divided: the heterogenic and the indivisible mode (1988, p. 64).

In Matte Blanco's work the fundamental antinomy is the arrival point of a long, tormented intellectual journey where it is necessary to examine three significant stages:

1. The formulation of the Freudian Unconscious as a Bi-logical structure, a cross between the principle of non-contradiction in classical and Aristotelian logic and what Matte Blanco called symmetrical logic. This is an application of the principle of symmetry according to which all asymmetrical relations are treated as if they were symmetrical–including fundamental relations such as order and belonging, at the basis of logic and mathematics. If A is the father of B, then B is the father of A; if A is part of B, B is part of A; is A is on the left of B, then B is on the left of A; if A is before A, then B is before A. The application of this principle to conscious logic implied a dissolution of its time-space organization, the violation of the Aristotelian principle of non-contradiction, and the impossibility of formulating general concepts as a result of the identification established between part and whole, element and class. Thus the principle of symmetry becomes the logical expression of the presence of the invisible world.

This principle is alien to thought and logic. It is, however, "circumscribed" within the broad networks of logical thought, and gives rise to various combinations, one of which - and the most important for our practical lives - is the biological structure of the unconscious.

This new concept of the unconscious develops a revolutionary bi-logical epistemology making use of both ordinary logic, bivalent or not—which characterizes scientific thought—and symmetrical logic. In *Thinking, Feeling and Being*, recently published in London, Matte Blanco states that:

> Classical and symmetrical logic entered into various types of relationships with one another. The result was a process of reasoning conforming not to one logic, as had hitherto been considered in science, but to two: a bi-logical process. In the end, therefore, we have three types of logic at our disposal to study the mind and the world: classical logic, symmetrical logic and bi-logic (1988, p. 64) . . . The Freudian unconscious is the realm of bi-logical structures and, as such, the realm of the antinomies (1988, p. 82).

2. The isomorphism between the logic of the unconscious an the logic of the infinite has led Matte Blanco to formulate mathematical infinity as a bi-logical structure. With Matte Blanco the infinite—which has been so fundamental for philosophic thought since its pre-Socratic origin—plays, for the first time, a decisive and operative role in psychology. The field of the Unconscious becomes the "site" of the mind, where processes and operations of infinitization are underway, which makes the whole class take the places of the individual element. For example, the concrete mother becomes Mother, the actual infinite of all possible, concrete and symbolic mothers. The element or part is subsumed into one of the totalities of all. Part and whole are identified as a consequence of the principle of symmetry, revealing the essential, structural aspect of the emotions, psychic qualities and basic perspectives on the dynamics and genesis of unconscious psychic conflict (Bria, 1989). The chain of isomorphism thereby increases the logic of the unconscious, the logic of the Infinite, the logic of the Emotions.

3. The Unconscious is formulated in multidimensional spatial terms, making space the essential coordinate of thought and its representative function. The Conscious is imaginative since its organizational reality seems to be based, by necessity, on perceptual space, on the three dimensional space of the image. With this premise, Matte Blanco revived a 1954 proposal by the mathematicians Courant and Robbins (Estudios de psicologia dinamica). He speaks of the possibility of representing an n-dimensional space in terms of a space of dimensions inferior to n. This proposal became the basis for an extraordi-

nary reflection on the relationships between space and mind, the final part of Blanco's *Unconscious as Infinite Sets* (1974).

When n-dimensional space is represented by means of a space of (n–1) dimensions the (n–l)dimensional spaces or those inferior to (n–1) are repeated in those representations. The simplest example is the triangle ACB proposed by Courant and reintroduced by Matte Blanco. The triangle ACB is a region of a plane, a two-dimensional space. If we rotate the side AC to the left and the side BC to the right so that they both form a straight line with AB, we have the line CABC. We can consider this line—which is a segment of a straight line that extends to infinity on both sides—as the representation of this triangle, a region of a two-dimensional space, in the line CABC, a segment of a one-dimensional space. As we can see in this representation, we had to represent the point C, a O-dimensional space twice.

In the case of a three-dimensional translating of a space with more then three dimensions, we can observe a multiplication or repetition of volumes where the number becomes greater by increasing the dimension of the space to be represented, until it becomes infinite. This multiplication is the three dimensional unfolding of a region of space with dimensions greater than three, in which n volumes of three-dimensional space are all together in what, to our three-dimensional "eyes"—connected to the image—appears as the same volume and therefore in the same space and the same time.

In a more recent work dedicated to the structures of oneiric space, Matte Blanco clarifies and develops the concept:

> An analysis in terms of space of more than three dimensions shows that the confusion of two or more volumes in a single one is the consequence of seeing an isomorphic reality of a space of more than three dimensions as three dimensional. Perhaps—but I am not certain—we can say that something which is one and only one thing in three dimensions —and thus our astonishment at discovering that the man is father and son of himself. In a space of more than three dimensions we can *put in* a lot of things, but there, like a space of only three dimensions, *there* we cannot put in more than a single thing (for example, two people cannot be contemporaneously seated in exactly the same place on a chair). The reasons could be that where we do not see any possibility of allowing another person to enter the concept of space

> of 6 or more dimensions, let's say, it allows us to find immense, *multi-dimensional caverns*, as it were, empty and hidden where everything seemed full because there were no other dimensions available to think about in a three dimensional space. It is just in these enormous emptiness/empty places of a pluridimensional space that we can comfortably fit three dimensional things where there was no place for them in a three-dimensional space . . . The result is that every region of a given space is unique while it is also more than one if this space is considered as a sub-space of a space of superior dimensions (1982, p. 94).

The three-dimensional Conscious (tied to the imaginative process) appears as a sub-space in contrast to the multidimensional Unconscious. For the latter to manifest itself in the Conscious, it must be subject to its laws—as Freud also believed—which are also laws (and limits) of the representative process. In *Studies on Hysteria* (1895), Freud intuited the profound sense of this dimensional dialectic:

> If it were possible, after the case had been completely cleared up, to demonstrate the pathogenic material to a third person in what we now know is its complicated and multi-dimensional organization, we should rightly be asked how a camel like this got through the eye of the needle. For there is some justification for speaking of the "defile" of consciousness. The term gains meaning and liveliness for a physician who carries out an analysis like this. Only a single memory at a time can enter ego-consciousness. . .The whole spatially extended mass of psychogenic material is in this way drawn through a narrow cleft and thus arrives in consciousness cut up, as it were, into pieces or strips. It is the psychotherapist's business to put these together once more into the organization which he presumes to have existed. Anyone who has a craving for further similes may think at this point of a Chinese puzzle (1892-95, p. 292, S.E.).

According to Matte Blanco the territory of the Unconscious is defined by the limits of our consciousness, which cannot work with more than three spatial dimensions. In his words:

> By its own nature, consciousness or the asymmetrical mode of being, when it functions in its fullness, cannot focus on more than one thing at a time. It must separate one thing from the next. Whereas by its own nature the symmetrical mode of being is all-embracing: it identifies the individual with the all, so that all individuals become identical to one another and to the class. Consciousness, in contrast, when confronted by a whole class, can only consider it in two ways:

> either it focuses on the limits (or definition) of the class, that is on those precise features which characterize it and distinguish it from all other classes, or it concentrates on the individuals which form the class. In both cases it must conform to its nature, which prevents it from seeing more than one thing at a time . . . No wonder then that a whole class, symmetrically grasped, cannot enter consciousness: the nature of consciousness prevents it. The situation can be compared to that of the jug in a painting which cannot contain water, because of the difference in dimension between the painted jug and the substance called water.

In this case, the repression, if we may still use the term, is structural: in a hypothetical, infinite-dimensional consciousness, the Unconscious would cease to exist, and the conscious would be absolute and occupy our entire mental potential. To use Matte Blanco's words the symmetrical being could enter and be grasped consciously. Thought and being would thus coincide.

In this context, the *oneiric imagination*, which Freud called the main road for the unconscious, becomes the site to study the process through which the multidimensional reality of the Unconscious (coinciding with the deep level of our affections, with "equations" and identity strange to logic) attempts to achieve representation, *unfolding* in the field of image and becoming three-dimensional. One of the authors reread Freud's *Interpretation of Dreams* from this point of view, and identified condensation and movement as the central mechanisms of this unfolding.

Thus, in Matte Blanco's theory, the process of becoming three-dimensional is accompanied by the more general function of thought, *translation*, or *unfolding*, and their relationship with the unconscious. Finally, Matte Blanco states:

> As a conclusion we may say that numerous facts which at first sight appear completely chaotic become perfectly well-ordered if we apply the concept of space of more than three dimensions. The dreamer (and the unconscious) behave like a geometrician who handles a number of variables superior to three and who is forced to use in his representation a space of dimensions not higher than three (1974, p. 433).

This reflection of the Unconscious through the mediation of the oneiric transformations is tied to the limits of consciousness. In contrast to the multi-dimensional nature of our emotional life, consciousness does what it can to be represented. Consciousness is important both for its cognitive value, for emotional development, and for the transformation of therapeutic significance.

The imaginary is an extremely powerful term for understanding the essential nature of a process that, making use of the image, attempts to substantiate an effective reality (the reality of the pure symmetrized class, according to Matte Blanco). This reality characterizes the deepest levels of the unconscious, which might be alien to any imaginative structure. In other words, the imaginary is an attempt to translate or unfold the unimaginable.

We believe that Melanie Klein used this term (although it had already been mentioned in Freud) within this problematic context to describe the vicissitudes of a child's emotional life. At first this term might appear contradictory, since the realm of fantasy seems incompatible with the structural laws of the unconscious. And yet, in light of what we have said, unconscious fantasy and the imaginary do coincide, and in their formulation they reflect a structural aspect of the reality they are attempting to describe: its antinomic nature, which is isomorphic to the unconscious.

Freud concludes, or rather suspends, his last theoretical writings with a discussion of this problem:

> Philosophy and literature have often toyed with it, but science could find no use for it. Psycho-analysis has seized upon the concept, has taken it seriously and has given it a fresh content. By its researches, it has led to a knowledge of characteristics of the unconscious psychical which have hitherto been unsuspected, and it has discovered some of the laws which govern it. But none of this implies that the quality of being conscious has lost its importance for us. It remains the one light which illuminates our path and leads us through the darkness of mental life. In consequence of the special character of our discoveries, our scientific work in psychology will consist in translating unconscious processes into conscious ones, and thus filling in the gaps in conscious perception . . .(1940 [1938], p. 286, S.E.)

SESSION IV

Chapter 7

The Imaginary in Psychoanalytic Metapsychology

Diego Napolitani

"...Octopus sliding
inky tentacles through the rocks
may use you. You belong to him
and you don't know it. You are him,
you believe you are yourself."
From "Indian Serenade," by Montale[1]

Foreword

The 36th Congress of the International Psychoanalytic Association (Rome 1989) heatedly discussed the theme "Common Ground in Psychoanalysis: Clinical Aims and Process," in an attempt to answer Wallerstein's question "One psychoanalysis or many?", which opened the previous Congress (1987, Montreal). The problematic approach to this subject revealed the uneasiness caused by the undefined range of theoretical models in which psychoanalysis is fragmented today. Before the 1970's, in metapsychological terms its identity was universally accepted, however wide its range of theoretical models. But today, there are signs of a strong break between adherents to the scientific ideal informing the metapsychological construction, and those who refer mainly to aesthetics, narratology and hermeneutics. This splitting of psychoanalytic culture reflects the profound epistemological crisis affecting all areas of modern knowledge. The dichotomy of a rigid scientific ideal and a deep humanistic vocation present in all of Freud's work can be viewed as an anticipation of this crisis.

In this paper I wish to show how my re-thinking of Freud, has led me to single out important contradictory structures at the basis of an unresolved epistemological conflict that pervades his entire work. The fact that I have recognized this conflict and have given it a subjective sense, in a historical, relativistic perspective, has prevented me from simply becoming its unconscious transmitter. Furthermore, I can no longer allow myself to be seduced by the idealizing assumption that psychoanalysis has its own pragmatic-cognitive order, which cannot be compared with, or criticized by, other fields of knowledge. This has prevented me from being swept up by the aging but still vital querelle over the scientific status of psychoanalysis as a traditional empirical deductive science, such as in Grünbaum's recent work (1984, 1986). When I compare Freud's scientistic ideal to his humanistic vocation, I do not mean that Freud's contradiction consists in a conflict between science and philosophy, but in maintaining, at times with dramatic insistence, his original metaphysical thought—positivistic scientism in its metahistorical and reductionistic perspective—even after he had been forced to question it because of his discovery of the relational historicity of neuroses. The relativistic, phenomenological tendencies that had appeared in his early clinical experiences reappeared, more or less explicitly, throughout his entire work in an obvious contradiction which, though, was never sufficiently worked through as a consequence of his fundamentally scientistic orientation.

Giving sense to a conflict pervading the cultural or familial origins of our identity does not mean giving it a definitive sense. Nor does it mean reaching an optimal distance from that conflict, or safeguarding one's future production from containing contradictory elements, new conflictual sequences, or new aporias. But *re-conceiving* our cultural origins implies bringing them back into the vital circle of our subjective configurations of the world, a circle of exchanges and symbolic responses from which all creative *contingency* emerges.

Freud's complex contradiction can be illustrated by the following metaphor: if a father deeply rooted in his cultural and familial tradition, but with a free and creative nonconformist spirit (in a letter to Fliess, Freud defined himself as an "adventurer") saw his own child—the product of his creative thought, his own intellectual "son"—grow and interact with the world around him according to this spirit, until the father himself becomes frightened and hands the child over to a religious institution or a military school to give him a strict, disciplined upbringing (the Church and the Army, as relevant social metaphors, recur in Freud's original work on the Super-Ego). But this child, while conforming to the Order to which the father has entrusted him, will always maintain an intimate disorder, a poetic disposition, and encounters with his father will always be characterized by moments of authenticity ambiguously mixed with strong calls to Prussian discipline.

Freud began his research in medicine, neurology and psychiatry according to the positivistic views of the academic culture of his time; he summarized this orientation in the "Project for a Scientific Psychology." But he found himself more and more involved with an experiential dimension in which the "truths" he faced appeared radically different from positivistic truths. Positivistic truths could be verified in experiments and explained in causal terms that accept the ontologic objectivity of things, and exclude anything irrational from the realm of scientific knowledge. The truths with which Freud found himself unexpectedly and intimately involved arose instead from subjective, partial, maimed, and contradictory narrations, which forced him to consider four fundamental questions:

1) the relational basis of every mental event, in contrast to the monadic representation of the anatomical-physiological individual;
2) casualness, which shocked him and which in his essay on Leonardo Da Vinci, he defined as "the scandal of the results of an investigation leaving to the casualness of the parental constellation such a decisive influence on the destiny of man";
3) the inapplicability of experimental verifications within this investigation, so that every statement was necessarily weighed down by the systematic doubt inherent in the arbitrariness of its construction (1937);
4) irrationality as the other face of rationality, both equally important in every process of communication and knowledge, as we see, for instance, in the transferential components of every relationship.

Today we can wonder why Freud avoided the huge question suggested by his experiences. Why did he abandon (though never completely and definitively) the phenomenological and hermeneutic approach?

A very difficult and taboo question, is the extent to which Freud's self-analysis, both in its procedure and results, can be considered the model for current clinical practice, and for the teaching methods of psychoanalytical institutes.

Is Metapsychology the Outcome of the 'Failure' of Freud's Selfanalysis?

In September 1897 Freud wrote a letter to Fliess in which he stated that he had given up his *neurotica*, and though this represented "a general catastrophe" for him, he confessed to being not at all depressed, for he felt "a sense of triumph rather than defeat." From this point on, he began his self-analysis, which would become the basis for *The Interpretation of Dreams*. His father's death and its influence on his entire self-analysis, are poignantly recalled by Freud in the preface to the second edition of that book:

> "[This book] appeared to me as a passage from my own autobiography, as *my reaction to the death of my father*, therefore to the most important event, to the most painful loss in a man's life." (my italics)

The "reactive" character of his enterprise consists in Freud's orienting his self-analysis, and its subsequent constructions toward a representation of the conflicted condition of human existence, which excluded any parental responsibility or guilt toward the child. In this representation the father's *auctoritas* is fully restored in the form of academic knowledge, which at the time was strictly anchored to scientific postulates. If Freud's turning point contains strong elements of a *Reaktionbildung*–a reaction formation to an inadequately worked through experience of mourning –Freud's selfanalysis could be considered the prototype for an unsuccessful analysis, which heavily affected the development of his thought and of all psychoanalytical culture.

But we do not want to call Freud's analytical treatment "a failure" on the basis of this scant biographical information, we can call it "successful". We only have to adopt the same assessment parameters used by psychoanalytic training institutes: an analysis is considered "successful", if the analysand shows he or she has achieved a "psychoanalytical conscience," and assumes as his or her own the "discoveries" of the unconscious and the method for reaching them suggested by the analyst throughout the course of the analysis. One result of this interpretation of psychoanalytical conscience is the multiplication of schools and sub-schools with their bonds of loyalty and their strong conflicts. This is one of the problems which arose from the start of the psychoanalytical movement and has been discussed by M. Balint (1947, 1953) and by J. Cremerius (1989), but has not led to changes in psychoanalytic institutions. In this perspective, analytical "success" does not simply consist in the analysand's generic acceptance of the analyst's ideology, but in the fact that the analysand structures his or her new "conscience" according to strong, objective, universal, and therefore presumably scientific, categories produced by the metapsychological "common ground" at the foundation of all psychoanalytic institutions.

The "success" of Freud's self-analysis consists in his reconversion to the scientistic ideal of his time, which Fliess personified in a most bizarre and literally deadly way (Masson, 1986). I stress the word "conversion" (with its obvious references to hysteria), recalling Kuhn's statement as quoted by Wallerstein, "what each takes to be facts depends in part on the theory he espouses, and ...an individual's transfer of allegiance from theory to theory is often better described as conversion than as choice." In *The Constructions in Analysis* (1937), Freud provides a particularly suggestive example of his metapsychological construction, which is characterized by an invasive and hegemonic thought that inhibits his creative freedom, typical of people who are subject to their own paranoical constructions. In the following passage he states that when facing difficulties that could lead to unbearable confusion and uncertainty:

> We must say to ourselves: and so-there is only the witch [citing a line from Goethe's *Faust*]. Well, this witch is metapsychology. We cannot advance even one step without speculating, theorizing–I was going to say, fantasizing–in metapsychological terms.

A Meaningful Example of Freud's Overcoming His Positivistic Ideal

In certain cases Freud abandoned his positivistic ideals and took a relational, non mechanistic approach to the problem of the decentered Ego. One of the most intense and comprehensive contacts with the world of the contingency and eventuality that he had "triumphantly" abandoned appears in the essay *Group Psychology and the Analysis of the Ego* (1921). This essay opens with a proposal for overcoming the ontological dichotomy between social psychology and individual psychology. Here the individual is no longer reducible to a set of drives and to an Ego, understood as that callousness which is produced on them in their friction with the world, but as a "subject"—in the sense of "subjugated"—to the indefinite complexity of history, traditions, and culture established in his or her language, and as the subject of his or her personal *poiesis*.

> Each individual is a constituent element of many masses, is subject to multilateral links and has built his own Ego ideal on the basis of the most varied models. Each individual is then participant of many collective souls...and he can rise, above these, to a minimum of autonomy and originality."

To this identificatory complexity, which is transpersonal, transgenerational, and consequently *relational*, Freud attributes an inductive power, similar to that of a hypnotist over the hypnotized subject, or of a charismatic leader over a subjugated crowd. The power of this identificatory complexity is *normally* exercised through judgments or reality testing voiced by the individual Ego but suggested by his or her intimate, overpowering prompter. This perspective gnoseologically summarized in Heidegger's question "Was heisst Denken?"(1954) (what does thinking mean, but also, what stimulates and orients our thinking?) warps the physiocratic (Napolitani, 1986) and metaphysical assumptions of metapsychology and simultaneously throws an oblique light on the "triumphant" turning point of Freud's thought. But while Freud in some way defines the imaginary universe and its power to replicate the Ego Ideal or Super-Ego, he does not define his intuition regarding the dimension of contingency and casualness -"autonomy and originality."

In my opinion, when Freud later wrote on autonomy in terms of saturations he framed the process from a positivistic, Enlightenment perspective; in this essay, autonomy and originality are not intended as the final outcome of a linear evolution, but as a significant moment of reorganization of mental life, according to Bion's concept of catastrophe.

Freud never returned to this thesis, which was so insidious for the congruence of his metapsychological rationality, and he minimized the transpersonal and historical relevance of the SuperEgo. He described the latter as a derivative of drives, as one of the "inner objects" (as M. Klein would later explain) produced by fantasmatical vicissitudes. These vicissitudes are all inscribed in the universal anthropological core that would take only its name from the tragedy of Oedipus (if you read the myth in its entirety). Freud precociously shows his uneasiness about having "raised himself above his collective souls" when he would later dedicate only two notes to this colossal issue. The first note was added to a 1923 re-edition of *Group Psychology and the Analysis of the Ego* in which he states:

> With regard to the validity of such an attribution [of reality testing to the Ego Ideal] it seems however permitted to raise a doubt which requires deeper discussion.

Not only would this discussion never be raised again, but in the second note in *The Ego and the Id* (1922), he completely dismisses the subject stating:

> The attribution I made of reality testing to this super-Ego is simply wrong and requires correction. The fact that reality testing remains a peculiar task of the Ego itself should without a doubt correspond to the relationships of the Ego to the world perception.

Freud's entire work can therefore be read in terms of the above example: an endless conflict between the overwhelming power of an implicit ideal "ordered" by its social, cultural, familial tradition and his early uncertain "vocation." From this vocation arose a prospect that the evils of the soul, and more generally, the human condition, were inevitably marked by the crushing power of the environment, which was *necessarily* intending, manipulative, seductive; dramatic conflicts may *con-*

tingently arise between this environment, once it has been internalized, and an obscure "autonomy and originality." This environment, does not consist in traumatic events that took place in childhood, but in the historical necessity of an individual's cultural growth.

Since metapsychology resulted from the false success of Freud's self-analysis, it has obscured, though never completely eradicated, its original historicist-relational vision. Freud's concept of "collective souls" as a transpersonal structure of the mind anticipates developments in psychoanalytical thought by various authors interested in the intrinsically relational quality of psychic events, such as Ferenczi, Fairbairn, Guntrip, Balint, Winnicott, Bion, and Foulkes. Despite their theoretical differences they have all stressed the relational foundation of individual identity and its possible transformations through a creative attitude. Today we could define this attitude as *autopoietic cognition*, a concept proposed by Maturana and Varela (1980). Some of the most meaningful developments in this area can be found in group analysis, founded by S. H. Foulkes (1975).

The Experience of Self in its Two Components

By the term "Self", I mean the complex representation arising from the intimate experience of one's own psychobiological organization–according to the paradigm of complexity–which has two sides.

a) The "Idem" and the Experience of Continuity

I call the identificatory complexity, which Freud refers to as "collective souls," the *imaginary universe*. This universe is made up of images, by which I mean not pure mnestic traces of sensitive impressions, but *configurations of relational complexities* in which the subject has been a constituent element since the beginning of his or her existence. These configurations are created in a series of encounters by the original psychobiological self-organization with the subject's intentional and affective environment. Each configuration maintains the characteristic traits of these encounters. Maintaining these traits means that each of these imaginary configurations persists as a prime element of personal identity, a *vital presence*, that shape the subject, the world, and the relationships between the Self and the world according to the affective, ideological patterns taught by the cultural environment (in Italian the word for *teaching*, *In-segnare* comes from the late Latin *in-signare*, to engrave one's signs on other's minds). Every subsequent contact with the world causes the imaginary devices acquired to resound, and express themselves through the most varied logical, affective and behavioral formalizations. These include ethical apriori imperatives, structures of the cosmologies of "common senses" (T. Reid, mentioned by D. Napolitani, 1982), particular behavioral or affective attitudes, and the so-called "free associations" in a transferential relationship. However different these formalizations may be, they are all *ordinative suggestions of the world and of the subject's relationships to it.* These imaginary, intentioning presences create a relational network that is the group matrix of personal identity, the identical component of the Self that I call the *idem*. The idem is fundamentally inert and apparently unitary. The transgenerational continuity of culture is secured, through its presumably innate status.

b) The "Autòs" and the Experience of Discontinuity

A second component of the Self experience induces the individual to re-construct the perceptive data of *both the outer and the inner world* in gnoseological terms. Any "natural" phenomenon enters into the typical human landscape by virtue of its *acculturation*–its being placed in a map of genetic meanings that is either already well established in one's culture, or partly recreated by the subject. Arnold Gehlen (1978) takes the anthropological view that "the natural environment of man is his culture", and therefore no datum is ever directly perceived or assumed as matter of transformation, but always assumed and only through the mediation of signification investing that datum and making it present as an event in the human universe. When this "making present" is not an accomplished process, the appearance of an opaque datum causes opaque responses, such as astonishment or anxiety. I use the term "autòs" for what E. Morin calls (1982) the *auto-re-organizational* component of the Self, a sort of "author" of the human world's occurrence, who could be referred to that mysterious subject of "autonomy and originality" which Freud contrasted with the subject subordinated to his "collective souls". But for Freud autonomy is manifested when the subject rises "above" his or her matrices–which seems to be related in some way to the concept of sublimation–whereas I think this undefinable "author" transforms the *subjectus–* that which is subjugated to the intentioning power of the idem–into *pro-jectus*, the subject-in-process–that is the subject of his or her own original symbolical narrations, in a word, into an *aesthetic* subject. The autòs must re-organize the configurations of sense that the imaginary device stores in its living archive in order to allow this existential transformation. *Authenticity* as a way of existing governed by the autòs is therefore the result of the dis-ordering/reordering traversing of *identicity*.

The "Innate Status" of Images and Their re-Birth: Conceiving What Is Already Conceived

Freud refers to the innate quality of images when he speaks about the mythical complex configurations (such as "the primitive horde") inscribed in the philogenetic mnestic patrimony. I refer not to a bio-genetic problem, but I want to confer a certain semantic ambiguity on *innate* images. The prefix *in* means both "in" and "not." In the word *intrude* it has a locative meaning, while in the word *in-valid* it has a negative meaning. If both meanings are applied to the word *innate*, then these intentioning presences can be seen as stirring and growing *within* ourselves, and that they did *not* originate from us, from our foundational or re-foundational attitude toward reality. If the autòs is the unrelenting and unpredictable author of the eventualization of the world, then it can compare the data emerging from both the inner and outer environment. If the objects of the inner world appear with the same opaque immediacy as inadequately symbolized natural objects, they provoke astonishment or anxiety. An anxious response leads to escape or to other survival mechanisms, while astonishment–that "perturbed and moved feeling," according to Vico–arouses curiosity and leads to an approach to the events emerging from one's inner or outer landscape. Gargani has recently written a book about the close relationship between astonishment and casualness (1985): his working through the phenomenology of creative thought is an important reference point for philosophy and for analytical practice.

Rethinking one's "innate" images, replacing them in a historical perspective, and questioning the exceeding sense by which they appear "obvious," rigidly hegemonize our subjective circuits of meanings, signifies bringing them to light, *conceiving* them. To conceive something that already exists in its completeness means our giving birth to what has already objectively been born, through that extraordinary logical paradox on which Winnicott (1971) built his own vision of a "transitional area". "Conceiving what is perceived" implies that intimate transitional experience from *sub-jectus* to *pro-jectus*, which may become a historic fact, or which may be denied, since this experience opens an intolerably catastrophic horizon of freedom and solitude.

The Psychoanalytic Praxis

a) Facing the Imaginary Game of Transference

The imaginary universe is reactivated every time the subject encounters the world, and is willing to follow the steps of *learning* set by the intentioning power of its original core (the Italian word for learning is *apprendere*, the opposite of *insegnare*, because it means *taking* the intentional signs of the Other *into* one's own mind). When elements from an individual's transpersonal matrix enter a new relationship, their inductive or suggestive power must be transferred. In this situation the relationship tends to assume the characteristics of the prevailing imaginary relationship, so the imaginary structures of one interlocutor are compared to those of the other, either in an antagonistically symmetrical or in a complementary way.

In this perspective, a subject who is pressured by the need for authenticity enters analysis following difficulty in accomplishing a reconceptive itinerary through the *idem* (or at least through those parts which compel him or her into a horizon of opaque necessities). The analytical relationship becomes the ambiguous setting for the most intense dramatization of the *idem*, which is exactly why it becomes their privileged place, where an original meaning of this dramatization can be built. This proves the Freudian assumption that analysis is substantially the analysis of transference, and any breach of its thick curtain reveals the prevalence of conceiving, transforming attitudes of the autòs in its *dis-continuity* toward the conservative attitudes of the *idem* in its *continuity*. This conflict is emotionally modulated by alternating moments of astonishment and anxiety at either the raw "naturalness" of the images or the possible break in the compactness of one's identicity.

b) The Double Circle of Symbolic Responses

Analytical practice does not consist therefore in rationalizing a crisis according to causal connections hypostatically attributed to an unconscious mechanism. Nor does it consist in defining borders and topography on a unitary and quasi- realistic map on the basis of archaeological finds (Spence, 1984). It consists in the construction of original symbolic significations of an individual's imaginary patrimony, which arises from a dialogical relationship facilitating the autopoietic or autoreorganizational mental processes. However analysis is not wholly the summation of single acts of signification, but rather the insertion of all such acts into a cycle of responses running among the most varied configurations of sense existing in one's diachronic and synchronic horizon. The intimate circularity of symbolic responses is established to the same extent as the circularity of interpretative responses between the analyst and the analysand. I do not mean that one symbolic circle *determines* the other, but that they reciprocally condition one another. Therefore when the analytical space is not what Winnicott calls the "area of transitional playing," or when the analyst pursues an objective, scientific model, and shirks a *relationship founded on an asymmetrical reciprocity* (Apel 1973), the establishment of an intimate circularity of symbolic significations is inhibited. Moreover, the joint relation between analyst and analysand–though functionally asymmetrical–should reproduce an analogous relationship among all the configurations of sense in their circular responses at the level of the interpersonal relationship.

The concept of inner or outer joint relation may be related to Whitebook's "pact of brothers," in his discussion of Freud's "*Totem and Taboo*." In my opinion this "pact" is not the result of renouncement-or repression-of infantile wishes (incest and parricide), but the only way for the symbolizing need of the human reorganizational core to express itself. In analytic practice this egalitarian, though asymmetrical dimension is therefore the final challenge to the attempt of both analyst and analysand to remain in a transferential parent/child relationship.

c) The Re-organizer Principles:
Concepts and Preconceptions

Although the circularity of symbolic returns constitutes an experience full of creative potential and symbolic exchanges with the Other, its trans-formative fluidity is disorienting, and episodic. Between any two episodes are moments of re-ordering one's intimate complexity as well as the interpersonal relationship in which the circularity of symbolic responses has taken place in conformity to any kind of legality[2]. The re-organizing principle can stem from the very product of the *conceptions* during the signification process. If a new idea is born, it will tend to prove itself by comparison with the world, and to submit all the relative configurations of sense to the world. This *conception* will always conserve the memory of birth and will thus be open to any possible transformation, to being jointly re-inserted in the circle of symbolic responses, and even to its own death.

A different situation exists when an *innate* ordering image, perhaps only superficially touched by the process of symbolic subjectivation, performs this function. We would then speak not of a *concept*, but of a *pre-conception*, of a configuration of sense installed in the *idem* at its origins and confused with them, which remains outside memory, time, transformation, decadence, and death. Because of its intrinsic ordinative power, the preconception does not tend to jointly enter the circuit of symbolic responses, but to hegemonize them, subordinating any other configuration of sense with the weakness of having been *born*, of having once been conceived by the subject (Gianni Vattimo's expression (1983) "weak thought" could refer not only to the situation of thought in an area deprived of "strong" ontological, objectivistic or metaphysical supports, but also to its creature quality, its knowledge of having been conceived and exposed to passing away). In this perspective we can speak of *paranoia* (not in strictly clinical terms) as the result of the hegemonizing process of a single imaginary segment over another configuration of sense. This hegemony develops through a hyper-rational argumentative procedure, in the everlasting search for clues that objectively certify the priority of the imaginary assumption over any other form of thought.

Paranoid objectivity is the most direct manifestation of the "naturalness" of the imaginary segments that were not born to one's subjectivity. The *rational certainty* related to this objectivity is in contrast to the *sentiment of truth*, whose peculiarly subjective character there is no reason to hide, which accompanies all authentically conceptual constructions, such as for any aesthetic experiences.

Why Does a Positivistic View Persist in Clinical Psychology?

The interpersonal experience of analysis can give a sense to the surprising persistence of a preconceptual thought, scientistic positivism, in most psychoanalytical culture. Introducing elements *exonerated from the order of necessity*, such as those referable to *auto-poietic casualness*, into this strictly deterministic culture, which might as well be strictly finalistic in terms of adaptativity and biological survival, means to radically subvert the entire cosmological vision to which psychoanalysis has always largely aspired to belong.

But why do psychology and particularly psychoanalysis resist the "revolution" (Kuhn, 1962) that modern thought has promoted? E. Morin maintains that the younger a science is, the more slowly and reluctantly it assimilates epistemological changes in its original discipline. Morin says that psychology still seems anchored to the strictly empirical-positivistic paradigms that the natural sciences have already long abandoned. I think that the psychoanalytic method itself can give a sense to this phenomenon.

Perhaps, unlike other pragmatic disciplines, psychology and psychoanalysis have a special reason for their reluctance *to conceive* their own origins, and to allow the ordering images of their progress to enter the dialogical circles of their scientific community. In reality "psychology" or "psychoanalysis" do not exist, but only "psychologists" or "psychoanalysts" who are systematically exposed to the *interpretative action* of colleagues and analysands within their institutions and professional practices. This summarizes the difference between the practices and methods relating to the knowledge acquired from inert objects, like literary texts, and knowledge acquired from active interlocutors. The reciprocity characterizing any human relationship tends to be simply ignored in "naturalistic" psychoanalysis, which calls "interpretations" the product of the analyst's thoughts about the analysand, and "free associations", "resistance", "narcissistic omnipotence" and so on the analysand's thought about the analyst, including the analysand's naive attempts at self-occultation, in which the analyst pretends he or she does not interfere. Still, the analysand's thought also is always an interpreting thought. In the analytical setting an invitation always arises to establish the circularity of responses constituting the open-ended playing of transitional conceptions. The fact that this game is replayed several times a day, with many patients, colleagues, and specialists of other disciplines means that analysts are exposed to a flow of conceptual experiences whose disordering quality can destabilize the continuity of their logical-operative Ego, and their professional *idem*.

This implies then that these professionals need a particularly efficient re-organizer of the elements: the imaginary patrimony available to each one of us. This is much easier if one's didactic analysis has been "successful" and if therefore one can rely on a "psychoanalytical conscience" that finds certainty in objective universalism and in medical ethics.

But the re-organizer can also be a product of the dis-order, an original concept that by maintaining its "weak" character, has sufficient orientational power to prevent unbearable disorientation or bewilderment. This conception-guide can be broad, explicit, and legal (with rules and regulations regarding the technical-methodological aspects of analytical practice), but the analyst producing it becomes a *unique author*, and will avoid the totalizing hegemony of his or her false conscience.

But the decline of a meta-psychological era in psychoanalysis implies a phenomenon similar to what Richard Rorty (1982) observed with the decline of the metaphysical era in philosophy:

> In 1951, a graduate student who (like myself) was in the process of learning about, or being converted to analytic philosophy, could still believe that there were a finite number of distinct, specifiable philosophical problems to be resolved—problems which any serious analytic philosopher would agree to be the outstanding problems... These were problems which fitted nicely into the vocabulary of the positivists...To recite this list of problems and paradigms is to evoke memories of a simple, brighter, vanished world...[Today] most philosophers are more or less "analytic," but there is no agreed-upon interuniversity paradigm of philosophical work, nor any agreed-upon list of "central problems." The best hope for an American philosopher is Andy Warhol's promise that we shall *all* be superstars, for approximately fifteen minutes a piece.

And a few pages later he adds: "We should let a hundred flowers bloom, admire them while they last, and leave botanizing to the intellectual historians of the next century."

His invitation is virtuous in its profound respect for any emerging Otherness, its suspension of any judgement on the eventuality of our common future, and its substantially aesthetic-narrative-dimension. This brings me back to the opening lines from Montale's poem. Questioning the existence of a metapsychological or metaphysical "common ground" means putting the octopus in its place in the historical-ecological complex we all share. It also means breaking the witch's spell, which consigns us to the octopus, under the illusion that we are using his "inky tentacles." Perhaps the "approximately fifteen minutes" of fame to which we all, as *authors*, legitimately aspire will give us enough time to tell ourselves: "Now you know you don't belong to him. Being yourself you become his *beyondness*."

References

Apel, O. (1962-1972). *Transformation der Philosophie*. Frankfurt: Suhrkamp Verlag, 1973.

Balint, M. (1947). "Training in Psycho-Analysis." International Journal of Psycho-Analysis. 1948:29

Balint, M. (1953). "Analytic Training and Didactic Analysis." International Journal of Psycho-Analysis. 1954:35.

(both these essays were published in: *Primary Love and Psycho-Analytic Technigue*. Enid Balint: 1965.)

Cremerius, J. (1989). *Analisi didattica e potere. La trasformazione di un metodo di insegnamento-apprendimento in strumento di potere della psicoanalisi istituzionalizzata*. Psicoterapia e Scienze Umane. 1989:23,3.

Foulkes, S.H.(1975). *Group Analytic Psychotherapy: Methods and Principles*. London and New York: Gordon & Breach, 1975.

Freud, S. (1897). *The Complete Letters of Sigmund Freud to Wilhelm Fliess* 1887-1904. Cambridge, Mass: The Belknap Press of Harvard University Press.

Freud, S. (1899). *Die Traumdeutung*. Gesammelte Werke 2-3; Standard Edition 4-5.

Freud, S. (191O). *Eine Kindheitserinnerung des Leonardo da Vinci*. G.W. 8:128; S.E. 11:59.

Freud, S. (1920). *Jenseits des Lustprinzips*. G.W. 13:3; S.E. 18:7.

Freud, S. (1921).*Massenpsychologie und Ich-analyse*. G.W. 13:73; S.E. 18:69.

Freud, S. (1922). *Das Ich und das Es*. G.W. 13:237; S.E. 19:3.

Freud, S. (1937). *Konstruktionen in der Analyse*. G. W. 16:43; S.E. 23:257.

Gargani, A.G. (1985). *Lo stupore e il caso*. Bari: Laterza.

Garroni, E. (1978). *Creatività*. In Enciclopedia, vol. 4, Torino: Einaudi.

Gehlen, A. (1978). *Der Mensch. Seine Natur und seine Stellung in der Welt*. It. tr., Milano: Feltrinelli.

Grünbaum, A. (1984). *The Foundations of Psychoanalysis*. University of California Press.

Grünbaum, A.(1986). "Reflections on the Foundations of Psychoanalysis. *Behavioral and Brain Sciences*. 9, 2.

Heidegger, M. (1954). *Was heisst Denken?* Tübingen: Max Niemeyer Verlag, 1971.

Kuhn, T.S. (1962). *The Structure of Scientific Revolutions*. The University of Chicago.

Masson, J.M.(1984). *The Assault on Truth*. J.M Masson. 1984

Maturana, H., Varela, F. (1980). *Autopoiesis and Cognition. The Realization of the Living*. Dordrecht, Holland: Reidel Publishing Company.

Morin, E. (1982). *Science avec conscience*. Paris: Fayard.

Napolitani, D. (1982). *Vita/Morte*. Enciclopedia, vol. 15, Torino: Einaudi.

Napolitani, D. (1986). "Crisi del paradigma fisiologico in psicoanalisi. Complessità identificatorie e gruppalità interne." *Rivista di Psicoanalisi*. 1986:32.3.

Napolitani, D. (1988). *Individualità e gruppalità*. Torino: Boringhieri.

Reid, T. (1764). *An Inquiry into the Human Mind, on the Principles of Common Sense*. Edinburgh: Kincaid and Bell.

Rorty, R. (1982). *Consequences of Pragmatism*. University of Minnesota. It. Tr., Milano: Feltrinelli, 1986.

Spence, D.P. (1982). *Narrative Truth and Historical Truth. Meaning and Interpretation in Psychoanalysis*. New York - London: Norton & Company. It. tr.,Firenze: Martinelli, 1987.

Vattimo, G., Rovatti, P. (1983). *Il pensiero debole*. Milano: Feltrinelli, 1987.

Winnicott, D.W. (1971). *Playing and Reality*. London: Tavistock Publications.

Notes

1. ". . . Il polipo che insinua / tentacoli d'inchiostro tra gli scogli / può servirsi di te. Tu gli appartieni / e non lo sai. Sei lui, ti credi te."

2. "When and only when legality exists, creativity exists (in other words, it makes sense to speak of creativity when and only when we can speak of legality) and viceversa, of course. A 'creativity' unrelated to a 'legality' is little more than a *flatus vocis*' (E. Garroni, 1978)

Chapter 8

Comments on Diego Napolitani's Paper

Alan Bass

For Diego Napolitani psychoanalysis is a process of "rethinking one's 'innate' images, replacing them in a historical perspective, questioning the exceeding sense by which they appear 'obvious' to us or through which they tend to rigidly hegemonize our subjective circuits of meanings . . ." Precisely so. However, I think that Napolitani's understanding of Freud's metapsychology is just such an "innate-image." In this discussion, I will question the "exceeding sense" which could make Napolitani's account of metapsychology "appear 'obvious'" and attempt to show that it is not so obvious if placed in "historical perspective."

Napolitani's main point is that the "metapsychological construction" is attached to a "scientist ideal" in conflict with the "deep humanistic vocation" also present in Freud's work. The resolution of this conflict would take psychoanalysis in the direction of "aesthetics, narratology, and hermeneutics." *Not* to go in this direction is to be "seduced by the idealizing assumption that psychoanalysis consists of a pragmatic-cognitive order in its own right." This epistemological seduction is itself the result of Freud's abandonment of the seduction theory. The seduction theory had the merit of being relational, relativistic, and non-conformist. Metapsychology represents a "reconversion to the scientist ideal," renewed submission to paternal authority, to "Prussian discipline."

Why does Napolitani need to seduce one away from what Freud always said about metapsychology? In one of his best known statements about metapsychological theorizing, Freud states that the "foundation of science...is observation alone" (1914, 77). Metapsychology, with all its energies and agencies, is a set of "nebulous, scarcely imaginable basic concepts." Such concepts "are not the bottom but the top of the whole structure, and they can be replaced and discarded without damaging it" (ibid.) If it is comparable to anything, metapsychology is like metaphysical speculation uneasily joined to observations calling for explanation. This is why Freud was willing to compare metapsychology to metaphysics and mythology from early to late in his career.

The first published use of the term, in *The Psychopathology of Everyday Life*, 1901, occurs in the context of a discussion of religion and myth. Freud speaks of how the "psychology of the unconscious" could "transform metaphysics in metapsychology," (259). On many occasions toward the end of his life, Freud was quite willing to say that metapsychology, the theory of the drives, is "our mythology" (see, for example, *New Introductory Lectures*, 1933, 95).

And if one further recalls the itinerary of Freud's metapsychological ideas, including such difficult topics as narcissism, the death drive, primary masochism, and telepathy, one hardly finds investigations geared to conformity with the paternal, "scientistic" order. Nowhere does Freud suggest, that metapsychology consists of a "pragmatic-cognitive order in its own right." In principle and in practice, Freud sees metapsychology as a kind of necessary evil for thinking about the relations between psychoanalytic observations and psychoanalytic theory.

The sense of metapsychology as a *necessary* evil informs one of Napolitani's citations of Freud. Napolitani writes: "Freud himself gives us in 'Constructions in Analysis' (1937 [sic, because the passage is from *Analysis Terminable and Interminable*]) a particularly suggestive example of his metapsychological construction, characterized by an invasive and hegemonizing thought, inhibiting his creative freedom, as happens to those who are subject to their own paranoical constructions. In the following passage he states that when facing certain difficulties (those which could lead to unbearable confusion and uncertainty) . . ." Before giving the citation, it is worth noting that the difficulty Freud is facing here is that of giving an explanation of how psychoanalysis brings a repressed drive "into the harmony of the ego" (1937, 225). While Napolitani is right that Freud finds himself possibly confused and uncertain, and says so here, the question he is uncertain about, is essentially *the* question he has spent his psychoanalytic life examining—the relation between clinical practice and the theory of drives and defenses. So, at a very late stage, after roughly forty years of working on this question, Freud admits to uncertainty. Again this is not the tone of someone using theory in a hegemonical way, of someone so certain that he appears subject to his own "paranoical construction." Here is Napolitani's citation of Freud, which I give in the *Standard Edition* version: "'If we are asked by what methods and means this result is achieved, it is not easy to find an answer. We can only say: '*So muss den doch die Hexe dran*!—the Witch Metapsychology. Without metapsychological speculation and theorizing—I had almost said 'phantasying'—we shall not get another step forward'".

Napolitani tells us that Freud is citing Goethe's *Faust*. Since we know how frequently Freud cited this work, we can assume that he knows the context of these lines, which is as follows: Faust, tempted by Mephistopheles, would like to find a way to restore his youth, but without resorting to magic and alchemy. Mephistopheles mockingly suggests that Faust could do so, if he were willing to lead a simple life of toil. Faust, of course, is unwilling, and so Mephistopheles has his way. Freud quotes Mephistopheles' response, "the witch must be called upon after all." So if Freud, near the end of his life, puts himself in the position of Faust when he reasons metapsychologically, his citation of Goethe means at the very least: I know that metapsychology is my pact with the devil. Since Freud did want to be a man of science, and could not comfortably admit metapsychology into his view of science, while simultaneously finding it *necessary*, he was willing to compare himself to Faust in thrall to Mephistopheles.

Freud clearly declares his-ambivalence by comparing the theoretical structure he had elaborated over a lifetime to a pact with the devil, making it inadmissible for Napolitani to read Freudian metapsychology as a rigid, paranoid certainty in conformity to the ideals of science. If anything, Freud's gesture here seems to me much more radical than Napolitani is willing to grant him: he is a rather unrepentant old Faust still trafficking with the devil; and not so concerned with the paternal order.

Napolitani links Freud's supposed allegiance to the "father's *auctoritas* . . . in the form of academic knowledge" to the failure of his self-analysis, as evidenced by his withdrawal of the seduction theory, which itself had challenged the paternal order with its insistence on parental guilt. Again, why does Napolitani ignore a much more complex picture? Freud had published the seduction theory in his 1896 paper, "*The Aetiology of Hysteria*." By 1905, with the publication of the *Three Essays on the Theory of Sexuality*, the theory of neurosis—allegedly *sans* seduction received its fullest exposition to date. Here is Freud, in the *Three Essays*, discussing the links between masturbation in latency and later neurosis:

> The reappearance of sexual activity is determined by internal causes and external contingencies, both of which can be guessed in cases of neurotic illness from the form taken by their symptoms . . . great and lasting importance attaches at this period to the accidental *external* contingencies. In the foreground we find the effects of seduction, which treats a child as a sexual object prematurely . . . An influence of this kind may originate either from adults or from other children. *I cannot admit that in my paper on 'The Aetiology of Hysteria' I exaggerated the frequency or importance of that influence* [my underlining], though I did not then know that persons who remain normal may have had the same experiences in their childhood, and though I consequently overrated the importance of seduction in comparison with the factors of sexual constitution and development (1905, 190).

Freud takes the position that in his earlier work he had not correctly conceptualized the effects of seduction, although the observation of its "frequency" and "importance" remains. This is why in the *Introductory Lectures on Psychoanalysis* (1916-17), Freud introduces the idea of the complemental series of endogenous and exogenous factors that produce neurosis. In this model, trauma and phantasy intermix. Thus, in discussing phantasy Freud asserts that sometimes stories of seduction are used to screen early masturbatory activity. He then immediately cautions his audience: "You must not suppose, however, that sexual abuse of a child by its nearest male relatives belongs entirely to the realm of phantasy. Most analysts will have treated cases in which such events were real and could be unimpeachably established . . ." (1916, 370). The question remains: why does Napolitani not want to know about Freud's position on seduction? It no more disappears from his theories than metapsychology can simply be equated with positivistic science.

The heart of the problem probably lies in Napolitani's understanding of hermeneutics and science. That one finds both "humanism" and "science" throughout Freud's work is indisputable. But Napolitani does not seem to consider that Freud's work, perhaps more than psychoanalysis in general, did a great deal to undermine the subject-object opposition on which the hermeneutics-science opposition rests. Although he accurately states that one would have to explain why psychoanalysis might remain within the "empirical-positivistic paradigms that the sciences of nature have by now abandoned," Napolitani seems not to understand that to choose hermeneutics over science is to remain within that paradigm. What is often so difficult to understand about Freud—again, Freud as distinct from psychoanalysis in general—is that while he often operates with the old concepts of interpretive versus scientific disciplines, his discourse constantly undermines that opposition. From beginning to end, metapsychology leads Freud in the direction of the literary and mythical, from the linkage of psychic energy to symbol formation in the *Project*, through the invocation of Oedipus in relation to drive and phantasy, to the reference to the Platonic myth of originally double beings seeking to reconstitute themselves as an illustration of the death drive, and to the late invocation of Empedoclean *philia* and *neikos* in relation to Eros and Thanatos—to say nothing about the problematic of the uncanny. From this perspective, Freud is simply consistent when he compares metapsychology to a Mephistophelean witch whose alchemy blurs the distinction between induction-deduction and phantasy. The unfortunate trend of many who support the hermeneutic position in psychoanalysis, as exemplified by Napolitani, is that in simply choosing "subjectivism" over "objectivism" they have to create a story about Freud—for example, that the "abandonment" of the seduction theory represents a commitment to positivism—that excludes complexity in the interest of narrative coherence.

Works by Freud Cited

The Psychopathology of Everyday Life (1901), S.E. 6.

Three Essays on the Theory of Sexuality (1905), S.E. 7.

On Narcissism (1914), S.E. 14.

Introductory Lectures on Psychoanalysis (1916), S.E. 15-16.

New Introductory Lectures (1933), S.E. 22.

Analysis Terminable and Interminable (1937), S.E. 23.

SESSION V

Chapter 9

Ethics and Aesthetics in the Definition of the Self: Freud and Wittgenstein

Aldo Giorgio Gargani

In our culture the notion of repetition is frequently accepted as a factor shaping linguistic, logical, mathematical and scientific procedures. This long tradition of acceptance includes the presumption that somehow everything is known, that all replies are symmetrically aligned to their questions, and that thinking, calculating and knowing are modes of retracing tracks which have been traced forever. "They are all numbers" for example, fails to distinguish between natural numbers and integers, and sweeps away with a bluster, as Wittgenstein says, the difference between the expression "two men entered the pub" and the expression "+two men entered the pub." This conceals the fact that while the law of monotony is of unlimited validity to multiplication for positive and negative integers, this law is circumscribed. "They are all numbers," we continue to say, as if the various extensions of the concept of number were merely specializations of a single identical and repeatable concept—the superconcept of number.

Our tradition has held the dominant assumption that our linguistic and cognitive operations are the incessant, monotonous repetition of a conceptional mechanism that has always existed, to anticipate any possible intellectual move. Dominated by the primal scene, we believe that our actions are merely linear repetitions of a past operation, and thus we assume the system of all things as a datum, which becomes the past and prehistory of our language and knowledge. This assumption becomes clear when we believe that the inferences or conclusions of a logical mathematical argument already exist in the super-mechanism of our concepts, from which they are drawn. Thus in *Principia Mathematica* Whitehead and Russell illustrate the *modus ponendo ponens* by observing that if p is true, and p implies q, then we can only *draw* the conclusion that q is true, as if we were pulling out change from a slot-machine. But if the conclusion derives from premises, the premises also derive their sense from the conclusions.

The reduction of our constructive procedure of knowing to the repetition of an identical content is reassuring, and suits a blinkered mode of thinking that seeks to exorcise whatever is new and original. For example, in what I call the *Zukunftsangst*, the patient shows a catatonic stupor, where defence against novelty and change is expressed through a refusal to give answers and a monotonous repetition of the question. By this means the patient arrests in time the sense of changelessness that he or she cannot give up.

Following Wittgenstein and Freud, we can recognize constructs just as mad as the compulsion to repeat in the conceptual super- mechanisms, the super-languages of philosophy and epistemology. The notions of the a priori, the transcencendental, and the analytic should be re-examined as symptoms of a particular form of the compulsion to repeat, by which we attempt to exorcise novelty and the risks of the present. Epistemological schemes of this kind assume that language and knowing are rooted in an early experience—the primal scene—which is defined by its own unchallengeability. And this operation of using something of *now* to refer to something *then* gives us our sense of security. This movement can be reduced—as Mach explained with reference to mechanical phenomena—to referring one unintelligible item to another. According to Mach explanation and demonstration within physical theory, do not bring the unintelligible to the intelligible, but the uncommon, unusual unintelligibility to another, more familiar and better-known unintelligibility.[1]

However we must ask if repetition is indeed the monotonous and unvarying retracing of an identical content. This notion of repetition is insufficient, whether we are referring to the compulsive repetition of obsessive neurosis, or to the repetitive schemes of the philosopher or epistemologist. The term repetition is used for procedures that do not consist in doing the same thing or inexorably replaying the same content. On the contrary, these procedures involve constructive reworking, in new, original decisions which have introduced into our knowledge such structures as infinitesimal notation, chemical symbolism or serial music. These structures are in no way inexorable, since they did not exist before their deliberate construction; without them, mankind had managed to live quite comfortably. Repetition disguises the operational aspect of language and knowing, and proposes the static image of a primal scene of objects, a representation of truth as object. We are profoundly moved by the performance of a ritual, but not because of the foundational character of a primal scene. Those epistemologists and anthropologists who derive the meaning of a ritual from its primordial point miss the point. It is the present resuscitation of a myth that produces the profound impression. If depth is characteristic of remote time, then we are struck by the depth of meaning that we attribute to a myth, retrospectively projecting its past as the memorable primal scene. In this sense myth does not provide causal explanation, but the indisputable evidence of its significance for us. The event described in a primal scene and in a myth depends on the retrospective capability of its meaning. This happens because myth has a terrible, unsettling, and fearful significance: this is what makes an event a myth. What represents perspicuity and evidence for us traces the event's remote depth. This then is not a genetic cause and effect problem of before and after, but a constellation of symbolic forms developing from each other, as the ellipse develops from the circle. No one would claim that the circle historically generated the ellipse.[2] In these terms, repetition does not develop as a replay of an identical content but as a progression of new, different reactions to the theme of a neurosis which originates in a primal scene but does not exist either as a necessarily historical event, or as a structure significant prior to and independently of men's reactions and reworkings. Instead one can state, with Wittgenstein and Freud, that the notion of origin deposited in the primal scene does not exist outside the elaboration of the theme it inscribes. Repetition does not derive from the primal scene through mechanical causality, nor does it instantly replay a content and all its recurrences. It is like the ellipse emerging from the circle; the ellipse is already contained in the circle, but it represents a variation on its form.

In Freud's *Jenseits des Lustprinzips* a child misses his mother. His game consists in throwing a bobbin to which a thread is attached, and then pulling it back, repeating first "fort" (away) and then "da" (here).[3] This child repeats the primal scene of his torment over and over again because he misses his mother. But his repetition is not a mechanical, linear replay of the content of that scene. How can this game repeat the absence and reappearance of the mother? This alternation does not fully explain the game. Instead the formal connection between both scenes illuminates them. One could say that the child has structured the mother's casual behavior into a perspicuous and methodical representation. As a repetition of the primal scene, the child's game shapes and clarifies it, as if it were an exercise to do. The repetition does not simply replay an observed and fixed content, but includes a variation: the child's reaction toward the mother, now that grief has entered his life.

In Freud's *Aus der Geschichte einer infantilen Neurose*, a child understands the primal scene of the parents' coitus that he witnessed at a year and a half when he is four, through *deferred thought*. The primal scene only begins to take on significance after the deferred, aesthetic, working out, and the deferment is therefore inside the primal scene. The celebration of a ritual does not refer to a remote event, for not all remote events have the effect of myth and ritual. As Freud observes in *Das Unheimliche*, "not everything which recalls repressed motions of desire and past modes of thought from the origins of individual or of collective history is for that reason necessarily disturbing.[4]"

The primal scene exists in the deferred thought, whose sounding the depths of distant time is a function of the significance added by the deferment itself. "This significance," writes Freud, "which was lacking in the memory, could be deduced with certainty from "concomitant associations"."[5] The entire representation of the "Clinical Case of the Wolf Man" in Freud's *Aus der Geschichte einer infantilen Neurose* consists of a cascade of symbols, a progression of references spreading out into an evolution of aesthetic development of symbolic forms which, I repeat, do not belong to the domain of mechanical causality but rather to that of the aesthetic development of symbolic forms one from the other.

The primal scene of the parents' coitus *a tergo more ferarum* that the child observes but which he might have simply imagined, is elaborated in a series of images: animals, mounting women crouching with their back parts in evidence more or less like the mother; a governess's threat of castration, echoed in the child's presumed observation of the mother's genitals, which he interprets as a wound; "Little Red Riding Hood" and "The Wolf and the Seven Little Goats"; the grandfather's tale of the wolf; the child's homosexual inclination toward his father; and the final transfiguration of the father through the religious topology of God and the son-made-flesh. These elaborations are not analytical relays of a single content, any more than the geometry of the cube is contained in the cube. As a geometrical entity, the cube is the origin of its own geometry, but does not exist independently of the geometric discourse which develops around it constituting its discourse and proofs, and by which we can refer to the cube.

Regarding the compulsion to repeat, Freud observes that "these infantile scenes are not reproduced in analysis in the form of memories but are the fruit of a reconstruction–in other words we cannot reach the most remote infantile episodes as such"[6]. No primal scene exists without repetition, in other words without retrospective aesthetic elaboration. As Freud observes in a note to *Aus der Geschichte einer infantilen Neurose*, the child understood the significance of his parents' copulation "at the stage of dreams, at four years of age, not at the moment of the observation. In other words, at a year and a half he gathered impressions the deferred understanding of which was made possible by his development, by his sexual excitement and sexual enquiries"[7].

In the repetition of a primal scene, Freud speaks of a prevalence of the general pattern over individual experience. In *The Case of the Wolf Man*, the father is the object of the sons' homosexual eroticism, but also his castrator. Here we also have, as Freud says, "the same victory of the pattern over the individual".[8] I believe that a structural theme exists in repetition, that is specific in an aesthetic variety of forms. This recurrence determines the throw-back to a primal scene, and hence to the prevalence of the general over the particular. In their entirety, these occurrences constitute the significance of the primal scene.

Wittgenstein says that the different proofs of a hypothesis are not different ways of verifying the same content as the hypothesis, but are themselves distinct sections of the hypothesis; that which is verified in a different way must have a different meaning. The hypothesis connects all its distinct space-time sections, and in psychic phenomena the primal scene connects the various repetitions of its theme. With both the scientific hypothesis and the repetition of the primal scene, we have not the verification of the same meaning, but different sections and symptoms of a single hypothesis and of a single primal scene. Each time we verify a different symptom of the original scene that established the theme of a neurosis. A hypothesis is not verified, but rather the single propositions that derive from it and correspond to its various sections; likewise a primal scene cannot be verified but rather its various symptoms.

When we perform a calculation or repeat a primal scene, we are not always doing the same thing, which is what we say when, as Wittgenstein observes, we are tricked by our modes of expression. This would seem to imply that the notions of identity and concordance precede what we in fact do. Following Wittgenstein, what we do establishes the meaning of the notions of identity and concordance. These are not static schemes of uniformity, pre- dating our actions; in mathematics we establish the meaning of "doing the same, identical thing" through calculations. We realize the meaning of identity and concordance at the same time as the practice of mathematical calculation. We create new mathematical entities through our operations, and say that we have established an identity between what we had already done and what we are doing now. Our actions show what it means "to do the same thing". So rather than multiply 16 by itself 15 times, I raise it to the power 15 and write 16^{15}. The proof of this calculation does not lie only in the fact that the multiplication of factors and the raising to a power give the same result; the proof itself must show that we take the number 16 as a factor 15 times and can obtain the same result by two different routes.[9] *We establish the meaning of the notions of identity and concordance while we construct and invent our mathematical entities.*

The primal scene is not an ontological basic, or a substantial presence, and it is not manifested as an opinion or belief. By the same token getting up from a chair does not manifest the opinion that we have two feet.[10] The primal scene is the vital, aesthetic element within which we elaborate our behavior and our attitudes. Men do not declare that they know that there are external objects such as chairs, tables, stars, books and trees. The existence of all the things does not constitute the content of an opinion or belief, but is implicit in all their actions. In other words, a man describes his primal scene through his actions. He now explains his primal scene not with *the grammar of his cognition* but with *the grammar of his actions*. Freud observes:

> The subject does not say that he has been stubborn and mistrustful towards his parents' authority, but behaves in just this way towards his analysts. He doesn't remember having been without advice and help during his infantile-sexual exploration, but carries with him a great many dreams and confused associations. He complains about being unsuccessful in everything he does and declares that it is his fate never to achieve the object that he undertakes. He doesn't remember having been deeply ashamed of certain sexual behavior and fearful that it was discovered, but he shows that he is ashamed of the treatment to which he is subjecting himself, tries to keep it hidden from other people, and so on.[11]

The Freudian notion of the primal scene reveals how truth does not consist in the representation of an object, but in the actions performed. Yet in another sense truth stands in front of us if we know how to seek it. The patient who cannot produce a word in the analyst's presence, and who cannot remember, is in reality producing his primal scene before our eyes. "In the end," says Freud, "one realizes that this is his way of remembering." Whenever we have patience and mental clarity, we should be able to discover the truth in the silence of his or her actions. These actions delineate something new: in their aesthetic development they trace the physiognomy of their origin.

The obsessed boy in *Aus der Geschichte einer infantilen Neurose* fills us with distress, but also with admiration for the huge, mad structure he had been erecting since grief entered his life and condemned him to compulsive repetition. Through his distressed, retrospective fantasizing he gathered, synthesized, the entire environment of his life. The people and objects that surrounded him, his fairy tales, the seductions of his sister, his nurse, the scullery-maid, and poor peasant women are elaborated into something as original as his life. Through repetition he was able to stare deep back at the remembrance of the primal scene that marked his whole life. And he did it all by himself. After all, was it not Freud who in talking about children said that they "have been underestimated, and truly we no longer know what may not be attributed to them?"[12].

Starting with the *Geheime Tagebücher* Wittgenstein gave voice to his striving for moral decency (*Anständigkeit*) and for a comprehensive aesthetical view (*Überblick*) capable of linking the scattered and disjoined aspects of life. The deepening of this inner experience, and his need to confess and to pull himself together (*sich sammeln*), aims to discover what he then called "das erlösenden Gedanken."[13] For Wittgenstein the difficulty of this achievement lies not in a deficiency of intellectual ability or talent, but in an ethical attitude centered on what one possesses rather than on what one precisely is, which consequently prevents people from delving into their own lives. Wittgenstein traced this difficulty back to the will superimposing its deceptive ideals upon a reality, instead of ascertaining reality as it stands, neither for better nor for worse. However, such a task would presuppose the individual settling accounts with him or herself, an undertaking which involves sacrifice and pain. Ethical reflection becomes something on oneself and one's own interpretation, as the condition for achieving sound human understanding. In 1931 Wittgenstein wrote:

> Working in philosophy ... is really more a working on oneself. On one's own interpretation. On one's way of seeing things. (And what one expects of them).[14]

In 1937 he combined ethical reflection and philosophical analysis with the recognition that the answer to philosophical problems is a new way of living, which will take the form of weeding out the disquietudes of the mind caused by the misconception of language practices. In 1944 Wittgenstein wrote "that man will be revolutionary who can revolutionize himself."[15] He meant that in order to achieve a clear philosophical view and sound human understanding, one must do away with images that have been turned into metaphysical representations of facts by the superstitious desire to grasp things once and for all. Our ability to wriggle out of the metaphysical picture that has held us captive depends on our assuming a deeper ethical attitude connected to a different form of life, and not a mere individual enterprise.

To write truthfully one must avoid the philosophical idealizations and arbitrary conceptual schemes we use to deceive ourselves about the place from which we speak, therefore dooming ourselves to failure. Wittgenstein wrote:

> You cannot write anything about yourself that is more truthful than you yourself are. That is the difference between writing about yourself and writing about external objects. You write about yourself from your own height. You don't stand on stilts or on a ladder but on your bare feet.[16]

These references to stilts and ladders are Wittgenstein's own criticism of his *Tractatus logico-philosophicus*. The *Tractatus* was an ambitious attempt at climbing a sort of theoretical ladder. Later on these stilts or ladders proved to be the idealizations and sublimations erected by philosophical theories.

The strict connection between Wittgenstein's striving after ethical rigor and his rejection of philosophical theorizing sheds light on the sublimation and distortion of analysis patterns which philosophers perform when they mistake their representations for objects and facts. In MS n. 213 Wittgenstein remarks that "the danger begins when we notice that the old model is inadequate and then instead of altering it as it were we sublimate it," and "all that philosophy can do is to destroy idols, without making new ones–say out of the 'absence of idols.'"[17] Instead of assuming patterns, images and words as models or objects of comparison with which they deal with the world, philosophers are often inclined to turn these images and patterns into *super-concepts of super-facts*.

They are often coerced into seeing the ideal in reality because they believe that the ideal must lie in reality itself.

The ethical discipline of delving into ourselves makes us climb down from the ladder on which our ideals and sublimations were set up, and implies a renunciation of feelings invested in those ideals. Getting off our ladder means coming down from the place of our false height and coming back to our true height. None of this implies any sacrifice of the intellect, but rather one of feeling and will. This reflects Wittgenstein's own development from the *Tractatus* to the positions taken in his later work. As he noted in his Manuscript 213:

> philosophy does not call me for any sacrifice, because I am not denying myself the saying of anything but simply giving up certain combinations of words as senseless. But in another sense philosophy demands a renunciation, but a renunciation of feeling, not of understanding. Perhaps that is what makes it so hard for many people. It can be as hard to refrain from using an expression as it is to hold back tears or hold in anger.[18]

Wittgenstein conceived philosophical analysis as a kind of linguistic therapy of those illnesses, cramps and disquietudes of the mind spawned by philosophical problems. In the *Philosophical Investigations* he writes: "The philosopher's treatment of a question is like the treatment of an illness."[19] In spite of his criticisms of Freud, although in an unpublished text he called himself a pupil of Freud, Wittgenstein shapes his logico-linguistic analysis as an activity and as a kind of therapy to bring out man's condition, bewitched and held captive by false representations that are characterized by death (*den Charakter der Tiefe*).[20] This depth is in contrast to the metaphor of height in the *Tractatus*.

Wittgenstein intends to raise the same questions that school children, for example, ask themselves while they are studying mathematics, and that schooling represses instead of answering. Wittgenstein purports to let these questions show themselves and speak for themselves.

> A mathematician is bound to be horrified by my mathematical comments, since he has always been trained to avoid indulging in thoughts and doubts of the kind I develop. He has learned to regard them as something contemptible and, to use an analogy from psycho-analysis (this paragraph is reminiscent of Freud), he has acquired a revulsion from them as infantile. That is to say, I trot out all the problems that

a child learning arithmetic, etc. finds difficult, the problems that education represses without solving. I say to those repressed doubts: you are quite correct, go on asking, demand clarification!.[21]

Wittgenstein's procedure and Freudian analysis are also similar in not being limited to pointing out a mistake or misunderstanding, but showing the source of it.

Wittgenstein assigns an important role to the acknowledgement expressed by a person faced with his or her philosophical misunderstanding and error, who then undergoes a deep-seated change. In the "Big Typescript" (MS 213, p. 410) Wittgenstein remarks that "we can bring someone's mistake home to him only when he acknowledges it as the right expression for what he feels. The point is: only when he acknowledges it as such is it the right expression (Psychoanalysis)."[22]

Wittgenstein also calls into question philosophical problems as such. Ultimately philosophy no longer exists outside of its own problems, which belong to individuals and must be dealt with from an ethical perspective, since they are embedded in the situations of our life. Wittgenstein asks himself what philosophical problems are like, and answers in the *Philosophical Grammar*: "For philosophy isn't anything except philosophical problems, the particular worries that we call 'philosophical problems' ".[23]

Rather than a theoretical construction, philosophy becomes an activity; philosophy is itself the philosophical action of descending into the depths of the grammar of language, in order to dissolve the false representations that are as deep as the problems of life. Just as a person who is unwilling to descend into him or herself will remain superficial in his or her writing, which is "a form of deceit" (*eine Art Betrug*),[24] and consequently become the victim of an illusion, so does one who sets up philosophical theories end up being caught by *surface grammar (Oberflächengrammatik)*, rather than descending into *deep grammar (Tiefengrammatik)*, and becoming the prey of superstition (*Aberglaube*) and grammatical illusions (*grammatische Täuschungen*).

According to Wittgenstein, the need for philosophical theorizing arises always from a neurotic attempt to get back behind what we have said in order to grasp a foundation, a cognitive constraint, that would account for why we say what we say. Wittgenstein instead demands that we find the courage to live without that foundation, while attributing to philosophy the task of *describing*, rather than *explaining*, linguistic practices and our undergrounded ways of acting, since words themselves are deeds. This is why he stresses the role of action, and shapes the notions of meaning, understanding and proving in the pragmatic terms of action and reaction as a test for language practices and interpretations.

In his analysis of language and mathematics, Wittgenstein excludes any possibility of absolute and final completeness and exactness. Furthermore, he excludes that every possible doubt must be taken into account. Freud takes a similar attitude. In certain theoretical writings, such as *Die endliche und die unendliche Analyse* and *Konstruktione in der Analyse* Freud states that an incomplete analysis is not necessarily an unsatisfactory analysis, if the incompleteness derives from having faced only the effective problems and real impulse conflicts. For Freud, as for Wittgenstein, an analysis is *terminable*, not because it has reached its final stage, but because it has achieved a practical success, *rebus bene gestis*.[25]

The activity of interpreting, that process of *seeing something as we interpret it*, accounts both for the circumstance underlined by Wittgenstein that "every view is significant for the one who sees it as significant"[26] and for the strict connection he makes between interpretation and inner experience. When he inverts Frazer's conception of rite and myth, Wittgenstein remarks that the depth of a ritual ceremony such as human sacrifice does not consist of historical evidence, origin, hypothesis or conjecture. The deep and the sinister elements inherent in the representation of a human sacrifice do not become apparent merely by our coming to know the history of external actions; rather it is *we* who ascribe them from an experience of our own.

This concept of the *inner nature* of a human practice excludes a kind of report that would reduce the practice to specific actions but it is not related to any psychological introspection either. The notion of inner nature refers rather to the context of all circumstances that, experienced as a whole, correspond to what might be defined as the spirit of a practice.[27] This inner nature of a practice lies in people themselves, in the community of the form of life they share.

The synoptic view, die *übersichtliche Darstellung*, consists precisely in connecting the aspects of events and things within a context, in what Wittgenstein calls the activity of a *poetic composition* (*dichten*): "I think I summed up my attitude to philosophy when I said: philosophy ought really to be written only as a *poetic composition*."[28] The synoptic view, the perspicuous representation, is not an already structured frame that is clear and visible by merely opening one's eyes; rather the synoptic view is as much made as discovered. There are as many aspects of a thing being looked at as there are ways of interpreting and speaking about it. As Wittgenstein writes in the *Philosophical Investigations*, "we can also *see* something now as one thing now as another: 'So we interpret it, and *see* it as we *interpret* it.' "[29]

Thinking is therefore for Wittgenstein also remembering. We could not perceive an event as terrible, disquieting, or anything except banal, if it did not echo something terrible and disquieting already inside us. This may be why, throughout his life, Wittgenstein insisted on saying that one must have the courage to descend into oneself. Wittgenstein's semantics and its technical development are rooted in an ethical attitude that breaks with false representations, and descends into the deep grammar of our saying and acting inside the form of life we share.

The strict relationship of different domains of intellectual life to aesthetics and ethics is a hallmark of contemporary Austrian culture, exemplified by men such as Otto Weininger, Arnold Schönberg, Robert Musil, Ingeborg Bachmann and Thomas Bernhard. A good deal of Austrian culture is the history of intellectuals who have had to fight against fear and cowardice. In a sense their idea has been that nobody can give voice to what is going on if he does not become the artist of his own life, and to shape his life and at the same time be prepared to break it up on changing job, work, and country. Such a man will not rest on his achievements, lest one day he should doze off and wake to find himself being swept away by an avalanche.

Notes

1 "Man führt ungewöhnliche Unverständlichkeiten auf gewöhnliche Unverständlichkeiten zürück", E. Mach, *Die Geschichte und die Wurzel des Satzes von der Erhaltung der Arbeit*,Prag:1872, p. 31.

2 Ludwig Wittgenstein, "Remarks on Frazer's Golden Bough", in C.G. Luckhardt (ed.), *Wittgenstein: Sources and Perspectives*, Hassocks, 1979, p. 69.

3 Sigmund Freud, "Jenseits des Lustprinzips" (1920), in: id., *Gesammelte Werke*, Bd. 13 (Frankfurt a. Main 1972), pp. 11-15.

4 Sigmund Freud, "Das Unheimliche" (1919), in: id., *Gesammelte Werke*, Bd. 12 (Frankfurt a. Main 1972), p. 259.

5 Sigmund Freud, "Aus der Geschichte einer infantilen Neurose" (1914), in: id., *Gesammelte Werke*, Bd. 12 (Frankfurt a. Main 1972), p. 129.

6 Sigmund Freud, (1914), p. 80: Freud, "Traumdeutung" (1899),in: id., *Gesammelte Werke*, Bd. 2-3 (Frankfurt a. Main 1972), p. 190.

7 Sigmund Freud (1914), p. 64.

8 Sigmund Freud (1914), p. 155.

9 Ludwig Wittgenstein, *Remarks on the Foundations of Mathematics*, Oxford: 1956, Part II, sect. 47.

10 Ludwig Wittgenstein, *On Certainty*, Oxford, 1969, sect. 148.

11 Sigmund Freud, "Erinnern, Wiederholen und Durcharbeiten", (1914), in: id., *Gesammelte Werke*, Bd. 10 (Frankfurt a. Main 1972), pp. 129-30.

12 Sigmund Freud (1914), p. 137.

13 See Ludwig Wittgenstein, *Geheime Tagebücher*, 21.11.1914, herausgegeben von W. Baum, in "Saber" (1985).

14 Ludwig Wittgenstein, *Culture and Value*, Oxford:1980, p. 16.

15 Wittgenstein (1980), p. 45.

16 Wittgenstein (1980), p. 33.

17 See A. Kenny, "Wittgenstein on the Nature of Philosophy," in: B.F.McGuinnes (ed.), *Wittgenstein and his Times*, Oxford: 1982, p. 5.

18 MS n. 213, p. 406, in: A. Kenny (1982), p. 16.

19 Ludwig Wittgenstein, *Philosophical Investigations*, Oxford: 1953, Part I, sect. 255.

20 See Wittgenstein (1953), Part II, sect. 111.

21 Ludwig Wittgenstein, *Philosophical Grammar*, Oxford: 1974, pp. 381-82.

22 See A. Kenny (1982), p.4.

23 Wittgenstein (1974), p. 193.

24 See R. Rhees, "Postscript," in: R. Rhees (ed.): *Recollections of Wittgenstein* (Oxford 1984), p. 174.

25 See Sigmund Freud, *Die endliche und die unendliche Analyse*, in: Id., *Gesammelte Werke*, Frankfurt a. Main 1972, Band 16, p. 79-80: *Konstruktionen in der Analyse*, in: Id., *Gesammelte Werke*, Frankfurt a. Main 1972, Band 16, p. 49.

26 Wittgenstein (1979), p. 71.

27 See Wittgenstein (1979), pp.75-6.

28 Wittgenstein (1980), p. 24.

29 Wittgenstein (1953), Part II, p. 503.

Chapter 10

Comments on Aldo Giorgio Gargani's Paper

Richard Rorty

I entirely agree with Professor Gargani's over-all point that Wittgenstein's criticisms of traditional philosophical notions help us understand Freud, and that Freud gives these criticisms a resonance they would not otherwise have. This is especially true in respect to Gargani's initial topic—the traditional notion that inference is a matter of repetition, of drawing out something that was already there in the premises, of reproducing in the visible world a pattern that already existed in an invisible world. Freud helps us see that the appeal of this notion is its suggestion that we remain subject to a power not ourselves—the power of logic.

I take Wittgenstein's criticism of this traditional account of inference to rest upon his claim that, as Gargani puts it, "it is what we do that establishes the meaning of the notions of identity and concordance". Logic, for the later Wittgenstein, is just a matter of abbreviating our actual practices, not of establishing contact with something that has the authority to correct those practices. To deny that valid inference is a matter of handling ourselves over to a mechanism larger and stronger than ourselves is to say, with Nelson Goodman, that a valid inference is simply an inference people will usually accept.

However, I think that Gargani goes a bit too far when early in his paper he says that the notions of the a priori, the transcendental, the analytic and the like are "symptoms of a particular form of compulsion." I agree that they are symptoms of the desire to believe that we cannot change our past practices and our past aims—the desire to protect those practices and aims by viewing them as deriving from something stronger and better than ourselves. But this is not to say, as Gargani does, that the "super-languages of so much philosophy and epistemology" are "as mad as the compulsion to repeat." Plato is obsolete, but not crazy.

The super-languages of philosophy should, I think, be seen not as the products of incipient madness but as outdated products of ingenuity—tools which we may now be able to set aside, ladders we have climbed and perhaps can now dispense with. We shall be able to set them aside just insofar as we become able to take "what we do"—our social practices—as sufficient ground for our projects. In the past, we have been unable to do this, and so have tried to think of our projects as assignments given us by God or Reason or History. But trying to see things this way was no more mad, and no more a product of compulsion, than seeing volcanic eruptions as resulting from the wrath of an underground deity. It was the best we could do at the time. It was not a matter of substituting appearance for reality, not a matter of deluding ourselves.

If one generalizes Wittgenstein's point along Nietzschean and Jamesean lines, one will say that what we do is the source of all our concepts, because no concept is more than a device for facilitating action, a device for getting us what we want. Once we drop the super-languages of philosophy, and adopt such a fullfledged pragmatism, we can no longer use notions like "unmasking" or "unveiling"—exhibiting what is *really* going on—for the relevant notion of "really" is a hang-over from those super-languages. So, in my view of the matter, we should not say that those super-languages, the ones Wittgenstein helped us discard, were masks or veils or delusions or symptoms. All we can say is that they are old tools that have now been replaced by better tools.

As applied to Freud, this means that there is not much point in asking whether the patient *really* witnessed his parents having intercourse, just as there is little point in asking whether black holes *really* exist or are just heuristic fictions, or whether sex is *really* as important as Freud thought. If talking about black holes is the best way we have of predicting stellar behavior, and if talking about memories of the primal scene is the best way we have of figuring out how to push the patient's buttons, then we can skip questions of reality. Freud gave us a set of tools for describing ourselves, and we have found them useful. But he did not substitute health for madness or reality for appearance. In Gargani's terms, Freud did not discover "truth as an object, as a determinate presence." He just suggested some new tools—some selfdescriptions which have turned out to be more useful, for some of our purposes, than traditional philosophical or religious selfdescriptions.

Gargani says that "one can state, with Wittgenstein and Freud, that the notion of origin deposited in the primal scene does not exist outside the elaboration of the theme inscribed in it" (p. 4). I would put the point slightly differently, and say that no notion exists outside of the practices to which it contributes. That is, no notion is of any use to us unless it can be connected with the details of what is going on in such a way as to give us better control over the situation. If we could not connect black holes with galaxies on the one hand and quarks on the other through a vast apparatus of astrophysical theory, the term "black hole" would be merely a name for our ignorance. If Freud had not shown us how to weave together reports of dreams, neurotic compulsions, behavior on the couch, and so on, with postulated infantile sexual fantasies, we would have no use for the notion of "primal scene".

Gargani also says that "the primal scene is the vital aesthetic element within which we elaborate our behavior and our attitudes". I would prefer to say that one useful tale about any person's over-all pattern of behavior is one which connects particular pieces of behavior with the person's relations to his or her parents, and with the person's attitudes toward various kinds of sex. I am not sure what Gargani's term "aesthetic" adds to the claim that Freud-style stories about parents and sex are useful in this way. Perhaps Gargani simply means that what is most interesting and idiosyncratic about a person—her individual style, the work of art she is trying to make of her life—is one of the things that are best explained by a Freud-style story about parents and sex. If so, I entirely agree.

But Gargani may have something more in mind when he uses the term "aesthetic" in this context. This is suggested by his contrast between "the domain of mechanical causality" and "that of the aesthetic development of symbolic forms one from the other." I am dubious about that distinction, since I think of a sequence of symbolic forms as just one more causal sequence, no more or less mechanically determined that any other such sequence. Wittgenstein's pragmatism and holism conspire, it seems to me, to make us drop Diltheyan distinctions between the mechanical and the symbolic. From a pragmatic angle, this distinction no longer looks like a reflection of the old metaphysical distinction between Nature and Spirit, but like a distinction of style. There is nothing more to the distinction between the mechanical and the symbolic than the distinction between the Galilean style, which looks for universal predictively useful, nomological statements, and the narrative style. From a pragmatist angle, these two are, once again, just alternative tools—tools that we pick up or lay down depending upon the requirement of the situation at hand.

I am not sure whether Gargani would agree with me here, or would instead agree with Ricoeur that Freud's work exhibits a tension between the mechanical and the symbolic. Ricoeur thinks that Freud was unable to integrate the quasi-physiological language of libidinal hydraulics and the language of hermeneutical interpretation. He and Gargani both make much of the distinction between reasons and causes, as do such interpreters of Wittgenstein as Anscombe and Kenny. I myself would follow Davidson in saying that reasons are just causes under a particular description, and that sequences of symbolic forms are just causal transactions described from a certain angle. To describe an agent's reason-giving or symbol-forming activities in narrative terms is useful for doing what Wittgenstein calls "knowing how to go on," seeing what it is like to be in the agent's shoes. To describe these activities in terms of impersonal libidinal hydraulics may be useful for doing other things such as linking the agent's actions up with certain biological or neurological facts about her. There is no tension to be overcome.

****

So far I have been confining myself to the first half of Gargani's paper. I have been trying to press his point further than he may wish to take it, by saying that Wittgenstein's critique of transcendence should be extended in the direction of a fullfledged pragmatism. When this pragmatism is applied to

Freud, we get a Freud who is useful for helping people get what they want, but not a Freud who tells us what people are *really* like, how they look when their self-delusions are set aside.

I turn now to the second half of his paper, in which he first concentrates on Wittgenstein's desire for "ethical rigor" and then goes on to say that such rigor demands that we make an aesthetic unity out of our life, become the artist of our own life. I am all for people being the artists of their own lives, but I am dubious about the quest for rigor. I am not as fond of this side of Wittgenstein as Gargani is. I find Wittgenstein's obsession with honesty and purity rather tiresome. I have trouble seeing the "moral beauty" which Norman Malcolm, Arthur Danto, Stanley Cavell and others have found in the pattern of Wittgenstein's life. I would happily credit Wittgenstein with sublimity, and with the courage to continually overcome himself, but "moral beauty" seems to me a term which has to do with the quality of a person's relations with other persons. Such relations were not Wittgenstein's strong point.

I admit that if Wittgenstein had not been obsessed with purity he would not have been the original thinker he was, nor have written the books he did. He might have been just a happy homosexual aeronautical engineer, rather than a tormented and chaste philosopher of language. But I do not think that his lifelong talk about purity and honesty can be reconciled with the drift of his later thought. Whereas the *Tractatus* can easily be seen as a work of self-purification, the *Philosophical Investigations* is most easily read as overcoming the need for purity.[1] The importance of Wittgenstein's later thought is precisely that it helps us give up the desire for starkness, purity, and rigor, and helps us accept the impure complexities of ordinary life.

If one emphasizes this side of Wittgenstein's later work, one can see it as complementing Freud's insistence that the desire for purity and cleanliness is just one more neurotic symptom—a bad tool for most people's purposes, though perhaps indispensable for the purposes of certain artists of their own lives, self-overcomers like Nietzsche and Wittgenstein. Then one can say that Wittgenstein served us well by warning us against the super-languages of philosophy, warning us against the sort of temptation to which he himself had succumbed when he wrote the *Tractatus*. But one will have to add that he himself never quite managed to wriggle free from the last residue of these languages—the idea that escaping from the transcendent to the ordinary is escaping from appearance to reality, going from dishonesty to honesty, from a false self to a true self.

Freud, as I read him, helped us give up on the idea of a "true self" as the aim of either psychoanalytic or philosophical therapy. He substituted the goal of a self which experienced rather more ordinary human unhappiness and rather less neurotic misery. He was almost completely free of the idea that therapy would lead you from appearance to reality, except in a pragmatic sense of these terms—the sense in which "appearance" just means a self-description which is less useful in helping you get what you want, and "reality" a self-description which is more useful. But Wittgenstein was not free of this idea. As Gargani says, he thought of his philosophical activity "as a kind of therapy purporting to bring out the condition of man being bewitched an held captive by false representations". He thought that this activity could help us in a process of askesis—process of moving from "an ethical attitude . . . centered on what one possesses" to one which centers on "what one precisely is" (Gargani).

This distinction between what one possesses and what one is, as I see it, is one more residue of the super-languages of philosophy. More specifically, it is one more residue of essentialism—the idea that a thing or a self divides into an inside and an outside, into what it is in itself and its relations to other things. If one abandons the languages Wittgenstein wanted us to abandon, there is no way to make such a division. So there is no way to separate "what one is precisely" from one's relations to one's parents, fantasies, lovers, teachers, money, car, record collection, and everything else that has influenced one's behavior. This means that purity and cleanliness are not very good descriptions of Wittgenstein's accomplishment. A better description would be that he succeeded in being the artist of his own life by redescribing his own youthful desire for purity in a novel, debunking, exemplary way. So, contrary to Gargani, I am happy to talk about the aesthetics of self-definition, and to see Freud as contributing to this aesthetics. But I should prefer to leave ethics out of it. I view Wittgenstein's constant chatter about "honesty" and "rigor" as the sort of static which a good psychoanalyst would have screened out.

Notes

1 I argue this point at length in "Heidegger, Wittgenstein, and the Reification of Language," in my *Essays on Heideggger and Others*, Cambridge: Cambridge University Press, 1991.

SESSION VI

Chapter 11

The Autonomous Individual and the Decentered Self

Joel Whitebook

If we were to enumerate the principal themes that distinguish the Latin reception of Freud, which is the topic of our symposium, the decentering of the subject would certainly have to be counted among them. Indeed, it is in large part through the impact of "Latinized" Freud that the theme of the decentered subject has come to occupy such a prominent position in the contemporary theoretical landscape. Today, who could disagree with the generally formulated proposition, which has become something of a commonplace, that Freud, by demonstrating that "the ego is not master in its own house,"[1] was a major contributor to the decentering of the modern subject? Disagreements begin to arise only when one attempts to determine the precise meaning of that decentration in Freud's theory. In the current discussions, the decentered self is often counterposed to the autonomous individual, which is both a product and a central ideal of modern European culture, as the proper norm for ethical Bildung and psychoanalytic practice. It is argued that the centered ego is a distorted mode of self-formation which reflects the distortions of the culture that produced it.

This opposition is part of the larger controversy concerning the fate of the Enlightenment and Freud's by no means uncomplicated relation to it. Indeed, because of the central and productive tension between Enlightenment and Romantic elements in his thinking, Freud has become a key figure in that controversy. On the one hand, he can be construed as a proponent of the Enlightenment—this, undoubtedly, is how he viewed himself—who was attempting not to extol the subterranean forces he had unearthed in mental life, but to appropriate them for the progress of scientific rationality as he somewhat naively conceived it. He can be construed, that is, as an Apollonian explorer of the Dionysian. Or it could be maintained that despite this self-understanding and intentions, his discovery of the unconscious unleashed consequences which could not be contained within "the project of enlightenment"[2] and which undermined the very project he was seeking to advance. In this case, Freud's efforts would be viewed as a last heroic attempt to extend the project of enlightenment to a new domain that was previously believed to be beyond its purview, but which ultimately served to explode that project from within.

With respect to the dimension of his thinking that can be traced to the German Enlightenment, it can be seen as providing an empirical concretization of Kantian practical philosophy. And, indeed, this is how the Frankfurt School interpreted him. They argued that while Kant had elaborated a theory of autonomy in strictly philosophical terms, Freud formulated an empirical theory which specified the concrete developmental accomplishments necessary for its actual attainment.[3] In this context, it is important to recall that, for Kant—as well as for Freud—the concept of autonomy is intimately linked to the concept of maturity, and both are connected with the emancipatory aspirations of modernity and the bourgeois-democratic revolutions. In a text that has received much attention recently,[4] "What is Enlightenment?," Kant described the process of enlightenment as the overcoming of one's self-imposed immaturity; he defined immaturity, in turn, "as the incapacity to use one's intelligence without the guidance of another."[5] Likewise, in a separate but related text,[6] Kant defined autonomy as self-determination qua self-legislation: one is autonomous to the extent that one is subject to laws of one's own making rather than to the heteronomous laws of nature. These include not only the laws of outer nature but of inner nature and of society as well, insofar as the latter functions in a nature-like (naturwüchsig) fashion. The larger issue behind these terminological considerations is Kant's characteristically—and perhaps uniquely—modern attempt to formulate a critique of traditional, dogmatic, paternalistic, and heteronomous authority. Once this critique has been established, it is no longer admissible, as Castoriadis has argued, to maintain that "the representations of the tribe"[7]—including its sacred core[8]—are valid simply by virtue of the fact that the elders, the parental generation, subscribed to them. Rather, it becomes legitimate to subject those representations to the scrutiny of critical reason. The establishment of this possibility constitutes an absolutely novel rupture in the course of human history; and it is simply an historical fact, not a piece of Eurocentrism, that this breakthrough occurred in the West.[9]

Although Freud's discussion of maturity is more prosaic, more familial and less intellectual than Kant's, the two accounts are, nevertheless, ultimately congruent. Freud writes:

> The liberation of an individual, as he grows up, from the authority of his parents is one of the most necessary though one of the most painful results brought about by the course of his development. It is quite essential that liberation should occur and it may be presumed that it has been to some extent achieved by everyone who has reached a normal state. . . . On the other hand, there is a class of neurotics whose condition is recognizably determined by their having failed in this task.[10]

The concept of maturity 's normative role in Freud's thinking is apparent: separation from one's parents, in a sense to be specified, is a crucial task of so called normal development; conversely, the failure to achieve that goal results in neurosis. For Freud, pathology in general, on both the collective and the individual levels, is identified with atavistic infantilism.[11] Freud, then, provides the intrapsychic, developmental, and affective dimension which is absent from Kant's theory by design. Maturity, in the Kantian sense of thinking for oneself, presupposes separation from one's parents, not in a superficial physical sense, but in the deep intrapsychic sense of relinquishing one's libidinal ties to incestuous objects. Only to the extent that an individual has undergone the painful process of relinquishing, mourning, and internalizing those infantile objects is his thinking (and acting) sufficiently uncontaminated by conscious or unconscious parental imagos and familial dramas[12] to be called his own.

Similar observations can be made about the concept of autonomy. Indeed, Freud's dictum, "Where id was, there shall ego become,"[13] can be taken as a programmatic statement for the Kantian move from heteronomy to autonomy. The formation of ego structure not only frees the individual from the heteronomous determination of the id—of inner nature—but, insofar as it also distances him from the ego's other "internal foreign territory," i.e., the super-ego—which is no less primitive and unreflexive than the id—it frees him from the nature-like compulsions of society as well. Indeed, paraphrasing Freud, we might say that the dictum "Where super-ego was, there shall ego become," could be taken as a programmatic statement for the move from acting "in accordance with" the law to acting "out of respect for" the law. Just as the sacred core of society is no longer systematically insulated from criticism in modernity, so post-conventional identity formation no longer takes place through the habitual socialization into traditionally delineated roles, which is to say, through the quasi-automatic internalization of the collective super-ego. The creation of psychoanalysis, in which no subject is taboo, and which seeks to maximize an individual's autonomy, only becomes thinkable after this rupture with tradition, and perhaps only in a decadent city like fin de siècle Vienna.

So much for the sympathetic interpretation of the notion of the autonomous individual. Let me now try to sketch one of the main critiques of that notion which combines elements from the philosophical discussion of alterity with elements from the psychoanalytic theory of narcissism. Its central thesis: the ego, far from being an agency of truth and emancipation, is a defensive structure, a submissive slave, sycophant, opportunist and liar[14]—"symptom" as Lacan put it[15]— that narcissistically seeks to protect the individual from otherness, and, in so doing, ultimately violates the otherness of the other. Or, stronger yet, it may be that the very notion of emancipation is simply one of the grandiose illusions of modernity which seeks to deny our finitude—our inescapable embededdness in nature, language, and tradition—through omnipotent mastery. According to this account, the ego, and, as Derrida has observed, the desire for a center in general,[16] is a product of anxiety.

The early work of Lacan has become a locus classicus for the critique of the autonomous ego. Drawing on Freud's theory of biological prematurity, Lacan traces its origins to a manic attempt to deny infantile helplessness (Hilflosigkeit). For Freud, it is a fundamental anthropological fact—and an essential feature of human finitude—that the human infant is born prematurely and is therefore helpless: because "its intrauterine existence seems to be short in comparison with that of most animals," the human infant "is sent into the world in a less finished," and, therefore, more helpless state than the young of other species.[17] Lacan locates that helplessness in the fragmented and unintegrated state of the child's bodily experience resulting from its "anatomical incompleteness," which manifests itself in "the signs of uneasiness and motor incoordination of the neo-natal months." During the mirror stage, the child anticipates a future situation in which its helplessness will have been overcome. In contradiction to its actual fragmented and uncoordinated state, in the mirror—the child perceives a synthesized image of itself as already integrated: "The uncoordinated, incoherent diversity of the primitive fragmentation gains its unity" in the fascination of the gaze.[18] This perception, moreover, is accompanied by a "flutter of jubilant activity" which evinces the child's manic excitement at believing itself to have escaped its helplessness qua fragmentation. The ego is constituted, then, through the identification with and the internalization of the unified imago, and this internalized imago, now set up in the psyche, provides the trajectory for further "maturation," namely, the further integration of the self.

Lacan's thesis is that this trajectory is "alienated" and "fictional" and the ego is more an agent of méconnaissance than of truth, the actual state of the child's corporeal and motor experience, which is in fact fragmented, and projecting an illusory image of him as whole. Moreover, Lacan considers the ego an "orthopedic" entity because of its imposition of this rigid and artificial unity on "the turbulent movements that the subject feels are animating him"—a unity it will also seek coercively to impose on the object. Finally, Lacan suggests that in the language of traditional psychoanalysis it might be more proper to refer to the ego thus conceived as an "Ideal-[ego]," as opposed to an "ego-ideal," in order to designate its idealized, grandiose and manic character. Today, we might compare it to Kohut's notion of the grandiose self.[19]

Time limitations allow me only to indicate, and not develop, two inter-related criticisms of this analysis of the ego. Both have to do with the purportedly "Fictional" and "alienated" status of the integrated imago. First: the imago is deemed fictional because its unity is only "virtual" or "anticipatory" when judged against the actually fragmented state of the child's existence. But why, it may be asked, should the temporal, developmental dimension be disregarded and the current state hypostatized into the true one? Why, in other words, should there be an essentialization of fragmentation? I believe this essentialization can be traced to Lacan's "Heraclitean"[20] predilection for deficiency, and discord fragmentation, his suspicion of all forms of finality, reconciliation, and synthesis. It is not simply that the infant's integrated image of himself is factually false at the present—Lacan's objection goes deeper: he objects to any future integration because he objects to integration as such. Similarly, Lacan's argument stems from a partly legitimate desire to prevent Freud's message of the "plague," that is, "the radical heteronomy . . . gaping within man,"[21] from being diluted by overly harmonistic and conformist theories of development. However, it becomes apparent in an interesting exchange with Hyppolite[22] that Lacan cannot incorporate the second moment of Freud's persistently and intentionally dualistic[23] thinking, namely, Eros—the creator of unities and the co-equal combatant in the battle of Titans—into his thinking; Lacan's theory, instead, tends toward a monism of the death instinct. For the other two major theorists of the mirror, Winnicott and Kohut, the integrating experience of the mother's smile, far from situating the child on an alienated trajectory, provides him with hope in a future when he would no longer suffer the pain and anxiety of infantile helplessness. To be sure, for such a notion of hope to avoid the obvious objections, and not constitute another variation on the imaginary, one would have to specify a concept of self-identity as non-coercive ego synthesis.

Be that as it may, let us examine one of the consequences of this analysis of the ego for the concept of the object. The ego's relationship to the object is no less narcissistic than its own formation; it apprehends the object not in its own right, but through "the grid of the narcissistic relation."[24] This is, of course, the psychoanalytically formulated counterpart to the central objection to the philosophy of reflection: the Cartesian subject constitutes the object according to its own internal schemata and can never reach the other independently of those schemata. The Being that "stands across from me in the circle of reflection" is, as Manfred Frank has put it, "my Being," and, in the Cartesian tradition, this "Being for-me" has been mistaken for Being as such.[25] This difficulty, moreover, is not confined to the theoretical plane alone, but has momentous consequences for practical life. Lacan argues that the object thus constituted is an object of domination, and that the form of knowledge corresponding to this objectification—which he terms "paranoic"—is a form of power. When the narcissistic ego constitutes the object in its own image—"egomorphically"[26] as he puts it—the orthopedic rigidity of the defensively constituted is conferred on the object; this reified object becomes an object of possible technical manipulation as a result:

> that which constitutes the ego and its object with attributes of permanence, identity, and substantiality, in short, with entities or 'things' . . . extends indefinitely [man's] world and his power . . . by giving his objects their instrumental polyvalence. . . .[27]

Lacan traces the desire for knowledge and the roots of rationality to the will to power: "the passionate desire peculiar to man to impress his image in reality is the obscure basis of the rational meditations of the will."[28] This line of argument has, as we know, been given a more concrete political direction in recent decades by a variety of thinkers who, in general, have argued not only that the "autocratic subject" (Adorno) cannot do justice to the Other, the different, the non-identical—e.g. nature, women, non-Western Cultures—but that by attempting to impose its grid of cognition actually violates the otherness of the Other.

For Lacan, Freud's "Copernican Revolution" consists in the "subversion" of the "pre-analytical notion of the ego"—the centered, self-present and transparent ego which is more or less shared by common sense, Cartesian philosophy and academic psychology.[29] More specifically, this subversion, according to Lacan, consists in the de-centering of the ego vis-à-vis the unconscious, which means that the unconscious, or the "subject of the unconscious" as he calls it, and not the ego, constitutes "the core of our being" [der Kern unseres Wesens].[30] Because it provokes such powerful resistances, later analysts have continually been tempted to recoil from this utterly subversive discovery and to rehabilitate the pre-analytic ego. The purpose of Lacan's return to Freud is to combat this temptation.

While it is true that Freud's Copernican revolution consists in the decentration of the subject, I would like to point to a curious fact concerning the context in which Freud situates his discovery—a fact already implicit in the reference to Copernicus. This observation will, I believe, begin to subvert the opposition between the autonomous individual and the decentered self as it has often been abstractly formulated in recent discussions. My point is the following: Freud proudly locates his discovery that "the ego is not master in its own house," in the trajectory defined by two great achievements of the modern scientific enlightenment, namely, Copernicus's discovery that "our earth [is] not the centre of the universe but only a tiny fragment of a cosmic system of scarcely imaginable vastness," and Darwin's discovery that "proved [man's] descent from the animal kingdom and his ineradicable animal nature." Freud, in other words, views the decentration of the subject not in opposition to, but as a major step forward in the "project of enlightenment." How then, are we to understand the deep and systematic connection between decentration and enlightenment in Freud's thinking? The answer is to be found in the theory of narcissism.

Indeed, this is already suggested by the fact that Copernicus's cosmological, Darwin's biological and Freud's psychological revolutions each dealt a major blow to humanity's "naive self-love," with psychoanalysis doing perhaps the most severe injury to "human megalomania."[31] The discovery of narcissism constituted more than the delineation of another stage of psycho-sexual development in psychoanalytic theory. Narcissism, as Ricoeur observes, introduced "a veritable evil genius, to which must be attributed our most extreme resistance to truth"[32] into the heart of psychic life, and therefore compelled Freud to confront the problematic of truth and reality more directly. Ultimately, the theory of narcissism provided Freud with the provocation as well as the terminology to articulate his psychoanalytic ethos, "the ethic of honesty," in Rieff's terms, or Freud's "truth morality," as Kohut refers to it[33].

I would like to develop my thesis by attempting a defense of two of Freud's perhaps most indefensible books, namely, *Totem and Taboo* and *The Future of an Illusion*. Now that the Enlightenment has fallen on hard times, these works appear hopelessly mired in nineteenth-century positivism, progressivism, Eurocentrism, and even utopianism. Nevertheless, I want to see whether there is a redeemable kernel that can be extracted from these admittedly often naive texts. Let me begin by examining Freud's attempt to translate a Comptean-style philosophy of history, with all its progressivist, Eurocentric prejudices, into psychological terms. Freud maintains that there are three stages of historical development—the animistic, the religious, and the scientific—and that these three historical stages correspond to the three phases of individual development, namely, narcissism, object-love and maturity. Ontogenetically and phylogenetically, the first phase, the narcissistic-animistic, is characterized by the "omnipotence of thoughts" resulting from the hypercathexis of the mind. The concentration of almost all the energy in the mind causes both the infant and the primitive to megalomaniacally "over-value" their thoughts and to mistake the order and connection of their wishes for the order and connection of things. In the second phase, object love and religion, the hyper-cathexis and resulting over-valuation is transferred from the self to the object, the gods or the parents. Using Kohut's terminology, we can say that omnipotence is not overcome but simply displaced from the grandiose self to the idealized object. According to Freud, only in the final scientific state, which "would have an exact counterpart in the stage at which an individual has reached maturity (Riefezustand)" would omnipotence as such have been surmounted: "The scientific view of the universe no longer affords any room for human omnipotence; men have acknowledged their smallness and submitted resignedly to death and to the other necessities of nature." Likewise, on the ontogenetic level, he maintains that the mature individual "has renounced the pleasure principle, adjusted himself to reality and turned to the external world for the object of his desires."[34] If the teleological philosophy of history, the ethnocentrism, and the energic explanations are disregarded, one crucial point nevertheless remains: for Freud, the desideratum is the overcoming of omnipotence.[35] And, correctly or incorrectly, he believes that desideratum to have been achieved in modern, post-theological, post-metaphysical, scientific society, which constitutes the maturity of the species, and in the mature individual who becomes a potential in that society and presupposes it as his precondition.[36] Freud's commitment to Science in the broad sense, as a Weltanschauung that embodies his truth morality, is distinct from his adherence to the specific tenets of nineteenth-century positivism. Science in the broad sense consists in the critique of illusion, with "illusion" being defined not simply as error, such as "Aristotle's belief that vermin are developed out of dung," but as "error derived from human wishes."[37] Freud maintains, *à la* Feuerbach,[38] that the projection of our wishes causes us to form distorted representations of the world, and that the most fundamental illusions—those of religion and, to a large extent, philosophy—grow out of one of the most elementary wishes, namely, the wish to be consoled in the face of an intrinsically harsh, almost intolerable, reality which "opposes human narcissism."[39] Science, thus conceived, defines a task that is not only cognitive but affective, and which requires the dynamic working-through psyche of the narcissistic resistances to truth. Freud rather naively believed that the specific procedures of nineteenth-century positivism, by, among other things, de-anthropomorphizing the world picture, had finally provided the methodology for realizing the program of Science in the broader sense: as Ricoeur observes, Freud, "like all his Vienna and Berlin teachers. . . sees and continues and continues to see in [modern natural] science the sole discipline of knowledge, the single rule of all intellectual honesty. . . ."[40]

However, after the critique of positivism and the rise of the post-empiricist philosophy of science, we now know—leaving the sense of the term "know" unspecified—that modern natural science did not provide a neutral, timeless methodology for the disinterested pursuit of truth, but constituted nature from a particular perspective. We also know that one of the innermost possibilities of that was technological domination: omnipotent mastery. Modern positivism, in short, turned out to be another idol that has fallen, at least in its hegemonic form. Moreover, a further inference is often drawn from the debunking of positivism, namely, that the project of Science in the broader sense—the critique of illusion—has been invalidated as well in a self-consuming process which leads toward "a perpetual play of mirrors" and "something like the experience of madness."[41] Suspicion, as Rorty has observed, has now been directed at the hermeneutics of suspicion itself.[42] Freud's truth morality would thus fall with the debunking of the positivist doctrine in terms of which he attempted to explicate it. However, a question can be raised against this self-liquidating dialectic: doesn't Kuhn's meta-discourse about positivism, for example—regardless of its validity—itself constitute a step forward in the critique of illusion, a step forward, that is, in an insufficiently radicalized project of enlightenment?

Strange as it may sound, there exists, as Castoriadis has recognized, a politically egalitarian and theoretically anti-foundational dimension, albeit elaborated in a mythical form, in *Totem and Taboo*. The connection between the two is the renunciation of omnipotence. Conservative interpreters of the text often assign more weight to the murder of the omnipotent father than to the pact between the brothers. But "the 'murder of the father' is nothing and leads to nothing (apart from endless repetition of the preceding situation) without the 'pact of the brothers',"[43] which, for Freud, constitutes the founding act of civilization. The significance of the pact—in which siblings are transformed into citizens and their association is placed on a non-kinship basis—is that to the extent that they renounce two of the most imperious wishes of childhood, incest and patricide, the brothers simultaneously renounce the right of narcissistic entitlement as such. Each standpoint is decentered vis-a-vis the others; the privileged center is left unoccupied and no one claims absolute entitlement for his wishes.[44] Indeed, the significance of the Oedipus complex, as Lacan has emphasized, remains virtually the same today: infantile omnipotence comes to grief in the encounter with that "absolutely unmasterable situation," and, with the renunciation of his incestuous wishes, the child is thrust into the law-governed world of equally decentered subjects. Any alternative gender arrangement will have to provide for a means of dislodging infantile omnipotence, which, to date, has been accomplished—perhaps contingently but nevertheless effectively—by the patriarchal family.[45] Likewise, the problematic of narcissistic entitlement also poses an ultimate limit to the right of Otherness. While the "right to particularity"[46] has been recognized in a modern world which has become irreversibly pluralistic, no form of life can claim absolute entitlement for itself and its interpretation of the world without creating a potential for violence: witness the Israelis and the Palestinians, the Christian and Moslem Lebanese, the Armenians and the Azerbeydjanis. Decentration, in this sense, is a condition of the possibility of a plurality of macro- and micro- lifeworlds.

If we take the fiction of the social contract[47] as a thought experiment that attempts to elucidate the founding not of civilization in general, but modern civil society—in this is its historical significance for Hobbes, from whom Freud borrowed it[48]— additional light can be thrown on the thesis that modernity comprises the maturity of the species. The murder of the primal father would symbolize the fact that no Absolute is available outside the decentered structure of mutual interaction to ground either that interaction or the interaction between that structure and external nature: no Absolute is available to ground either practical or theoretical reason. The phallus as the transcendental signifier is, as Lacan argues, an imaginary entity. Modernity would be mature, then, insofar as it has in principle renounced the father, that is, insofar as it has structurally "stripped any paternal coefficient"[49] from its disenchanted worldview. Mutatis mutandis, immaturity would consist in the prolonged "longing for the Father"[50] as a source of ultimate authority and consolation in the face of meaningless, indifferent and cruel *Ananke*. Freud tells us that his "sole purpose" in writing *The Future of an Illusion* is to promote the completion of this process of maturation qua disillusionment, which was structurally and programmatically initiated by modernity's critique of tradition, religion, and metaphysics, but which remains empirically unfinished.[51] In his most utopian, and perhaps—but only perhaps—most uncharacteristic passage, which has certainly been challenged by the recent rise of neofundamentalist movements, Freud declares that". . . infantilism is destined to be surmounted. Men cannot remain children forever. . . ." Someday, "like a child who has left the parental house where he was so warm and comfortable," they will "admit to themselves the full extent of their helplessness and insignificance in the machinery of the universe" and "go out into 'hostile life'."[52]

Freud's ironic reference to "our God Logos"[53] indicates his awareness of the difficulty of justifying his adherence to the scientific *Weltanschauung*–of justifying his faith in Reason once access to the Absolute has been foreclosed. Indeed, Freud, "the master of suspicion,"[54] raises the possibility that he too may be "chasing an illusion."[55] He grasps the fact that the invalidation of religion and metaphysics makes it impossible to ground his adherence to science in the unconditional manner formerly required by the theological and ontological traditions. He does not, however, allow this lack of an ultimate ground to let him fall into nihilism, either in its depressive or manic form.[56] While he cannot provide a demonstrative deduction, he is satisfied with enumerating a number of good reasons, ranging from the progressive nature of science to the course of human evolution, which justify his adherence to the Logos. Chief among these is the fact that science, unlike religion does not have "the character of a delusion"[57] and can be unlike religion, corrected. This strategy of justification does not satisfy the post modern skeptic who, insisting that the foundations of science themselves be strictly scientific, often lodges his critique of the Enlightenment in its inability to provide an unconditional ground for its program. And, an earlier, more naive and more heroic stage of the Enlightenment, which sought to secure the natural light of reason with the same certainty as divine revelation, invited this criticism. An Enlightenment, however, which had become consistent with its own learning experience, that is, with its own maturity, would have worked through the fact that its "god Logos is . . . not a very almighty one,"[58] and would not therefore seek to ground itself apodicticly. Psycho-philosophically speaking, the skeptic, who repetitively insists on the criterion of the Absolute only to demonstrate that it cannot be fulfilled, continues to "long for the father" in disappointment rather than to mourn his loss.

The contemporary critique of rationality and the subject is abstractly negative in its failure to appreciate the residuum that remains after it has ended. Freud reminds us that although the human intellect is weak, "there is something peculiar about this weakness,"[59] which means there is also something peculiar about its strength. And it is this peculiarity that seldom gets thematized in current discussions. Thus the methods of psychoanalysis are often turned back against Freud himself, to undermine the knowing subject and discredit psychoanalysis. However, reflection on the peculiar status of Freud's standpoint and the magnitude of his achievement can produce a different result. As Ricoeur observes, ". . . the same doubter who depicts the ego as a 'poor wretch' dominated by three masters (the id, the superego, and reality or necessity) is also the exegete who rediscovers the logic of the illogical kingdom. . . ."[60] The strength of the investigator who has the courage to document the weakness of the ego and map the kingdom of the unconscious cannot itself be negligible. While the decentered ego of psychoanalysis may be humble in comparison to the more grandiose ego of idealist philosophy, it nevertheless requires austere strength of a certain order to tolerate the narcissistic injuries demanded by psychoanalytic knowledge and to master one's grandiosity to the extent such mastery is possible. To conclude: the ego may no longer be master in its own house, but it hasn't been evicted either.

Notes

1 S. Freud, "A Difficulty in the Path of Psycho-Analysis," S.E., Vol. XVII, p. 143. (emphasis in the original).

2 See Jurgen Habermas, "Modernity–An Incomplete Project," *The anti-Aesthetic: Essays on Postmodern Culture*, ed. Hal Foster, Townsend, Washington: Bay Press, 1983, pp. 3-16.

3 Castoriadis makes the following similar but broader point: "Without prejudice to the new depth dimension revealed by Freud, this is the program proposed by philosophical reflection on the individual for the past 25 centuries, at once the assumption and the outcome of ethics as it has been viewed by Plato and the Stoics, Spinoza or Kant. (It is of immense importance in itself . . . that Freud proposes an effective way to attain what, for philosophers, had remained an 'ideal' accessible through abstract knowledge.)," *The Imaginary Institution of Society*, trans. Kathleen Blamey, Cambridge, Mass: The MIT Press, 1987, p. 102.

4 See Michel Foucault, "What is Enlightenment?," *The Foucault Reader*, ed. Paul Rabinow, New York: Pantheon Books, 1984), pp 32-51; Jurgen Habermas, "Taking Aim at the heart of the Present," *Foucault: A Critical Reader*, ed. David Couzens Hoy, New York: Basil Blackwell, 1986, pp. 103-109; Hubert Dreyfus and Paul Rabinow, "What is Maturity? Habermas and Foucault on "What is Enlightenment?'" *Foucault: A Critical Reader*, pp.pp. 109-123.

5 Popper observes that in the opening paragraph of "What is Enlightenment?" Kant "is saying something personal . . . It is part of his own history. Brought up in near poverty, in the narrow outlook of Pietism–a severe German version of Puritanism–his own life was a story of emancipation through knowledge. In later years he used to look back with horror to what he called 'the slavery of childhood,' his period of tutelage," *Conjectures and Refutations*, New York: Harper Torchbooks, 1965, p. 177.

6 See Immanuel Kant, *Groundwork of the Metaphysics of Morals*, trans. J.J. Paton, New York: Harper Torchbooks: 1964), p. 100.

7 Cornelius Castoriadis, "The First Institution of Society," *Free Associations*, 12, 1988, p. 42.

8 See Jurgen Habermas, *Theory of Communication: Reason and the Rationalization of Society*, Vol. I, trans. Thomas McCarthy, Boston: Beacon Press, 1984, pp. 61ff.

9 Castoriadis, "The First Institution of Society," p. 41.

10 "Family Romances," S.E., Vol. IX, p. 237. In the same passage Freud notes that "Indeed, the whole progress of society rests upon the opposition between successive generations."

11 See Edwin R. Wallace: *Freud and Anthropology: A History and Reappraisal*, New York: International Universities Press, 1983, p. 25.

12 Se Joyce McDougall, *Theaters of the Mind: Illusion and Truth on the Psychoanalytic Stage*, New York: Basic Books, 1985.

13 New Introductory Lectures on Psycho-Analysis, S.E., Vol. XXII, P. 80. (translation altered)

14 Freud, *The Ego and the Id*, S.E., Vol. XIX, p. 56.

15 *The Seminar of Jacques Lacan*: Book I, Freud's Papers on Technique 1953-1954, trans. Sylvana Tomaselli, New York: W.W. Norton & Co., 1988, p. 16.

16 Jacques Derrida, "Structure, Sign and Play," *The Structuralist Controversy: The Languages of Criticism and the Science of Man*, ed. Richard Macksey and Eugenio Donato, Baltimore: The John Hopkins Press, 1972, p. 248.

17 Freud, *Inhibitions, Symptoms and Anxiety*, S.E., Vol. XX, pp. 145-5.

18 Jacques Lacan, *The Seminar of Jacques Lacan*, Book II: The Ego in Freud's Technique of Psychoanalysis 1954-1955, trans. Sylvana Tomaselli, New York: W.W. Norton & Co., 1988, p. 50.

19 Unless otherwise specified, all the quotes in this paragraph are from, Jacques Lacan, "The Mirror Stage," in *Écrits: A Selection*, trans. Alan Sheridan, New York: W.W. Norton & Co., 1977, pp. 1-7.

20 Jacques Lacan, "Aggressivity in Psychoanalysis," *Écrits*, p. 21.

21 Jacques Lacan, "Agency of the Letter in the Unconscious," *Écrits*, p. 172.

22 See *Seminar II*, pp. 78-79.

23 See for example: *Beyond the Pleasure Principle*, S.E., Vol. XVIII, P. 53.

24 *Seminar II*, p. 167.

25 *What is Neostructuralism?*, trans. Sabine Wileke and Richard Gray, Minneapolis: University of Minnesota Press, 1989, p. 297.

26 *Seminar II*, p. 166.

27 Lacan, "Aggressivity in Psychoanalysis," p. 17.

28 "Aggressivity in Psychoanalysis," p. 22.

29 *Seminar II*, p. 3.

30 Freud, *The Interpretation of Dreams*, S.E., Vol. V, p. 603, Lacan, *Seminar II*, p. 43. It should be pointed out that despite the innovations of ego psychology and the structural model (second topography) in the twenties, and the theoretical reorientation brought about by those innovations, Freud uses the very same phrase to describe the id in "An Outline of Psycho Analysis," (p. 197) thirty-eight years later in *The Interpretation of Dreams*. See S.E., Vol. XXIII, p. 197.

31 Freud, *Introductory Lectures on Psycho-Analysis*, XVIII, S.E., Vol. XVI, pp. 284-5. See also "A Difficulty in the Path of Psycho-Analysis," passim.

32 *Freud and Philosophy: An Essay on Interpretation*, trans. Dennis Savage, New Haven: Yale University Press, 1970, p. 426.

33 Philip Reiff, *Freud: The Mind of the Moralist*, Chicago: The University of Chicago Press: 1979, chap. IX, and Heinz Kohut (1984), "How Does Analysis Cure?," ed. A. Goldberg, Chicago: University of Chicago Press: 1984, p. 54.

34 All of the quotes in the preceding paragraph come from "Animism, Magic and the Omnipotence of Thoughts," which is the third chapter of *Totem and Taboo*, S.E., Vol. XIII, pp. 75-99.

35 See Ricoeur, *Freud and Philosophy*, p. 236 ff.

36 See Castoriadis, *The Imaginary Institution of Society*, p. 107 and Jurgen Habermas, "Toward a Reconstruction of Historical Materialism," *Communication and the Evolution of Society*, ed. Thomas McCarthy, Boston: Beacon Press: 1979, p. 154.

37 Freud, *The Future of an Illusion*, S.E., Vol. XXI, PP 30- 31.

38 The influence of Feuerbach on Freud has not been adequately appreciated. See Wallace, *Freud and Anthropology*, pp. 12-15.

39 "The key to illusion is the harshness of life, which is barely tolerable for man, since he not only understands and feels pain but yearns for consolation as a result of his innate narcissism," Paul Ricoeur: *Psychoanalysis and the Movement of Contemporary Culture, The Conflict of Interpretations*, Evanston: Northwestern University Press: 1974, p. 131.

40 *Freud and Philosophy*, p. 72.

41 Michel Foucault, *Nietzsche, Freud, Marx. Transforming the Hermeneutic Context: From Nietzsche to Nancy*, ed. Gayle Ormiston and Alan Schritft, Albany: State University of New York Press, 1990, pp. 61 & 65.

42 Richard Rorty, *Habermas and Lyotard on Postmodernity, Habermas and Modernity*, ed. R. Bernstein, Cambridge, Mass: MIT Press, 1985, p. 161.

43 See *Psychoanalysis: Project and Elucidation. Crossroads in the Labyrinth*, trans. Kate Soper and Martin Ryle, Cambridge, Mass: MIT Press, 1984, pp. 62-63.

44 Winnicott makes the following observation which is pertinent in this context: "We can share a respect for illusory experience, and if we wish we may collect together and form a group on the basis of the similarity of our illusory experiences. This is a natural root of grouping among human beings. Yet it is a hall-mark of madness when an adult puts too powerful a claim on the credulity of others, forcing them to acknowledge a sharing of illusion that is not their own. *Transitional objects and Transitional Phenomena. Through Paediatrics to Psycho-Analysis*, ed. M. Masud R. Khan, London: The Hogarth Press, 1978, p. 231. See also Jean Piaget, *The Moral Judgment of the Child*, trans. Marjorie Gabain, New York: The Free Press, 1965, pp. 276ff.

45 Castoriadis, *The Imaginary Institution of Society*, pp. 309-11.

46 Se Hegel, *The Philosophy of Right*, Trans. T.M. Knox, Oxford: the Clarendon Press, 1952, Addition Paragraph 182.

47 For Freud's extensive knowledge of Hobbes see Wallace, *Freud and Anthropology*, pp. 54-5, n. 18.

48 See Albrecht Wellmer, "Model's Freedom in the Modern World," The Philosophical Forum, Vol. XXI, Winter 1989-90, p. .

49 Ricoeur, *Freud and Philosophy*, p. 327.

50 Freud, S.:*Civilization and its Discontents*, S.E., Vol. XXI, p. 72. Limitations of space prevent me from taking up the enormous question of Freud's tracing the oceanic feeling and the origins of religion to the father alone and disregarding the maternal dimension completely.

51 See Habermas, "Modernity–An Incomplete Project."

52 *The Future of an Illusion*, p. 49.

53 *The Future of an Illusion*, p. 54.

54 Ricoeur, *Freud and Philosophy*, 33.

55 *The Future of an Illusion*, p. 43.

56 See Freud "Lecture XXXV: The Question of a Weltanschauung," New Introductory Lectures on Psychoanalysis, S.E., Vol. XXII, p. 176.

57 The Future of an Illusion, p. 53.

58 The Future of an Illusion, p. 54.

59 The Future of an illusion p. 53

60 "Psychoanalysis and the Movement of Contemporary Culture," *The Conflict of Interpretations*, ed. Don Ihde, Evanston: Northwestern University Press, 1974, p. 150.

Chapter 12

Comments on Joel Whitebook's Paper

Jacqueline Amati Mehler

First of all I would like to thank the organizers of this meeting for giving me the opportunity to discuss Dr. Joel Whitebook's very scholarly work.

Last spring I received the preliminary draft of the paper I was asked to discuss, "Scrap of Independence–The Problem of the Ego in Freud." Then, shortly before I left Rome, I received instead of the final version of that paper, a different paper entitled "The Autonomous Individual and the Decentered Self."

In the time allocated for this discussion, I shall of course be unable to do justice to both of these most interesting and challenging papers. I will, however, try to include the second paper in the discussion I had addressed to the first one which, in a certain way, can be considered the pre-history of the one presented today.

The first question I would like to raise is: what prompted Dr. Whitebook to shift focus from the concept of an *autonomous ego* in relation to the decentered self, to that in his second paper, of the *autonomous individual*, linked to philosophical, social and psychological concepts of maturity? Perhaps the displacement reflects the author's internal course in an attempt to place his discourse within the larger arena of current psychoanalytic debate over different models of ego, subject or self. The autonomous individual–unless improperly used as a synonym of the autonomous ego–is not really a psychoanalytic concept; it needs to be contextualized–as Dr. Whitebook tries to do in his second paper.

The main point raised in the first paper—and with which I agree entirely—has to do with the need to mediate dialectically between two extreme positions in response to the question: what are the relative forces of the ego and the id *vis-à-vis* each other? In one position the ego is at the mercy of superior, uncontrollable forces; in the other it is considered an autonomous functional entity. While ego psychologists claim that structural theory recognizes in the ego progressive strength and independence from the id, Lacan claims that Freud never abandoned the notion that the uncontrollable forces behind the ego are the core of our being. However, Dr. Whitebook correctly points out that Freud refused the notion that unkown forces always remain the commanding factor in psychic life, although "upon close examination, the text *The Ego and the Id* is weighted on the side of the ego's 'depended relations'."

Both followers of ego psychology and followers of such contemporary critics of the subject as Lacan invoke Freud to support their view. As we know, different authors are able to demonstrate opposite theses, using Freudian formulations to sustain their own viewpoints.

Dr. Whitebook uses a similar technique to demonstrate that Freud's position allows for a much more sophisticated discussion of the main question. And I shall do the same in support of Dr. Whitebook's position—mainly by stressing a concept of Freud's which, though not explicitly mentioned by Dr. Whitebook, is nevertheless implicit in most of his arguments.

A crucial formulation, already foreshadowed in Freud's letters to Fliess and in the "Project," views the psychic apparatus as a complex system which can only be dealt with in its totality from a temporal, developmental, and topic-structural viewpoint. To my mind this is a fundamental milestone of psychoanalysis, but unfortunately it is almost completely neglected in current psychoanalytical literature.[1]

This has enormous implications for the clinical perspective, and for the ideological position towards the therapeutic aim of psychoanalysis, generally represented by Freud's famous phrase: "*Where id was, there ego shall be.*"

But, as Lacan has frequently insisted, the English translation of the German phrase "*Wo* es *war, soll* ich *werden*" is very reductive (as if this were a simple substitutive operation of the ego replacing the id).

In colloquial German—and Freud used a very colloquial mode in his writings—*Ich* means *I*, the personal pronoun in all its subjective complexity, and it also possesses a structural meaning. While *it (Es)*, a neutral pronoun, hints at indifferentiation, *soll (ich) werden* implies a kind of project, meaning not exactly "ego shall be" but rather "I (ego) should become." What I want to emphasize is the sense of unending process—a continuous integration and transformation rather than a substitution. (In his second paper, I noticed, Dr. Whitebook replaced *the ego shall be* with *the ego shall become*.)

Appropriately, Dr. Whitebook recalls (in both papers) that Lacan's absolutism led him to state that Freud was not only alien to, but repudiated the notion that there was a tendency in nature to produce superior forms, more and more elaborated and integrated. I am not going to dwell on arguments of Hyppolite's response to Lacan which are very well illustrated by Dr. Whitebook.

However, I do wish to point out a peculiar contradiction in Lacan's reasoning: very few authors have stressed more than Lacan himself one of Freud's most militant concepts in favour of progressive integration and development of a complex psychic apparatus.

I refer here to the notion of "*Nachträglichkeit*," translated as "deferred action" which again alters its meaning somewhat: "deferred revision" or "retroactivity" would perhaps be more appropriate. Freud often mentions this mechanism, which allows the resignification of new experiences or memories to suite new stages of development. By development I am not merely implying a simple temporal evolution; Freud conceived of the psychic apparatus as the result of a constant interaction between past and present, outside and inside, and between different levels of perceptual organization of representations, in progressive and regressive moves towards differentiation of a tripartite structure.

In his letter to Fliess of December 1896 (S.E.) (Vol. I, p. 233) Freud states: "I am working on the assumption that our psychical mechanism has come into being by a process of stratification: the material present in the form of memory traces being subjected from time to time to *rearrangement* in accordance with fresh circumstances—to a *re-transcription*. . . . I postulated a similar kind of rearrangement . . . (*Aphasia*) . . . (for the paths leading from the periphery (of the body to the cortex)."

I agree with Laplanche and Pontalis's definition of the concept of *Nachträglichkeit* as that which undergoes revision, or rather acquires meaning (and constant resignification): that which—because of a lack of sufficient psychic maturation—could not be incorporated, in the first instance, into any meaningful context.[2]

I would like to suggest another view which is not really in contradiction, but adds perhaps a more clinical perspective of development. Rather than as a process for relinquishing drives (and we know that sometimes this is not in the service of differentiation or growth, but in order to avoid conflict), maturation could be viewed as a constant striving toward drive differentiation and tolerance of aggression and conflict as a means of recognizing not only the Other, but also the Unlike.

My point is that just as life is studded with more than one psychological birth, so, too, is triangulation, alterity, and maturity a constant, unending process.

Here we face a crucial Freudian paradox, mentioned by Dr. Whitebook as well, but from a different perspective. Growth and maturation imply autonomous thought and autonomous identity, separate from that of parental figures. But precisely those objects from which we have to separate and whose loss we must mourn are the ones we have internalized (through incorporation, introjection and identification), and transformation, transcription and transition contribute to the configuration of a psychic space within a pluralistic view encompassing what separates me from not me, inside from outside, phantasy from reality. Separation and individuation, processes enhancing the passage of primary to secondary process, together with symbolization, thinking, and the capacity to "subjectively objectivate" the object, are, of course, crucial to the issues of truth and reality testing that Dr. Whitebook discusses in his work.

As he rightly mentions, Freud described the Id as the core of our being while Lacan used this phrase to claim the eccentricity of the subject in relation to the ego. This is precisely where the concept of complex structure comes in, endorsed by Lacan himself when he posited that the pre-verbal ground of imaginary relations related to body images–source of symbolization–fuses and melts in language, while conserving its own particular modalities of communication.

Lacan says in 1953-4 (*Le Seminaire*, Livre 1, ch. XII) that the unconscious is ". . . something that will be carried through in the symbolic dimension, or more precisely it is that which, in virtue of the symbolic progression in analysis, will have been" (coming close, by the way, to the alternative translation mentioned above of Freud's phrase about where the id was, the ego shall be). It is thus a complex paradoxical structure where transformation occurs and where different levels co-exist.

Dr. Whitebook touches upon the important issue of "culture" in its psychoanalytic sense. Freud's concept of the intermediate space between *Vorstellung*, or creativity, on one hand, and culture, ethics, and civilization on the other, is inhabited by the move from the pleasure principle to the reality principle and by the integration of the perceptual system's archaic experiences into more elevated hierarchies of mental functioning through the development of thought processes.

The triumph of culture over nature is, thus, again a process of integration and transformation.

Lacan often reminds us that Freud insists far more on the conservation and overlapping of different stages in all different psychic levels than on a concept of linear evolution–thus contradicting what at other times appears to be an essentialization of fragmentation. I think that Lacan would hardly disagree with Dr. Whitebook's illuminating statement where he says that . . . "The fact that *Eros* is a vehicle for *Logos* need not serve to invalidate *Logos*; on the contrary, it can serve to indicate a more sensuous conception of rationality, which critical theory, in one form or another, has always been searching for."

Nevertheless, Lacan's position toward Freud's concept of mental apparatus remains contradictory; perhaps because concepts like regression, historical data, biological evolution and its relationship with psychic development were very controversial for him. The collapse of the distinction–in the second topographic scheme–between ego and sexual drives, and the concept of an ego irremediably deceived—and thus incapable of hosting the truth—are very well illustrated by Dr. Whitebook when he points out that Lacan's monolithic and completely undialectical view of the ego prevented him from recognizing its simultaneous accommodation of "rationalization and insight, resistance and curiosity, deception and truth." (Low.)

The problem of truth and its relationship to knowledge is a fundamental question that I have no competence to deal with from a philosophical viewpoint. Although Lacan derived many of his concepts from philosophy, we should remember that the source of his formulations about the ego was eminently clinical. Were we to solve only philosophical controversies, I think we would miss the main point which, to me, is how all of this affects our clinical work, and how our clinical experiences orient our theories.

Lacan never interpreted resistance; since he considered the ego itself as a symptom—the seat of *méconnaissance* and deceipt—there would have been no point in doing so. Ego psychologists strive for an alliance with the ego, endeavouring to enlarge the healthy part of the personality. Whether treating neurotics or psychotics (though, to my knowledge, ego psychologists rarely treat such patients in analysis), the analyst's position is that of reinforcing the ego. Lacan refused to make any alliance with a deceived ego and only addressed the unconscious, structured as a language, through the interpretation of dreams, the play of words, the parapraxis, etc. Let me give two examples:

One of Lacan's patients, tired of hearing the same interpretation repeated to him said: "You persevere" (in French, "Vous persévérez"), and Lacan responded: "Oui, je suis un père sévère" ("I am a severe father").

The second example has an anecdotal flavour. As you probably know, in his later days Lacan would have patients come and sit in his waiting room until he picked one of them at random. A very patient lady who had been coming for several days was finally invited by Lacan to follow him to the consulting room. She said she wanted to tell him a dream—a dream she had carefully preserved in her memory. She made several attempts to speak, but was so overcome that she had forgotten the dream. In great despair she uttered the words: "Oh God, it's terrible; I realize that I have a big hole." Lacan said: "Very well, Madame, that's all you needed to know; your analysis is over."

These are examples of a technique that tends to shift continuously to the unconscious, illustrating what Lacan considers the revelation of the truth, which has almost the quality of a religious revelation. The main objection to this technique is, I think, that it neglects the concept of *working through*, that microscopic, continuous flux of hide-and-seek, of memory and repression, of defence and insight that pursues sense and meaning. But on the other hand, does the therapeutic alliance with the ego guarantee sufficient working through?

I would partly address this issue by recalling another term of Freud's that has been neglected: reconciliation (*Versöhnung*). In reconsidering its importance, I am indebted to J. Canestri (Rome) who has written a paper on the difference between restoration, reconciliation and reparation.

By "reconciliation," Freud refers to the task of adaptation to reality that constrains individuals; according to J. Smolovich (1978), he first mentioned it in his work on Schreber's case. As Canestri points out, the interest of its use lies in the fact that it is connected with the concept of cure through the acceptance by Schreber of his repressed homosexual phantasies. In his almost contemporaneous paper on "The two principles of mental functioning," Freud mentioned reconciliation in relation to the growing sophistication of thought processes as instruments capable of opening up new spaces to renew sources of pleasure and to secure a fate for wishes. But reconciliation also seems capable of mediating between the pleasure and the reality principle through artistic creativity. Reconciliation thus appears to be: 1) a mechanism of acceptance of repressed material, and 2) a regulating principle of the complex whole psychic system mediating between reality and phantasy.

Actually, the concept had already appeared by the time of the Project, and would re-emerge at different stages of the construction of psychoanalytic theory. But what interests us here is the use that ego psychologists made of Freud's speculation about reconciliation between the different ego dependent relations.

They view reconciliation as a function or activity of the ego, resulting from its strength and organization. And in fact many of Freud's arguments could support his view. However, this becomes a controversial issue when taken in the context of his core concept of the psychic apparatus as a complex system, which determines the totality of the personality.

If, on the one hand, the outcome of reconciliation is subordinated to the strength of the ego, what risks being neglected, on the other hand is the fact that the ego, provided it succeeds in reconciling its various dependent relations (with superego, es and reality), is ready to undergo all sorts of alterations, deformations or perversions, thus sacrificing its unity due to more or less damaging splitting mechanisms. As Dr. Whitebook, albeit with other arguments, Lacan would insist that such a partial point of view on the ego can only deny truth; under these conditions, he would certainly refuse any such thing as a therapeutic alliance–a principal tenet of ego psychologists.

The above arguments lead Canestri to suggest that reconciliation ought to be considered: a) not as a *function* of the ego but rather as a . . . "*principle* specifically linked to the functioning of the *entire psychic apparatus*–one of the principles that regulate the "solutions" that the apparatus allows the subject to achieve; therefore not a mechanism"; and b) as a *neutral principle* that does not necessarily function in the service of progress or growth.

In this sense, reconciliation can lead to a cure, but also to a state of equilibrium, with illness becoming part of the total personality. Were we to endorse the ego as the sole agent of reconciliation, we would, in a dynamic and structural sense, be denying the comprehensive and complex quality of the psychic apparatus.

In conclusion, I would like to make two more brief comments linked to the more general theme of this conference. First–and I wonder if Dr. Whitebook would go along with this–I think that it would be misleading to identify "Latin" psychoanalysis (whether European or South American) with Lacan and American psychoanalysis with Ego psychology. Time does not allow me to mention all the possible arguments in favour of Dr. Whitebook's theses that could be provided by contributions form M. Klein, Bion, Winnicott, Greenacre or M. Mahler–just to mention a few who are well-known and influential here and abroad.

Secondly, when considering the influence of Freudian theory and the difference of its impact in the Unted States and in Latin cultures, I would like to recall the statements mentioned in this conference's introductory remarks. I agree that in the United States psychoanalysis has had a much larger influence in its therapeutic applications; although nowadays a part of the psychoanalytic world strives to validate its explanatory powers by shifting the experiential psychoanalytical situation to an experimental one. In my mind, this risks disqualifying the setting as psychoanalytical by modifying the core interaction between the analyst and the patient, which is the main source of our psychoanalytic hypotheses.

In France and Italy, the impact of psychoanalysis has enormously influenced all branches of culture, in conjunction with the 1968 movement, and long before the medical, psychiatric or allied helping professions gave up opposing it and actively tried to take possession of it. Lack of time prevents me from touching upon the fascinating contrasts of the 1968 movement, with its re-edition of patricide and its rupture of tradition that featured, along with authentic trends of growth, a kind of pseudo-growth and pseudo-renunciation of parental figures, taking transgression for a mark of independence, and taking psychoanalysis, for a *passe-partout* to internal and external liberation, rather than an omnipotent scientific *Weltanschauung*.

While this has brought about an enormous expansion of psychoanalysis, it has also obscured the boundaries between psychoanalysis as a therapy requiring specific training, and psychoanalysis as a theory of the mind, which is a patrimony of all cultures.

Notes

1 And "Since the mind is something that can only be studied starting from its totality (that is, it cannot be recomposed if you study it starting from its parts or details), every absolutization of a particular mechanism, mode, or mental phenomena is the sign of a denial of its totality." (A. Semi, 1989)

2 In his description and critique of the analogies between Kant's and Freud's concepts of autonomy, Dr. Whitebook discusses, in his second paper, the issue of maturity, linked to separation from the parents, with resolution of the Oedipus Complex viewed as a turning point.

SESSION VII

Chapter 13

Lacan and the Crisis of Ocularcentrism

Martin Jay

[The eye may be prophylactic, but it cannot be beneficent—it is maleficent. In the Bible and even in the New Testament, there is no good eye, but there are evil eyes all over the place. Jacques Lacan[1]]

"During the night before my father's funeral," Freud wrote in *The Interpretation of Dreams*, I had a dream of a printed notice, placard or poster—rather like the notices forbidding one to smoke in railway waiting rooms—on which appeared either, 'You are requested to close the eyes', or, 'You are requested to close an eye.' "[2] In his exegesis, Freud dwelt on the ambiguity manifested in the dual formulation of the request, which he used to illustrate the willingness of the dream-work to tolerate undecidability or even outright contradiction.

With a certain amount of license, we can interpret this ambiguity as also expressing the psychoanalytic attitude towards vision. For at times, Freud seems to suggest that understanding the workings of the unconscious requires shutting both our eyes, while at others he relents and allows one eye to remain open. But even the latter may have an anti-visual implication, if we interpret it, as Freud did in *The Interpretation of Dreams*, as implying "winking at" or "overlooking" an unpleasant visual experience.

Whatever the degree of hostility to the visual in Freud's work, an appreciation of its importance seems to have played a role in the long-delayed French reception of psychoanalysis.[3] For it was only when an anti-ocular discourse came into its own in the 1960's that psychoanalytic thought began to permeate the general intellectual climate in France.[4] Here the major figure was undoubtedly Jacques Lacan, whose celebrated dictum that the unconscious was structured like a language meant, among many other things, that the hope of understanding the constitution of the subject through a philosophy of perception alone was moribund. Lacan absorbed many of the negative lessons of that project's failure which he combined with others he had derived from the interwar Surrealist interrogation of the visual. The result was a radical recasting of Freud's thought, which focused unprecedented attention on the issue of sight.

Although psychoanalysis became self-consciously anti-visual, only with Lacan's linguistic turn were there tendencies in Freud's work that lent themselves to a similar interpretation. Before proceeding to Lacan, we must consider the ways in which classical psychoanalysis also implicitly requested that we close an/the eye(s). "The invention of hysteria," to borrow Georges Didi-Huberman's phrase,[5] took place in the theatricalized amphitheater and photographic studio of Charcot's clinic at Salpêtrière. Freud, whose scientific curiosity was mightily aroused by what he witnessed during his stay there, later admiringly spoke of Charcot's observational skills: "He was, as he himself said a '*visuel*,' a man who sees."[6]

Freud's own intellectual curiosity remained insatiable, and he steadfastly continued to value clinical observation. But he gradually distanced himself from Charcot's ocularcentric method, for he recognized that the very desire to know, rather than being innocent, was itself ultimately derived from an infantile desire to see, which had sexual origins.[7] Sexuality, mastery, and vision were thus intricately intertwined in ways that could produce problematic as well as "healthy" effects. Infantile scopophilia (*Schaulust)* could result in adult voyeurism or other perverse disorders, such as exhibitionism and scopophobia (the fear of being seen).[8] Some of his most celebrated case studies, such as that of the Rat Man, centered on obsessional visual fantasies, and he came to interpret obscene jokes partly in terms of displaced scopophilic desire. *Witz* (wit) and *Wissen* (knowledge) thus revealed a common root, as Samuel Weber has observed, in the Latin *videre* (to see).[9]

Freud also explores the powerful symbolic resonance of the eyes. Blindness, for example, could imply castration, as in the Oedipus legend or in E.T.A. Hoffmann's story, "The Sandman." Freud's discussion of the latter appeared in his celebrated 1919, essay "The Uncanny," which he followed Schelling in defining as "the name for everything that ought to have remained secret and hidden but has come to light."[10] The sadistic implications of the penetrating "phallic" stare were also evident in such phenomena as the "gaze of Medusa."[11] Here the eye was the source of castration rather than the symbol of its enactment. And finally, the absorption of the self in its mirror image was a basic characteristic of the varieties of narcissism, primary and secondary, which Freud examined from 1910 on, and which psychoanalysts have never tired of trying to interpret.[12]

On an even more speculative level, Freud explained the phylogenesis of the species as the triumph of the eye over the nose. In *Civilization and its Discontents*, he conjectured that civilization was "a consequence of man's raising himself from the ground, of his assumption of an upright gait; this made his genitals, which were previously concealed, visible and in need of protection, and so provoked feelings of shame in him." Man's erect posture thus led to "the devaluation of olfactory stimuli and the isolation of the menstrual period to the time when visual stimuli were paramount and the genitals became visible, and thence to the continuity of sexual excitation, the founding of the family and so to the threshold of human civilization."[13] Civilization was thus based on the shame produced by the visibility of the genitalia and the need to distance ourselves from the "dirtiness" and unpleasant odors of our nether regions.

Freud foreswore any hope for the radical undoing of the ocularcentric civilization produced by the assumption of an upright stance, despite its manifold discontents. In many ways he remained very much a man of the Enlightenment, though more sober and disillusioned than his 18th-century predecessors. The metaphors he frequently used of casting light on the dark recesses of the mind or illuminating the "dark continent" of feminine sexuality were of a piece with his hope to map the uncharted topography of the psyche.[14]

And yet, Freud's stoic commitment to the enlightened values of the scientific tradition was often tempered by a realization of the limits of its ocularcentric premises. His thought was thus enough of a departure from that of the *visuel* Charcot for later French thinkers to consider him an ally in their critique of visual hegemony. Most obviously, his stress on the interpretation of verbally reproduced phenomena, such as dreams or slips of the tongue, rather that the mere observation of hysterical symptoms or physiognomies, meant that listening was more important than seeing.[15] The visual representations in dreams had to be rearticulated in linguistic form before they could become available for analysis. Freud admitted that even the most thorough exegesis of dreams confronted a blind spot, which he called its "navel": a place "which has to be left obscure . . . the spot where it reaches down into the unknown."[16] Still more evidence of Freud's turn away from the visual could be found in his insistence on the couch as a way to avoid direct eye contact between patient and analyst. Not only did this device diminish the perceptual stimuli interfering with the patient's free association in the "talking cure," it also thwarted the scopophilic-exhibitionist potential of face-to-face therapy.

French admirers of Freud often praised precisely these anti-visual implications. For example, Michel de Certeau applied to all of his own work the notion of his novel that Freud had introduced in *Moses and Monotheism*. He concluded: "To adopt the style of the novel is to abandon the 'case study' as it was presented and practiced by Charcot in his Tuesday sessions (*ses Mardis*). These latter consisted of 'observations,' that is to say coherent charts or pictures, composed by noting the facts relevant to a synchronic model of an illness."[17] Derrida approvingly noted the movement away from optical metaphors in *The Interpretation of Dreams* to more scriptural ones in the later work, such as the "mystic writing pad" (a transparent piece of celluloid over a wax slab that erases, but keeps traces of what disappears.)[18]

The French appreciation of Freud's anti-visual implications could also be detected in their greater willingness to acknowledge in a positive way his Jewish background. Whereas in its early years, psychoanalysis was often stigmatized as a "Jewish science,"[19] in recent French thought the same attribution has become a source of explicit praise. A major reason for the shift was the growing appreciation of the Jewish taboo on graven images, which Freud was assumed to share. By the early 1980's colloquia on the themes *Is Psychoanalysis a Jewish Story?* and *The Interdiction on Representation*[20] were bringing together a wide-range of Jewish and gentile scholars to discuss the link between psychoanalysis and Jewish iconoclasm. This outcome was prepared by the linguistically inflected "return to Freud" initiated by Lacan, who, in the words of Susan Handelman, took "to their utmost extreme the antivisual and antimimetic aspects of Freud's thought."[21]

*****

The story begins with a famous crime. After a winter thunderstorm in February, 1933 in Le Mans, a lawyer's wife and her daughter returned to their home and found it in darkness. They unfairly blamed their maids, the sisters Christine and Léa Papin, for the power failure, an accusation whose gruesome consequences were vividly described in an essay in the December issue of the Surrealist journal *Minotaure.*

> [The sisters] each grab an adversary, and tear out her eyes from the socket while she is still alive—a hammer, a pewter jug, a knife—they fling themselves on the bodies of their victims, smashing in their genitals, lacerating their thighs and buttocks, and daubing them with each other's blood. They then wash up the instruments they used for their atrocious rites, clean themselves up and go to sleep in the same bed.[22].

Not surprisingly, the two sisters became instantaneous heroines to the Surrealists, whose fantasies of enucleation were now actually realized by victims of apparent social oppression.[23] Years later the horror of the act would continue to haunt the French collective psyche, as evidenced by the sisters' reappearance as Claire and Solange Lemercier in Genet's play *The Maids* in 1947.[24] What makes it of exceptional importance for the story we are telling is that the writer of the article in *Minotaure* was thirty- three year old Jacques Lacan, and the lessons he wrested from the obscurity—both metaphorical and literal—of the Papin sisters' crime were of prime importance in the development of the most powerful concept in the French reception of Freud: the "mirror stage", in which the role of vision in the constitution of the self was given a hitherto unimagined prominence.

Lacan had already been drawn to another celebrated instance of savage crime committed by a woman, the attempted knifing of an actress by a railway clerk called Aimée. Diagnosed as a paranoiac, Aimée was the main case discussed in his doctoral dissertation, directed by Gaëtan Gatian de Clérambault in 1932.[25] Lacan's interest in the visual dimension of paranoia was likely stimulated by Clérambault, whose own visual preoccupations were extraordinarily intense.[26] In his clinic, Roudinesco reports:

> the cult of the gaze reached its paroxysm. In Clérambault, the art of observation was mixed with a story of the eye reviewed by Charcot and corrected by Roussel . . . Without a private clientele, he passed his life perfecting his eagle's gaze; he manipulated and observed sickness without ever hearing it."[27]

Clérambault, however, reserved his most dramatic visual act for the last. Having lost his eyesight through cataracts, he decided to end his life on November 17, 1934. Sitting in an armchair in front of a mirror, he shot himself in the mouth. In a document found after his death, he invited any interested colleague to examine his eyes.

Lacan, who had worked with Clérambault from 1928 and who called him his only master in psychiatry, was thus already sensitized to the links between vision and aggression, which were reinforced by the criminal episodes he pondered. He drew on a wide variety of sources in his efforts to interpret them, including the then fashionable theories of auto-punishment, erotomania and mental automatism.[28] The Surrealist musings of Salvador Dali on the links between paranoia and hallucinatory images were also in evidence.[29] But his analysis was unified by his adoption of Freud's explanation of paranoia as an unsuccessful defense against repressed homosexual desire.[30]

According to Freud, the defense failed because it entailed a disavowal of the anxiety-producing wish and a projection of it onto an allegedly persecuting other, who was often felt to be watching the self. Such hallucinatory "delusions of observation,"[31] as Freud called them, were complicated by the paranoid's confusion of the projected persecutor with his loved object, which ultimately reflected a narcissistic failure to distinguish self from other.

In the case of the Papin sisters, who were emotional Siamese twins, Lacan emphasized their inability to endure separation. Aimée, was inseparable from a string of different figures, including the assaulted actress, all of whom were surrogates for a strong primary identification with her mother. In both instances, psychosis followed an overly intense and close identification with another, and the concomitant inability to escape a kind of narcissistic doubling. Or rather, the only way to "escape" was through the violent destruction of the double, a kind of self-punishment akin to self castration. "They plucked out their victims' eyes," Lacan noted of the Papin sisters, "as the Bacchantes castrated their victims."[32] But here the victim was ultimately the self, punished because its narcissistic identification with the projected persecuting other implied intolerable homosexual desire.

Lacan's complicated explanation of the crimes to which he was so drawn is of special importance because it provided the kernel of a more ambitious argument, whose impact on the antivisual discourse would prove enormously powerful. Just as Freud had found clues to the workings of the "normal" psyche in his studies of hysteria, so Lacan's analysis of paranoid psychosis led him to posit a universal stage through which all humans pass, a stage displaying marked similarities to the pathological crimes of specular violence committed by the Papin sisters and Aimée.

On August 3, 1936, Lacan read a paper to the 14th Congress of the International Psychoanalytic Association entitled "The Mirror Stage: Theory of a Structuring and Genetic Moment in the Constitution of Reality, Conceived in Relation to Psychoanalytic Experience and Doctrine."[33] A later version of this unpublished work was read at the 16th Congress in 1949 and included as the opening essay in *Écrits*, the immensely influential collection of Lacan's work that appeared in 1966.[34] Although the precise relation between the two versions remains a source of some contention among students of Lacan's often enigmatic *oeuvre*, the main rudiments of the "mirror stage" argument seem to have been in place by the mid-1930's.[35]

The universalization and normalization of the mirror stage—his greatest heresy against conventional psychoanalysis, according to Didier Anzieu—was abetted by Lacan's absorption of several other influences, some narrowly psychological, others more generally cultural. Among them were scientific studies of imitation in animals and Roger Callois's remarkable comparison of insect with human behavior in the pages of *Minotaure*.[37] These works seemed to have alerted Lacan to the importance of visual fusion with the other through morphological mimicry. According to Callois, such a fusion was accompanied by a loss of psychic energy. Borrowing a term from Pierre Janet, Callois called this condition "psychasthenia," which meant a drop in ego strength.[38] Here visual experience meant a crisis of the boundaried well-formed self, which invites comparison with Georges Bataille's notion of *informe*.[39]

Lacan, however, was interested more in the formation of that self than in its dissolution, and he turned to child psychology for help in explaining it. In 1931, the French psychologist Henri Wallon had published a paper entitled "How the Child Develops the Notion of His Own Body."[40] Although the published version of Lacan's "mirror stage" essay mentions Wallon only in passing, Lacan was deeply influenced by Wallon's paper and by his lectures from 1928 to 1934. Wallon had tested the differences between animal and human infant behavior in front of a mirror, demonstrating that the animal did not identify its reflections itself, while the human did. Thus was born a visually constituted notion of the self. Wallon also noted that children often identified very closely with the feelings of others, for example by crying when another child felt pain. This phenomenon, known as "transitivism," suggested that the temporary confusion of self-image and the image of the other could be understood as functional in the creation of a healthy self.

Whereas Wallon conceived of these experiences in essentially positive terms, as advances in the maturation of consciousness, Lacan interpreted them more darkly. Before investigating how he arrived at this conclusion, let us be clear about the description of the mirror stage posited by Lacan in its final formulation in the 1949 essay. Born before it has overcome its organic insufficiency, the human infant is initially in a state of postnatal "fetalization." Between the ages of six and eighteen months, however, the infant achieves a compensatory sense of selfhood through visual identification with its image in a mirror.

What Freud had called primary narcissism was thus achieved through taking an image for the reality of a coherent self, an image which compensates for its still dependent and immature body. This *gestalt* of corporeal wholeness also anticipates the child's later upright posture, which recapitulates on an individual level the fateful step in the history of the species that Freud identified with the privileging of sight over smell or touch. Because the child experiences this new sense of wholeness as an overcoming of "motor incapacity and nursling dependence,"[41] he enjoys what Lacan calls a "jubilant assumption of his specular image."[42] Although this image might be understood as the source of the Ideal-I (the term Freud introduced in his 1914 essay "On narcissism," or the super-ego, coined nine years later in *The Ego and the Id*), Lacan was careful to claim that the ego itself was at stake. The sight of a specular image, he wrote, "situates the ego, before its social determination, in a fictional direction, which will always remain irreducible for the individual alone . . ."[43]

We must now ask, how the mirror stage related to the psychotic violence shown in the cases of the Papin sisters and Aimée, and how Lacan shifted Wallon's positive description of specular identification in a negative direction. The answer lies in Lacan's absorption of the analysis of Hegel's master-slave interaction, presented in Alexandre Kojève's lectures at the École des Hautes Études in the mid-1930's.[44] Kojève's influential anthropological reading of *The Phenomenology of Spirit* as a dialectic of desire, violence and intersubjective recognition left a strong mark on Lacan, as it did on an entire generation of French intellectuals.

According to Kojève, human consciousness emerges over time in response to a primordial desire to overcome a lack, a felt sense of incompleteness on the part of the biological proto-subject. But what defines human as opposed to animal desire is that its realization entails an interaction with the desire of the other, and interaction which is the basis of history. The initial attempt to achieve a coherent sense of selfhood is made by reducing the other to an image of the self, in a manner similar to the projective transitivism noted by child psychologists like Wallon. This violent de-realization of the other however, proves unsatisfactory, for only when the other is truly separate from the self can the self benefit from recognition. A second stage of the dialectic thus entails acknowledgement of the ineradicable otherness of the non-self, which resists reduction to a specular double. In Kojève's terms, a "higher" self is constituted by a dialectic of desire in which achieving the other's recognition supplants solipsistic visual projection. This negative dialectic resists the ultimate *Aufhebung* of difference in Hegel's system as it is normally understood; otherness remains unrecuperable in a grand unity of subject and object.[45]

The role of language in preserving otherness and thwarting specular identity was essential to Lacan.[46] But first, we must clarify the extent of Lacan's critique of the visual constitution of the self. Here a comparison with another ember of Kojève's audience, Sartre, will be useful, for the similarities in their attitudes toward the gaze have been widely acknowledged.[47] In the 1949 article, Lacan specifically criticized Sartre for positing an irreducible core of subjective autonomy, a "self-sufficiency of consciousness"[48] prior to the intersubjective dialectic of desire. The residual Cartesian *cogito* latent in phenomenology, he implied, must be sternly rejected. But what Lacan did not spurn was Sartre's radical demolition of the transcendental ego created by the internalized look of the other. As Macey has noted, "the parallel [in Sartre] with the ego of the mirror stage is startling; in both cases the ego is viewed as an illusory representation, as a source of alienation. Both authors make use of optical metaphors, and both relate their theorizations to Rimbaud's formula [*Je est un autre*]."[49] Sartre and Lacan also shared a deep distrust of the spatialized self created by the reifying look, a distrust traceable to the revaluation of temporality in Bergson and Heidegger. Both posited a desiring subject, whose primordial lack could not be filled by internalizing the look of the other or by accepting the "misrecognition" of the mirror.

The term *méconnaissance*, also translatable as misprision, was introduced by Lacan specifically with reference to the constitution of the ego.[50] Insisting that the ego was nothing more than an illusory construct based on a false faith in a mirror image of corporeal wholeness, Lacan set himself resolutely against ego psychology, one of whose leading advocates had in fact been his own analyst, Rudolph Loewenstein. The therapeutic goal of a strong, integrated ego, he claimed, is misguided, for rather than proving an escape from the vicissitudes of alienation, it is itself the greatest alienation of all. Produced by identification with a specular mirage, a dead image of a body like a film "suddenly stopped in mid-action,"[51] it is nothing less than an instantiation of what Sartre called "bad faith."[52] Indeed from a clinical point of view, Lacan claimed, "the ego represents the center of all the *resistances* to the treatment of symptoms."[53]

We are perhaps now better able to understand the link between Lacan's work on paranoid violence and his discussion of the mirror stage failure. For if specular identification meant the rigid, "orthopaedic" constriction of the psyche, to move beyond the mirror stage could lead to a repetition of its aggression. That is, if the self were narcissistically projected onto the other, then the other was construed as being of the same sex and self-punishment for disavowed homosexual desires could produce violence toward the projected source of those desires. Once the idealized other lost its ideal status, the unity of the self based on identification with the ideal would be threatened, and aggression could be unleashed "outward." Aimée could knife the actress and the Papin sisters could kill their employers, acts that seem to be intersubjective, but in fact were intrasubjective instead.

Such a dynamic is not confined to psychotics, Lacan reasoned but is also evident in everyone's passage through the mirror stage, because of such virtually universal experiences as sibling rivalry, which he dubbed the "intrusion complex".[54] As a result, what Lacan called "the Imaginary," the dimension or realm of images, perceived or imagined, conscious or not is a constant dimension of the psyche, which can never achieve unimpeded access to "the real," that unknowable, but irreducible "outside" of human consciousness. But there is nonetheless, a difference between normal and psychotic behavior which depends on the partial transition from the imaginary to a further stage, which Lacan termed "the Symbolic." Concurrent with the resolution of the Oedipus Complex, the Symbolic meant the child's entry into language.

Lacan's clear preference for the Symbolic over the Imaginary has been widely recognized.[55] Despite the similarities between public seminars and Charcot's theatricalized presentations of hysteria, his debts to Clérambault's psychiatry of the gaze, and his fascination with topographical representations of the unconscious in his later years, Lacan remained preeminently a critic of ocularcentrism. Even in his most scientistic moments, he resolutely rejected the residues of disinterested observation in Freud.[56] And for all his debts to the structuralist linguistics of Saussure and Jakobson, he never assumed the coolly detached perspective of the disinterested spectator reducing the *délire* of linguistic practice to neatly opposed binary oppositions. The only *clarté* in Lacan's own language, as one commentator has remarked, was similar to Magritte's deceptively lucid canvases, replete with visual puns.[57]

This is not the place to hazard yet another heroic explication of Lacan's complicated, ambiguous and slippery analysis of the Symbolic. Suffice it to say that for Lacan, only when the illusory *dyadic* specularity of the mirror stage is surpassed by the *triadic* interaction of the Oedipal drama can a nonnarcissistic intersubjectivity become possible, an intersubjectivity in which the alterity of the non-self is preserved rather than destroyed. The creation of the superego through the *introjection* of the prohibition of the father against incest, creates a secondary identification, which supplants the primary identification, based on specular *projection*.

Only that is when the desire for fusion (either with the image of the self in the mirror or at an earlier stage with the mother) is replaced by the acceptance of the prohibition of that desire, represented by the father's "no," can a healthy subject replace the "misrecognized" subject of the mirror stage. Because the father's "no" is a speech act, and one which in French is conveniently homophonic with his name (the "*non-du-père*" and the "*nom-du-père*"), the introjection is a fundamentally linguistic phenomenon. This is why entrance into the Symbolic is related to the Oedipus complex. The healthy subject thus produced, however, paradoxical it may seem, is thus split and decentered: it accepts the condition of infinite desiring, which the mirror stage had tried to overcome through primary narcissistic identification with the image of wholeness in the glass. Or more precisely, the subject leaves behind mirror-stage primary desire for the secondary "metonymic" desire that Lacan called "demand."[58]

The splitting of the ego helps to defuse the mirror stage's, aggressive potential, which is still evident in paranoid psychosis. The split self is no longer in danger of projecting its ideal of wholeness onto another that it confuses with itself. Nor is it prone to punish itself in that other when it feels threatened by the projected transgressive homosexual desires. The resolution of the Oedipus Complex means overcoming castration anxiety, for the child introjects the father's phallus as a symbolic signifier, rather than trying to *be* the imaginary phallus that will complete the mother's "castrated" body. "Having" the phallus as an internalized object of linguistic desire is thus superior to confusing the self with the image of it. This secondary identification with a word rather than an image means that the self-castration evident in such acts as tearing out the eyes of the specular double is no longer a threat. In sum, only when the unconscious is like a language and not like a mirror can the healthy subject, split and introjecting the other, rather than projccting itself on to it, be achieved.

But what if the unconscious could never completely transcend its non-linguistic, visual dimension, even when the subject successfully negotiated passage through the mirror stage? What if the persistence of the eye in the mind/psyche remained, even in the midst of the Symbolic? What, in other words, if instead of experiencing two distinct temporal stages in developmental process, the unconscious was structured synchronically, without any absolute break between before and after the resolution of the Oedipal phase?

The answers to these questions were spelled out elsewhere in Lacan's work. For his animadversions on the dangers of visual primacy did not end with his influential characterization of the mirror stage and the Imaginary. In at least two other moments, Lacan returned to the theme of vision: when he integrated the concept of "scotomization" into his analysis of psychosis; and when he critically appropriated Merleau-Ponty's chiasmic ontology of the visible and the invisible. In both cases, Lacan interrogated the implications of vision in the constitution of the self and for its vicissitudes.

Scotomization was a term first borrowed from opthalmology by the French analysts René Laforgue and Eduard Pichon in the mid-1920's.[59] Technically it refers to a retinal lesion producing a visual blindspot. Laforgue and Pichon used the term to designate a mode of psychotic unawareness that was different from repression as Freud had defined it. Repression meant denying an instinct or its mental derivative any access to consciousness; scotomization, by contrast, was a "process of psychic depreciation, by means of which the individual attempts to deny everything which conflicts with his ego."[60]

In a series of exchanges with Laforgue, Freud rejected this distinction. Although he apparently won the argument and the term was dropped from orthodox psychoanalytic parlance, it seems to have had a sustained impact on Lacan. The term would explicitly resurface in such texts as "Aggressivity in psychoanalysis;" where Lacan tellingly referred to Freud's failure to recognize the ego's ability to scotomize as a *Méconnaisance*.[61]

In the interim Lacan had also adopted another technical term from Pichon that did much of the same work as scotomization: "foreclosure." [62] *Forclusion* was proposed as the French translation of Freud's *Verwerfung*, which was different from repression (Freud's *Verdrängung*, translated into French as *refoulement*). The difference consisted in the non-integration of foreclosed signifiers into the unconscious, their "casting out" in the literal sense of *ver-werfen*, which prevented them from reappearing as neurotic symptoms. Instead, they resurfaced in the realm of the real, most often as hallucinations, the classic case being that of Schreber.[63] Thus, foreclosure rather than repression is the defense mechanism of psychosis, especially paranoia.

Another way to describe the difference is to note that while repression translates perceptual experience into the realm of the Symbolic, scotomization and foreclosure do not. Psychosis can thus be triggered by the failure to resolve the traumatic experience of castration anxiety produced by the child's perception of the mother's visible lack of a penis; a resolution could only take place through the introjection of the father's linguistic prohibition. The child remains instead in a dyadic union with the mother, in which he or she identifies with the assumed object of maternal desire, the imaginary phallus. This identification during the mirror stage is abetted by the jubilation the child feels when it sees its erect and plenitudinous image in the mirror, as one Gestalt of tumescence slides into another. In striving to *be* the object that can fulfill the mother's apparent lack, the child never comes to accept the law against incestuous coupling laid down by the father. The name-of-the father, representing Symbolic castration, is thus a signifier whose integration into the unconscious is thwarted. As a result, the child never really enters the Symbolic, where the phallus operates as a signifier of unfulfillable desire, splitting the ego, remaining instead trapped in an Imaginary relationship in which image and reality are conflated.

The ultimate source of psychosis seems to be the mother's insistence that the child serve as the fulfillment of her lack. In Lemaire's summary of Lacan's argument, "if the mother treats the child as the complement of her own lack, as the phallus with which the child is in any case trying to identify, if, therefore, the child is everything to her and merges with her in a diffuse union, then the child cannot dispose of his own individuality."[64]

Based on the assumption that "castrated" mothers feel such a lack, Lacan's account of the origin of psychosis betrayed a gender bias that his feminist critics would come to question. However they were less willing to dispute his devaluation of visual experience, which is evident in the residues of scotomization in the concept of foreclosure. Scotomization suggests that an actual blindspot occurs when something is too threatening to be seen. Foreclosure goes further in suggesting that the sight of the mother's apparent castration triggers a casting out of the rejected image, or more precisely an inability to integrate it in symbolic, linguistic terms, and its reappearance as a hallucination in the order of the real. In both cases, psychosis is connected to a disturbance in sight, while health is identified with linguistic introjection of the visual or Imaginary that causes psychological damage.

That such a disturbance may be more than the mere return of an earlier phase, as the stage argument would suggest, is shown by the hidden premise of the child's alleged visual perception of a lack in his mother's body. Vision alone cannot produce the sense of a lack, which is already a Symbolic concept. Therefore the synchronic imbrication of the verbal and the visual is implied by Lacan's conflation of scotomization and foreclosure.

No less resistant to the assumption that the visual constitution of the self was left behind with entrance into the realm of language, and even more influential in the subsequent antiocular discourse in France, were Lacan's remarkable seminars on the chiasmic intertwining of the eye and the gaze collected in *The Four Fundamental Concepts of Psycho-analysis* under the rubric "Of the Gaze as *Objet Petit a*." Lacan began the first seminar, "The Split Between the Eye and the Gaze," by paying tribute to Merleau-Ponty's pioneering interrogation of vision in particular the recently published *The Visible and the Invisible*, praising it for going beyond Merleau-Ponty's earlier *Philosophy of Perception* because of its rejection of the constitutive, form-giving powers of the intentional subject, Lacan nonetheless reinterpreted its significance in his own terms. Merleau-Ponty was right to divide the scopic field, but wrong to interpret it as a chiasmus of visibility and invisibility; it would be better to conceptualize it in terms of the eye and the gaze.

To explain what he meant by these terms, Lacan drew once again on the work of one of his co-contributors to *Minotaure*, Roger Callois. In a work concerning animal mimicry titled *Méduse et Compagnie*, Callois had raised the question of whether the imitated eyes, *ocelli*, employed by certain animals to frighten predators or victims achieve their effect because they resemble real eyes or vice versa. In other words, do real eyes fascinate on their own terms or because they imitate their simulacrum? The implication was that the real eye was intersected in the scopic field by the "gaze" of a fake one. Callois's example was thus "valuable in marking the preexistence to the seen of a given-to-be-seen."[65]

Returning to his critique of the Imaginary, Lacan went on to explain the problem of remaining hostage to the mirror stage, a problem that characterized Western philosophical ocularcentrism as the inflation of the role of the eye at the cost of recognizing that of the gaze. That is, if fails to register what Merleau-Ponty had pointed out: "That we are beings who are looked at, in the spectacle of the world. That which makes us consciousness institutes us by the same token as *speculum mundi*.[66] This failure can be understood if we contrast waking and sleeping experience. The awakened consciousness only operates with a looking eye, while in our dreams, images show themselves to our unconscious: "In the final resort, our position in the dream is profoundly that of someone who does not see . . . in no case will [the subject] be able to apprehend himself in the dream in the way in which, in the Cartesian *cogito*, he apprehends himself in thought."[67] Because of the privilege normally given to wakened consciousness, it is necessary in analysis to bring to the surface the crossing of eye and gaze, avoiding the alibi of visual plenitude and mastery. "It is not, after all, for nothing," Lacan noted, "that analysis is not carried out face to face. The split between eye and gaze will enable us, you will see, to add the scopic drive to the list of the drives."[68]

To explore the implications of that drive, Lacan turned to the theme of anamorphosis, whose importance had been brought home to him by Jurgis Baltrusaitis' influential study.[69] Before treating it directly, he began by commenting on Valéry's *La Jeune Parque*, in which the main character talks of seeing himself seeing. The problem with this formulation, Lacan suggested, was that it was indebted to a Cartesian notion of the subject as constituted by the eye alone: "The privilege of the subject seems to be established here from that bipolar reflexive relation by which, as soon as I perceive, my representations belong to me."[70] Merleau-Ponty's phenomenological alternative, with its deprivileging of the Cartesian subject, was superior, but according to Lacan, it lacked the courage to take its chiasmic conclusions to their non-reciprocal end. Merleau-Ponty, he charged, had fallen back on an alleged substratum prior to reflection.

Psychoanalysis, however, calls into question the search for a primordial state, anterior to the split between the eye and the gaze, because it regards "consciousness as irremediably limited, and institutes it as a principle, not only of idealization, but of *méconnaissance*, as—using a term that takes on new value by being referred to a visible domain—*scotoma*."[71] Here Lacan reintroduces the visually inflected category Freud had banished as superfluous, now not merely as an explanation for psychosis, but as a dimension of the psyche *per se*. Blind spots, he implied, were incurable. The misprision of visually constituted consciousness operates, as Lacan had earlier claimed for the mechanism of foreclosure, by seeking to overcome its sense of incompleteness through identification: "The interest the subject takes in his own split is bound up with that which determines it—namely, a privileged object, which has emerged from some primal separation, from some self-mutilation induced by the very approach of the real, whose name, in our algebra, is the *objet a*."[72]

The *objet a* (object small a) was Lacan's term for the object of lack or the missing object that would seemingly satisfy the drive for plenitude, "a" is the first letter of the french word for "other," (*autrui*). At its most fundamental level, it is the phallus which the child wishes to be in order to make up for the mother's alleged lack, her apparent castration. It can then be transformed into the Symbolic register as the metonymic object of desire, which motivates the split subject's interminable search for a unity it can never achieve. But it also operates in the realm of the Imaginary, where "the object on which depends the phantasy from which the subject is suspended in an essential vacillation is the gaze"[73].

To explicate his cryptic assertion that in scopic relations the gaze functions as the *objet a*, Lacan turned to Sartre's *Being and Nothingness* in which the reifying power of the gaze was explored. Although he challenged Sartre's claim that the eye cannot see the eye that looks at it, he agreed that the gaze had the quality of being unseen: "the gaze I encounter—you can find this in Sartre's own writing—not a seen gaze but a gaze imagined by me in the field of the Other."[74] It is for this reason that "*le regard*" can include non-visual phenomena like the rustling of the leaves. More importantly, the unseen character of the gaze meant it was not necessarily that of another subject looking threateningly at the original subject, but might rather be understood as a function of the desire of the original subject, the desire for the *objet a*.

For further help in explicating this relationship, Lacan turned to anamorphosis, as exemplified by Hans Holbein's *The Ambassadors*. Normal perspective, he noted, corresponded to the Cartesian subject's geometrical mapping of space, a geometricalization that could be based, as Diderot had noted in his *Letter on the blind*, on a sightless man's touch. Such a rigid and linear reduction of vision invited comparison, Lacan suggested, with an erect penis. In *The Ambassadors*, this phallic gaze of the dominant Cartesian perspectivalist was challenged by another, which was expressed by the distorted skull at the bottom of the canvas, a skull whose natural shape could only be restored by an oblique glance from the painting's edge. Such an object expressed another kind of desire than that which seeks phallic plenitude. Instead, it suggested the desire of the Symbolic realm in which the subject is decentered, split, and comes to terms with its own incompleteness. The eye is that of the specular, Cartesian subject desiring specular plenitude and phallic wholeness, and believing it can find it in a mirror image of itself; the gaze is that of an objective other in a field of pure monstrance. To believe that these two chiasmically crossing dimensions of the scopi field could ever be reconciled harmoniously is to forget the lesson, which Lacan had absorbed in Kojève's lecture hall, that true reciprocity is only an illusion.

In his next seminar, "The Line and the Light," Lacan reformulated and expanded his argument, using triangulated schemas to illustrate the chiasmic intertwining of eye and gaze. The first, that of the eye signified Cartesian perspectivalist vision. The viewer's monocular eye was at the apex, and the object at the far wall of the triangle. The image was on another line parallel to the wall, but halfway between the wall and the eye/apex. The second schema, that of the gaze, put a point of light at the apex, the picture on the far wall, and what Lacan called "the screen" halfway between. Here the subject is placed not at the apex, but in the middle, as if it were an image on a screen in a generalized perceptual field, not a seeing eye. This subject, Lacan contended, "is caught, manipulated, captured in the field of vision."[75] Holbein's anamorphosed skull, with its invocation of the nothingness of death, expresses a subject trapped in a visual field it cannot master. Indeed, Lacan insisted, "in this matter of the visible, everything is a trap. . . .There is not a single one of the divisions, a single one of the double sides that the function of vision presents, that is not manifested to us as a labyrinth."[76]

Yet another figure introduced by Lacan's friends on *Minotaure*, Roger Callois, resurfaced in Lacan's attempt to clarify the relation between eye and gaze: the dihedron, intersection of two planes. Callois had used the dihedron in his 1935 essay, "Mimétisme et psychasténie légendaire," to explain animal mimicry, a piece whose impact on Lacan's "mirror stage" has already been mentioned.[77] Lacan used the dihedron to superimpose his two visual triangles in inverted form. The chiasmic interposition of the two planes created a new figure in which the middle sections of both triangles, the image in that of the eye, the screen in that of the gaze, coincided in the form of a divided subject. At its center was an opaque line very different from the transparent window typical of the Albertian subject's view on the world.[78]

To clarify its implications, Lacan moved from the realm of visual schema to that of narration and told an anecdote, which he claimed was true. Years ago when he was fishing off Brittany, a friend pointed to a sardine can in the water and said laughingly, "*You see that can? Do you see it? Well, it doesn't see you.*"[79] Ruminating on the lesson his friend had drawn from the floating can, Lacan concluded that it was mistaken, for the can "was looking at me, all the same. It was looking at me at the level of the point of light, the point of light, the point at which everything that looks at me is situated—and I am not speaking metaphorically."[80] Lacan, in other words, felt that he was indeed in the center of a conflictual visual field, at once the eye looking at the can and the screen in an impersonal field of pure monstrance. His subjectivity was thus split between the apex at the end of the triangle of the eye and the line in the middle of the gaze's triangle.

Another variation on this unsublated dialectic was evident, Lacan claimed, in the realm of painting, to which he turned at the end of this seminar and that which followed, entitled "What is a Picture?" It was by looking at the art of painters like Cézanne, he reminded his audience, that Merleau-Ponty had overthrown the traditional identity of eye and mind. In pictures, something of the gaze is always manifested, he argued, but the spectator is invited by the artist to lay down his gaze there as one lays down one's weapons. This is the pacifying Apollonian effect of painting. Something is given not so much to the gaze as to the eye, something that involves the abandonment, the *laying down*, of the gaze."[81] There is a certain duplicity in all of this, which Lacan suggested with the concept of the "lure"(*leurre*, which also means enticement, decoy and bait; Lacan related this concept to *méconnaissance*). In *trompe l'oeil* painting, the gaze triumphs over the eye. The result is similar to the negative dialectic of lovers described by Sartre.

After some cryptic remarks on icons, on the Jewish taboo on images, and on the role of painting in communal settings, Lacan concluded by returning to the link between desire and vision, which he called the "appetite of the eye." "Modifying the formula I have of desire as unconscious—*Man's desire is the desire of the Other*—I would say," he explained, "that it is a question of a sort of desire *on the part of* the Other, at the end of which is the *showing* (*le donner-à-voir*)."[82] In other words, the gaze was brought about by the Other's desire to show itself, a desire matched only by the eye's desire to see. But showing and seeing do not harmoniously complement each other or overcome the split in the subject. The violence of their struggle is shown in the ubiquitous existence of myths of the evil eye, which Lacan interpreted as that "the eye carries with it the fatal function of being in itself endowed—if you will allow me to play on several registers at once—with the power to separate."[83] The evil eye operates as the *fascinum*, "that which has the effect of arresting movement and, literally, of killing life."[84] This power may be metaphorical, but it captures the aggressive potential of vision, to which Lacan had been sensitive ever since his earliest studies of the links between paranoia and the mirror stage. Significantly, the transcription of this last seminar on vision ends with a question from Jacques-Alain Miller, who wondered if anything in Lacan's critique of Merleau-Ponty's celebration of a healthy visual ontology had been changed by the publication of *The Visible and the Invisible*, acknowledgment of the non-dialectical chiasmus of sight. "Absolutely nothing," replied the intransigent Lacan.

Although it is impossible to summarize Lacan's complicated dialectic of the eye and the gaze in any simple formula, it is clear that his thinking had moved beyond his early discussion of the mirror stage. First, whereas in the mirror stage argument, vision was involved in an imaginary identification with a gestalt of corporeal wholeness, an identification due to a specular projection of narcissistic sameness, now it connected to desire for the other. As Jacqueline Rose has noted, Lacan understood Freud "in terms of the gradual intrusion of the axis of desire onto the axis of identification, an intrusion which can be measured against the shift from the drives of demand (oral, anal) to those of desire (scopic, invocatory) in which the physical distance of the object reveals the relation between subject and object to be necessarily disjunct."[85] That is, the *objet a* Lacan called the gaze is not a mirror image of the subject; it is, as we have seen chiasmically crossed with the subject's eye. The dyad of specular projection is replaced by a dual and inverted triangulation, even more complicated than the triadic introjection of the father's name associated with the resolution of the Oedipus Complex.

Not only have we moved beyond the Imaginary realm of specular doubling into that of the disjunction between desiring subject and its unattainable object, we are also now on the threshold of intersubjective relations as well. As Lacan's evocation of Sartre makes clear, vision may be understood as a conflictual field in which the looker is always a body to be observed. On one level, the impersonal gaze is a function of the split subject's internal dynamics, his desire for the *objet a* as a way to compensate for a lack, on another, it expressed the unsublated dialectic of intersubjective gazes, that dihedron of superimposed visual triangles Lacan had borrowed from Callois and used to redescribe Kojève's dark version of Hegel.

Vision necessarily enters the realm of the Symbolic, in which language is paramount.[86] A lack, after all, is precisely that which cannot be seen; it must exceed the realm of the visual. One recent commentator, Joan Copjec, has contended that the two triangles in the dihedron can be understood as counterposing optics and semeiotics. As a result, she argues,

> Semeiotics, not optics, is the science that clarifies for us the structure of the visual domain. Because it alone is capable of lending things sense, the signifier alone makes vision possible. There is and can be no brute vision, no vision totally devoid of sense. . .the field of vision is neither clear nor easily traversable. It is instead ambiguous and treacherous, full of traps.[87]

Copjec's claim is made in the service of a critique of French film theory's appropriation of Lacan, which she faults for conflating his mirror stage theory with his later work on the gaze. But however correctly Lacan's often cryptic work was understood, it was invariably adopted as a powerful weapon in the dismantling of ocularcentrism on the part of a wide variety of French intellectuals, from Louis Althusser and Luce Irigaray to Christian Metz and Jean-Louis Comolli.[88] Indeed, if we live in a climate deeply distrustful of the time-honored nobility of sight, if we have become suspicious of its claims to provide enlightenment and clarity, if we have lost our faith in the innocence of the gaze, Lacan's relentless critique of what he called "the maleficent eye" must be accounted a major source of that outcome.

Notes

1 Jacques Lacan, *The Four Fundamental Concepts of Psycho- analysis*, ed. Jacques-Alain Miller, trans. Alan Sheridan, New York, 1981, pp. 118-119.

2 Sigmund Freud, *The Interpretation of Dreams*, trans. James Strachey, New York, 1965, p. 352.

3 The most extensive history of the French reception is Elisabeth Roudinesco, *La Bataille de cent ans: Histoire de la psychanalyse en France*, vol. I, 1885-1939, Paris, 1982, vol. 2, 1925-1985 (Paris, 1986); for a critique of its teleological reading of that history as a prelude to Lacan, see Paul Bercherie, "The Quadrifocal Oculary: The Epistemology of the Freudian Heritage," *Economy and Society*, 15, I (February, 1986), pp. 23-70. See also Sherry Turkle, *Psychoanalytic Politics: Freud's French revolution*, New York, 1978.

4 For an account of the anti-ocular discourse see Martin Jay, "In the Empire of the Gaze: Foucault and the Denigration of Vision in Twentieth-Century French Thought," in David Couzens Hoy, ed., *Foucault: a Critical Reader*, New York, 1986.

5 Goerges Didi-Huberman, *Invention de l'hysterie: Charcot et l'iconographie photographique de la Salpêtrière*, Paris, 1982.

6 Sigmund Freud, "Charcot" (1893), *S.E.*, vol. 3, London, 1962, pp. 12-13.

7 Freud, "Five Lectures on Psychoanalys," *S.E.*, vol. II, p. 44.

8 For a recent psychoanalytic discussion, see David W. Allen, *The Fear of Looking: Or Scopophilic-exhibitionist Conflicts* (Charlottesville, Va., 1974). He notes that the translation of *Schaulust* is sometimes scoptophilia, but says that scopophilia is preferable.

9 Samuel Weber, *The Legend of Freud* (Minneapolis, 1982), p. 172. Weber, Drawing on recent French thought, has many pertinent observations about Freud's critique of vision.

10 Freud, "The Uncanny," *S.E.*, vol. 17, p. 224.

11 Freud, "Medusa's Head," (1922), *S.E.*, 18. For a critical analysis of Freud's use of the Medusa legend, see Tobin Siebers, *The Mirror of Medusa* (Berkeley, 1983), chapter 5.

12 For a recent summary of the debates, see C. Fred Alford, *Narcissism: Socrates, the Frankfurt School, and Psychoanalytic Theory* (New Haven, 1988).

13 Freud, *Civilization and its Discontents*, trans. James Strachey (New York, 1961), pp. 46-47.

14 For an analysis of these metaphors, see David Macey, *Lacan in Contexts* London, 1988), chapter 6.

15 For a good discussion of this issue, see Weber, *The Legend of Freud*, p. 17f.

16 Freud, *The Interpretation of Dreams*, p. 564.

17 Michel de Certeau, *Heterologies: Discourse on the Other*, trans. Brian Massumi, foreword Wlad Godzich (Minneapolis, 1986), p. 20.

18 Derrida, "Freud and the Scene of Writing," in *Writing and Difference*, trans. with intro., Alan Bass (Chicago, 1978).

19 For a discussion of its impact on the French reception, see Roudinesco, vol. I, p. 395f.

20 Adélie and Jean-Jacques Rassial, eds. *La psychanalyse est- elle une historie juive* (Paris, 1981); *L'Interdit de la représentation* (Paris, 1985).

21 Susan A. Handelman, *The Slayers of Moses: The Emergence of a Rabbinic Interpretation in Modern Literary Theory* (Albany, N.Y. 1982), p. 155.

22 Jacques Lacan, "Motifs du crime paranoïaque: le crime des soeurs Papin," *Minotaure*, 3/4 (December, 1933), p. 25. For discussions of the episode and its implications, see Roudinesco, vol. 2, p. 138f; Macey, *Lacan in Contexts*, p. 69f.

23 Macey, *Lacan in Contexts*, p. 69.

24 For a discussion of the similarities and dissimilarities between the two sets of sisters, see Philip Thody, *Jean Genet: A Study of His Novels and Plays* (New York, 1970), p. 164f. Sartre also comments on Genet's appropriation of the crime in *Saint Genet: Actor Martyr*, trans. Bernard Frechtman (New York, 1963), p. 617f.

25 Lacan, *De la psychose paranoïaque dans ses rapports avec la personnalité* (Paris, 1932).

26 For example, he staged and collected some 40,000 photographs of draped figures during his trips to Morocco. Some are reproduced in the special issue on Clérambault in *Tumult: Zeitschrift für Verkehrwissenschaft*, 12 (1988). For a brilliant and imaginative attempt to interpret these photographs using Lacanian categories, see Joan Copjec, "The Sartorial Superego," *October*, 50 (Fall, 1989), pp. 55-95.

27 Roudinesco, vol. 2 pp. 120-121.

28 For a helpful account of these concepts and their role in the development of French psychiatry, see Carolyn Dean, "Law and Sacrifice:

Bataille, Lacan, and the Critique of the Subject," *Representations*, 13 (Winter, 1986), pp. 42-62.

29 Roudinesco, vol. 2, p.125.

30 Freud, "Psychoanalytic Notes on an Autobiographical Account of a Case of Paranoia (Dementia Paranoides)," (1911) in S.E., vol. 12, trans. James Strachey (London, 1953-74).

31 Although primarily visual, these delusions could be auditory, as Sartre also noted in his discussion of "the look" in *Being and Nothingness*. For a psychoanalytic treatment of auditory delusions of observation, see Otto Isakower, "On the Exceptional Position of the Auditory Sphere," *International Journal of Psychoanalysis*, XX, 3/4 (July-October, 1939), p. 346. Lacan, to be sure, seems to have stressed the visual rather than the auditory dimension of the cases he studied.

32 Lacan,"Motifs du crime paranoïaque," p. 28.

33 The paper was indexed as "The Looking-Glass Phase" in *The International Journal of Psychoanalysis*, 18 (1937), p. 78, but contrary to the claim of the editors of *Écrits: A Selection*, trans. Alan Sheridan, New York, 1977, p. xiii, it was not published in English translation. For an interesting discussion of the mysterious history of this text and its citations, see Jane Gallop, "Lacan's 'Mirror Stage': Where to Begin," *SubSTance*, 37/38 (1983), pp. 118-128.

34 The title was now "The Mirror State as Formative of the Function of the I as Revealed in Psychoanalytic Experience."

35 In 1936, Lacan published a paper entitled "Au-delà du 'Principe de réalité,'" *Evolution psychiatrique*, 3 (1936), pp. 67- 86, in which the mirror-stage theory was outlined.

36 Cited in Anthony Wilden's prefatory note to Lacan, *The Language of the Self*, p. xiii. What makes this claim especially interesting is Anzieu's identity, which Wilden does not mention. According to Roudinesco. vol. II, p. 135, he was the son of Aimée, who was then analyzed by Lacan many years later without Lacan's knowing (or repressing) who he was! Anzieu subsequently became an analyst himself.

37 Roger Callois, "Mimétisme et Psychasthénie Légendaire," *Minotaure*, 7 (June, 1935); for suggestive analyses of its relevance to Lacan's argument, see Rosalind Krauss, "Corpus Delicti" *October*, 33 (Summer, 1935), p. 46f; and Paul Foss, "Eyes, Fetishism, Text," *Art and Text*, XX (February-April, 1986), p. 27f.

38 For an analysis of this argument, see Denis Hollier, "Mimesis and Castration, 1937," *October*, 31 (Winter, 1985), pp. 3-16.

39 Krauss, "Corpus Delicti," p. 49.

40 Henri Wallon, "Comment se développe chez l'enfant la notion du corps propre," *Journal de Psychologie,* (Nov.-Dec., 1931), pp. 705-748.

41 Lacan, "The Mirror Stage as Formative of the Function of the I as Revealed in Psychoanalytic Experience," *Écrits* p. 2.

42 *Ibid.* For a critique of the empirical validity of this claim of jubilation, and much else in the mirror stage argument, see Raymond Tallis, *Not Saussure: A Critique of Post-Saussurean Literary Theory*, London, 1988), p. 142f.

43 *Ibid.*

44 For an account of their impact on him see, Roudinesco, vol. II, p. 149f. See also, Wilfried Ver Eecke, "Hegel as Lacan's Source for Necessity in Psychoanalytic Theory," and Edward S. Carey an J. Melvin Woody, "Hegel, Heidegger, Lacan: The Dialectic of Desire," both in Smith and Kerrigan, *Interpreting Lacan.*

45 Roudinesco notes that the difference between Wallon and Lacan can be understood in part as a contrast between a more optimistic Hegelian version of the unity of the self and a pessimistic Kojèvian one. (vol. 2, p. 157).

46 For Kojève, who was a marxist, labor was even more crucial than language, but Lacan ignored its role.

47 See, for example, Macey, *Lacan in Contexts*, p. 103; Anthony Wilden, notes to Lacan, *The Language of the Self: The Function of Language in Psychoanalysis*, trans. Anthony Wilden, New York, 1968, p. 160f; Leo Bersani, *Baudelaire and Freud*, Berkeley, 1977, p. 112; and Fredric Jameson, "Imaginary and Symbolic in Lacan: Marxism, Psychoanalytic Criticism, and the Problem of the Subject," *Yale French Studies*, 55/56 (1977), p. 379.

48 Lacan, "The Mirror Stage," p. 6.

49 Macey, *Lacan in Contexts*, p. 103. The Rimbaud formula seems to have been taken to mean that the "I" was the product of the internalization of the other's look. In Lacan's fluid vocabulary, however, the "*ie*" often meant as well the speaking subject. For its complicated relations to the "*moi*" in his thought, see Ellie Ragland-Sullivan, *Jacques Lacan and the Philosophy of Psychoanalysis* (Urbana, 1987), p. 58f. Roudinesco points out that the splitting of Freud's *Ich* into the *ie* and the *moi*, which she identifies with the subject of the unconscious and imaginary self, was anticipated by Eduard Pichon. (vol. II, p. 311).

50 Lacan, "The Mirror Stage," p. 6. Surprisingly, Lacan, who reveled in the play of language, neglected to tie *voir* and *non- savoir*. The reason may have been that *connaissance* has the connotation of knowledge as recognition, which fits better with the Kojévean dialectic of recognition.

51 Lacan. "Aggressivity in Psychoanalysis," *Écrits*, p. 17.

52 Lacan, "Aggressivity in Psychoanalysis," p. 15.

53 *Ibid.* p. 23.

54 Lacan, "La Famille," *Encyclopédie Francaise*, VIII (Paris, 1938), p. 840. For a discussion, see Alphons De Waelhens, *Schizophrenia* (Pittsburgh, 1978), p. 76-79.

55 For example, by Antoine Vergote, Foreword to Anika Lemaire, *Jacques Lacan*, trans. David Macey (London, 1977), p. xix.

56 For a discussion of the differences, see Shoshana Felman, *Jacques Lacan and the Adventure of Insight: Psychoanalysis in Contemporary Culture* (Cambridge, Mass., 1987), p 61f.

57 William Kerrigan, "Introduction," *Reading Lacan*, eds. Smith and Kerrigan, p. xxiv.

58 According to Lemaire, "in Lacan, demand appears to be a generic term designating the symbolic, significant site in which the primordial desire is gradually alienated." *Jacques Lacan*, p. 165.

59 For a discussion, see Roudinesco, vol. I., p. 388f, and Macey, p. 35f.

60 Laforgue, "Scotomization in Schizophrenia," *International Journal of Psychoanalysis*, 8 (1927), p. 473, cited in Macey, p. 35.

61 "Aggressivity in Psychoanalysis," p. 22.

62 For a helpful account, see John P. Muller, "Language, Psychosis and the Subject in Lacan," in Smith and Kerrigan, *Reading Lacan*.

63 For Lacan's treatment of it, see "On a Question Preliminary to Any Possible Treatment of Psychosis." *Écrits*.

64 Anika Lemaire, *Jacques Lacan*, trans. David Macey (London, 1970), p. 234. Lacan also explains perversions in a similar way. "The whole problem of the perversions," he writes, "consists in conceiving how the child, in relation to the mother, a relation constituted in analysis not by his vital dependence on her, but by his dependence on her love, that is to say, by the desire for her desire, identifies himself with the imaginary object of this desire insofar as the mother herself symbolizes it in the phallus." ("On a Question Preliminary to Any Possible Treatment of Psychosis," *Écrits*, p. 198).

65 *Ibid.*, p. 74.

66 *Ibid.*, p. 75.

67 *Ibid.*

68 *Ibid.*, p. 78. Freud had suggested oral, anal and genital drives; besides adding the scopic, Lacan also posited an invocatory drive related to the voice. According to Lacanian theory, "the drives represent the cause of sexuality in the psychic; they do so only partially and yet they constitute the only link of sexuality to our experience." ("The Phallic Phase and the Subjective Import of the Castration Complex," in *Feminine Sexuality: Jacques Lacan and the École Freudienne*, eds. Juliet Mitchell and Jacqueline Rose, trans. Jacqueline Rose, New York, 1982, p. 119. This article was an unsigned contribution to Lacan's journal *Scilicet* in 1968). The importance of construing vision as a scopic drive is that it then must seek an erotic object outside of itself for fulfillment; this is the role of the gaze. For Lacan, drives cannot be realized, which is why the eye and the gaze are shown in perpetual disharmony. For an useful gloss on Lacan's drive theory, see Juliet Flower MacCannell, *Figuring Lacan: Criticism and the Cultural unconscious*, Lincoln, Nebraska, 1986, p. 161f.

69 Jurgis Baltrusaitis, *Anamorphoses: ou Perspectives curieuses* Paris, 1955; the third edition, Paris, 1984, mentions Lacan's appropriation, as well as others by contemporary intellectuals such as Roland Barthes, Jean Cocteau and Jean-François Lyotard.

70 *Ibid.*, p. 81.

71 *Ibid.*, pp. 82-83.

72 *Ibid.*, p. 83.

73 *Ibid.*

74 *Ibid.* This passage nuances Ragland-Sullivan's otherwise accurate observation that "existentialist philosophers demonstrated that the *regard* is always 'out there.' Lacan connects it to dreams and shows that it is also always 'in here': the gaze of the Other (A)." *Jacques Lacan and the Philosophy of Psychoanalysis*, p. 44.

75 *Ibid.*, p. 92.

76 *Ibid.*, p. 93.

77 *Minotaure*, 7 (June, 1935). For discussions of its importance, see Denis Hollier, "Mimesis and Castration, 1937," *October*, 31 (Winter, 1985), pp. 3-16, and Rosalind Krauss, "Corpus Delicti," *October*, 33 (Summer, 1985), pp. 31-72.

78 The comparison is made by Kaja Silverman, "Fassbinder and Lacan: A Reconsideration of Gaze, Look and Image," *Camera obscura*, 19 (January, 1989), p. 74.

79 Lacan, *The Four Fundamental Concepts of Psycho-analysis*, p. 95.

80 *Ibid.*

81 *Ibid.*, p. 101

82 Lacan, *The Four Fundamental Concepts of Psycho-analysis*, p. 115.

83 *Ibid.*, p. 115.

84 *Ibid.*, p. 118.

85 Rose, *Sexuality in the Field of Vision*, p. 182. For a discussion of the difference between demand and desire in Lacan's vocabulary, see Lemaire, *Jacques Lacan*, p. 166f.

86 According to Julie Flower MacCannell, Lacan "reduces the drive to its minimal equation in the passion of the signifier to become the signified–of the image to become the concept. (*Figuring Lacan*, pp. 67-68).

87 Joan Copjec, "The Orthopsychic Subject: Film Theory and the Reception of Lacan," *October*, 49 (Summer, 1989), p. 68.

88 Their concerns have now become widely shared outside of France, as demonstrated by the vigorous debate over the gaze in feminist film criticism in Britain and America.